WITHDRAWN

ILLINOIS CENTRAL COLLEGE
PS3531.A764Z73
STACKS
Kenneth Patchen :

A12900 389583

PS
3531
.A764
Z73   Kenneth Patchen

DATE			

WITHDRAWN

© THE BAKER & TAYLOR CO.

WITHDRAWN

Kenneth Patchen:
A Collection
of Essays

Kenneth Patchen: A Collection of Essays

EDITED
AND WITH AN INTRODUCTION BY

Richard G. Morgan

FOREWORD BY

Miriam Patchen

AMS PRESS INC.
NEW YORK, N.Y.

63873

I.C.C. LIBRARY

FIRST AMS PRESS EDITION: 1977

Library of Congress Cataloging in Publication Data

Main entry under title:

Kenneth Patchen: a collection of essays.

Bibliography: p.
1. Patchen, Kenneth, 1911-1972 — Addresses, essays, lectures. 2. Authors, American — 20th century — Biography — Addresses, essays, lectures. I. Morgan, Richard G.
PS3531.A764Z73   811'.5'4 B   77-78319
ISBN 0-404-16005-0

Copyright © 1977 by Richard G. Morgan.

The following illustrations are copyright ©1976 by Miriam Patchen: "Imagine seeing you here" (on dust jacket), "In Perkko's Grotto," and "The one who comes to question himself"

ALL RIGHTS RESERVED

PRINTED IN THE UNITED STATES OF AMERICA

For Lissa

Contents

III. General Critical Analyses

List of Plates and Illustrations

Foreword

Because the words describing Kenneth Patchen as an ordinary man, an "extraordinary, ordinary man," startle people, the use of them has to be explained. They are truly fitting, appropriate. As a man he was ordinary yet most extraordinary in his sensitivity and creative talents.

No one could speak more plainly, live with less flair, or tell a more "corny" joke. Yet no one could, with one or two words, get at the heart of the matter more succinctly or with greater thoughtfulness if that were needed.

"Tell a more corny joke . . ." Yes, but also his straight-faced delivery usually fooled one. He enjoyed dead-panning an outrageously impossible statement. Invariably he caught even me who should have been prepared for this after so many years. That facet comes out quite clearly in his work. His drawing and painting-poems, his puns, his double twists and back flips with what at first glance appear to be straight statements are so much, by now, a recognized part of the Patchen character. That form of humor is clearly visible not only in the drawing and painting-poems, but in the writing almost from the beginning.

From the time of his early childhood Kenneth Patchen's advice and help were sought. His suggestions were invariably followed for it was known that his quiet, calm reasoning mind and manner looked into a problem fully and came out with a solution worthy of respect. A young person is very serious when faced with all the problems of the world compounded by the difficulties of living needs. Patchen was especially so because of his nightmarish years on the road and because his Miriam was unused to humor or laughter, was heavily concerned with all the ills of the world. But after a while the young man's innate, irrepressible humor began to become visible in all possible — and even impossible — ways.

So it was. Poor, ill, wracked with pain, he still had to create laughter. There were times when handling the visual material was nearly excruciating for him, yet he'd chuckle at "Grandfather Foof" or his *Chief-Son-Of-A-Gun*, "last surviving member of the Blackfeet Tribe" with feet painted blue and the notation "Boston Branch." Examples could go on endlessly. Some of his painted covers made us laugh. One I always said was a portrait of his mother-in-law, my mother. It was a happy, ludicrous-looking thing.

Although there were usually difficulties with the materials used for the painting, there was no difficulty with the creative flow. He never encountered that dead period writers dread. His production of work was interrupted only by medical blocks in his path. There was always material on the instantly ready tape in his head. It poured out as fast as he could physically handle it. The work of creation went on all the time, even when he was asleep. I'd hear him saying the words which would soon be on paper.

Kenneth Patchen was a poet; he was that all the time; he is that still. That is what is meant by "Poet." The poetry never stops working if it is real.

Miriam Patchen

Chronology

1911   Kenneth Patchen born, December 13, in Niles, Ohio, to Wayne and Eva McQuade Patchen, into a lower middle-class family of steel mill workers and coal miners. Taken to Edgehill Drive in Warren, Ohio, to live.

1923   Starts a diary and begins writing poetry.

1928   Spends the summer working in the steel mills.

1928-1929   Scholarship student at Alexander Meiklejohn's Experimental College at the University of Wisconsin.

1930   Attends Commonwealth College in Mena, Arkansas, for several months. This marks the end of his formal education.

1931-1933   Travels around the U.S. and Canada taking odd jobs and working as an itinerant farm laborer, eventually coming to rest at 228 West 13th Street in New York City.

1932   Publication of "Permanence," a sonnet, in *The New York Times*, April 10.

1934   Moves to 20 Bullfinch Street, Boston, Massachusetts, where he meets and is sponsored by Conrad Aiken and others. Meets Miriam Oikemus, a young student, at a party, and marries her on June 28, a marriage which is to last his entire life. Begins reviewing books for the *New Republic*. First major periodical appearance in *Poetry*.

1935   Lives in New York City and Rhinebeck, New York.

1936   First book, *Before the Brave,* is published by Random House, reviewed by over fifty publications.

Awarded Guggenheim fellowship. Travels west, living at 3 Placita Rafaela, Santa Fe, New Mexico, and in Phoenix, Arizona.

1937 Lives at 1414 North Las Palmas, Los Angeles, California. Suffers disabling back injury.

1938 Lives at 5526-½ Virginia Avenue and 427 South Figueroa Street, both in Los Angeles.

1939 *First Will and Testament* published. Spends time in Concord, Massachusetts, then moves to Norfolk Connecticut where he and Miriam become, respectively, the accounting and shipping departments of James Laughlin's New Directions.

1940-1941 Lives at 81 Bleecker Street, New York City. Writes *The Journal of Albion Moonlight*.

1941 After failing to find a publisher who will risk bringing it out, the Patchens publish *The Journal of Albion Moonlight* by subscription. It is printed by Peter Beilenson at the Walpole Printing Office in Mt. Vernon, New York, and "launched" at the Gotham Book Mart in New York City.

1942 *The Dark Kingdom,* the limited edition of which is the first of the "painted books," each carrying a different original work painted directly onto the cover by Patchen, is brought out. *The Teeth of the Lion* published in New Directions' "Poet of the Month" series. Lives at 265 Avenue A and 317 West 4th Street in New York City. *The City Wears a Slouch Hat,* a radio play, produced on Columbia Radio Workshop.

1943 Moves to 333 West 22nd Street, New York City. Harper publishes *Cloth of the Tempest.*

1944 Visits Concord, Massachusetts. Receives Ohioana Book Award for *Cloth of the Tempest.* Moves to 336 West 12th Street, New York City.

1945 *Memoirs of a Shy Pornographer* published.

1946 Spends the summer in Mt. Pleasant, New York, then returns to 336 West 12th Street. *An Astonished Eye Looks Out of the Air, Outlaw of the Lowest Planet, Panels For the Walls of Heaven, The Selected Poems* of Kenneth Patchen, *Sleepers Awake, They Keep Riding Down All the Time,* and *Pictures of Life and of Death* are published.

1947 Moves to a house in Old Lyme, Connecticut, where he and Miriam remain for five years.

1948 *See You in the Morning, To Say If You Love Someone,* and *CCLXXIV Poems* published.

1949 Publication of *Red Wine and Yellow Hair.*

1950 First major operation on spine. Many benefit readings and concerts to raise money, through a fund headed by T. S. Eliot, Thornton Wilder, W. H. Auden, and Archibald MacLeish, and supported by E. E. Cummings, Marianne Moore, William Carlos Williams, Edith Sitwell and others. The surgery is unsuccessful.

1951 Moves to west coast for health reasons.

1952 Moves into 377 Green Street, San Francisco. *Orchards, Thrones, and Caravans* published.

1953 *Fables and Other Little Tales* published.

1954 Receives Shelley Memorial Award. The City Lights Bookshop publishes *Poems of Humor and Protest* in their "Pocket Poets" series. *The Famous Boating Party* is published.

1955 *Glory Never Guesses,* a silkscreen portfolio of picture-poems, is brought out.

1956 Lives at 852 Bryant Street, Palo Alto, California. Spends much time at the Palo Alto Clinic, finally undergoing a spinal fusion operation, which gives him some relief from pain for the first time in almost twenty years. The Patchens buy a house at 2340 Sierra Court, Palo Alto, in March, their final home. *Surprise for the Bagpipe Player,* another silkscreen portfolio, is produced.

1957 Begins the poetry-and-jazz movement, reading with jazz groups up and down the West Coast until 1959. *Hurrah for Anything, Kenneth Patchen Reads With the Chamber Jazz Sextet* (recording), *When We Were Here Together,* and *The Selected Poems, Enlarged Edition* all appear.

1958 *Poemscapes* is published. *The Journal of Albion Moonlight* (recording) is brought out.

1959 A "surgical mishap" destroys the benefits of the 1956 operation, leaving Patchen in great pain, and rendering him almost constantly bedridden for the rest of his life. *Don't Look Now,* his only full-length play, produced by the Troupe Theatre in Palo Alto. *Kenneth Patchen Reads His Selected Poems* (recording), and *Kenneth Patchen Reads With Jazz in Canada* (recording) brought out.

1960 *Because It Is* and *The Love Poems* are published. Also *The Moment,* a bound edition of *Glory Never Guesses* and *Surprise for the Bagpipe Player.*

1961 *Kenneth Patchen Reads His Love Poems* (recording) is produced.

1966 *Hallelujah Anyway* and *Doubleheader* published.

1967 Receives $10,000 award from the National Foundation on the Arts and Humanities for "life-long contribution to American letters."

1968 *The Collected Poems of Kenneth Patchen, But Even So,* and *Love and War Poems* are published.

1970 *Aflame and Afun of Walking Faces* and *There's Love All Day* published.

1971 Publication of *Wonderings.*

1972 Dies January 8. *In Quest of Candlelighters* appears. *Patchen's Funny Fables* (recording) brought out posthumously by Miriam Patchen. Memorial readings in San Francisco and New York.

Everything That Lives

Kenneth Patchen died in 1972, the victim of a crippling spinal ailment which had raged almost unabated through his body for over thirty years and of a heart scarred and broken by the moral indifference of the world about him. In death, his literary legacy belies his own fate.

Patchen was the son and grandson of coal miners and mill workers who spent their lives pitched on the edge of industrial darkness and desolation. His voice was torn from the very fiber of the earth, and raised into steeltown eloquence by intense emotions of both love and hatred striving passionately to halt the sorrow and depravity of socialized man while saving and enhancing the music of the soul.

Between the publication of his first book, *Before the Brave*, in 1936, and the year of his death, he wrote over forty books of poetry, prose, and drama. In addition, he produced hundreds of individually hand-painted books, and innumerable silkscreen prints, original paintings, papier-mâché animal sculptures, and drawings. He also pioneered the poetry-and-jazz movement, reading his words with noted musicians around the country, and making several recordings in that genre.

Each of Patchen's works is marked by a combination of horror and wonder. Aside from his personal demon of disease, he incessantly combatted the larger monsters of war and inhumanity. His prose work, *The Journal of Albion Moonlight*, perhaps his masterpiece, is his strongest and most overt statement on these evils. Written in 1940, but as relevant to our time as to World War Two, it represents one of the central concerns of Patchen's career. The war never left him, and each successive cataclysm of

hate, each new outburst of economically-motivated murder con-
firmed in him a sense of outrage and of mission.

If *Albion Moonlight, Sleepers Awake,* and many of his
poetic works were intended to "stop the war," other of his efforts
were designed to open a pathway into a new world, a world where
the angels and green deer of *Memoirs of a Shy Pornographer* were
visible to all, where faith and love built lives and saved
civilizations. This is the world of the *Fables*, the love verses, and
above all, the picture-poems. It is inhabited by unheard-of and
legendary creatures, by people with odd and wonderful vocations,
and by a nature which is beneficent and always within reach, a
reflection of the love embodied by its inhabitants.

It is away from the "dark kingdon" and toward this country of wonder where the movement in Patchen's work occurs. His
intention was to create a sanctuary in his books where the war
would not exist and where a new world could be seen and felt. The
countless lives which have been entranced, delighted, amazed,
and transformed by their contact with that world, and who have
emerged with a greater sense of the beauty and of the painful
fragility of life, are the legacy of Kenneth Patchen.

In the title poem of *Red Wine and Yellow Hair,* Patchen
wrote these lines, which might serve as an epigraph to his collected
works:

> Come cry come in wrath of love and be not comforted
> Until the grave that is this world is torn asunder
> For human the lock and human the key
> O everything that lives is holy!

This is the first critical book on Patchen to be published,
though other scholarly and critical works will doubtless follow.
With the publication of his plays *Don't Look Now* and *The City
Wears a Slouch Hat* (Capra Press, 1977) the corpus of his work is
now available in print, and interest in him should increase. My intention here has been to collect as many of the significant essays
on Patchen as possible, and to provide material for further
inquiry by interested readers and scholars.

In terms of the latter aim, I have provided a general
chronology of Patchen's life and work and a selective bibliography
and resource guide. The chronology is an effort both to correct

past inaccuracies relating to Patchen's life and put the writing in a biographical framework. The bibliography lists both primary and secondary works, enumerating all books and recordings by Patchen, major collections of his manuscripts and correspondence, and selected works about him grouped by subject.

The essays include most of the important writing of any length which has been done on Patchen from 1936 to 1977, some in print here for the first time. I have divided the collection into three general parts: Reviews and Explication, Biographical and Personal, and General Critical Analyses. Also included are a number of photographs and reproductions of several of Patchen's picture-poems. Miriam Patchen, the author's widow, to whom each of his books was dedicated, has written the foreword.

The arrangement of the collection should speak for itself, and the essays should need no intermediary; I will thus forebear from an extensive discussion of the contents and permit each individual work to assert its position independent of my introduction. My own critical perspective on Patchen should be adequately revealed by my essay on *The Journal of Albion Moonlight* in the final section of the book.

* * * *

This project has had a number of friends, and I would like to acknowledge their part in it.

The fact that this book is at this moment in your hands is a result of the belief and interest in Kenneth Patchen's work by the staff of AMS Press.

I have benefited from the wisdom and perspective of Professor Leon Howard, without whose guidance my essay within this book and the book itself would be less than they are.

Also to be thanked are Professors Hamlin Hill, Robert Fleming, Lynn Bloom and Morris Eaves, who have created a professional atmosphere conducive to the success of my efforts. Mrs. Fern McLean has greatly helped the passage of this book from idea to object by her continued kindness.

Without the friendship and assistance Miriam Patchen has shown me from the moment we met one another, neither this book, nor any other work of mine, including my current writing of the critical biography of Kenneth Patchen, would ever have been possible, and I despair of ever being able to fully repay her.

The path of this book has been smoothed by many people I have never met in person. New Directions Publishing Corporation has been of enormous help, specifically in the persons of Mrs. Else Albrecht-Carrie, Ms. Griselda Ohannessian, and Mr. James Laughlin. I am equally grateful to all those who granted permission for the printing or reprinting of work in the collection.

Tessie Segal, Robert and June Fischer, Jerome and Helen Sharlach, and Donald and Etta Van Greenby have shown me great love during the year of work this book required. Lissa Fischer and M.C. have each given me, in their own ways, greater gifts than I believed existed. I thank you.

And I thank Kenneth Patchen, for his heart, and his anger, and his hope.

Richard G. Morgan

Williamstown, West Virginia
April, 1977

Acknowledgments

Quotations from the works of Kenneth Patchen:

Collected Poems. Copyright 1963, 1942, 1945, 1946, 1952, 1968 by Kenneth Patchen. Copyright 1939, 1942, 1949, 1954, 1957, 1967 by New Directions Publishing Corporation.

Hurrah for Anything (Doubleheader) Copyright 1958, 1957, 1946 by Kenneth Patchen.

Reprinted by permission of New Directions Publishing Corporation, (All Rights Reserved.)

Picture-Poems:

Hallelujah Anyway. Copyright 1966 by Kenneth Patchen.

But Even So. Copyright 1968 by Kenneth Patchen.

Reprinted by permission of New Directions Publishing Corporation. (All Rights Reserved.)

William Carlos Williams, "A Counsel of Madness," from *Fantasy*, X, 26 (1942). All Rights Reserved. Reprinted by permission of New Directions Publishing Corporation, agents for the estate of William Carlos Williams.

Babette Deutsch, "A Poet of the Steel Works," first appeared in the *New York Herald Tribune, Books,* March 15, 1936. Copyright 1936 by *New York Herald Tribune.* Reprinted by permission of Babette Deutsch.

Frajam Taylor, "Puck in the Gardens of the Sun," first appeared in *Poetry Magazine,* August 1947. Copyright 1947 by the Modern Poetry Association. Reprinted by permission of the Modern Poetry Association.

James T. Hall, "Patchen's Angry Shoes," first appeared in *Poetry Magazine* in November 1949. Copyright 1949 by the Modern Poetry Association. Reprinted by permission of the Modern Poetry Association.

Kenneth Rexroth, "Kenneth Patchen, Naturalist of the Public Nightmare," from *Bird in the Bush*. Copyright 1959 by Kenneth Rexroth. Reprinted by permission of New Directions Publishing Corporation.

John Ciardi, "Kenneth Patchen: Poetry, and Poetry with Jazz," first appeared in *Saturday Review*, XLIII (May 14, 1960). Copyright 1960 by *Saturday Review*. Reprinted by permission of John Ciardi and *Saturday Review*.

Henry Miller, "Patchen, Man of Anger and Light," first appeared in 1946. From *Stand Still Like the Hummingbird*. Copyright 1962 by Henry Miller. Reprinted by permission of New Directions Publishing Corporation.

Holly Beye and William McCleery, "The Most Mysterious People in the Village," first appeared in *P.M.* in 1946. The Library of Congress has discovered no evidence of copyright in force.

Alan Neil, "Alan Neil's Account of the (recording) session," from Folkways Record FL 9718. Copyright 1959 by Folkways Records. Reprinted by permission of Folkways Records.

Jonathan Williams, "Out of Sight, Out of Conscience," first appeared in *Contact*, II (February 1961). Copyright 1961 by *Contact*. Reprinted by permission of Jonathan Williams.

Anonymous, "An Interview With Kenneth Patchen," first aired on KUOW Radio in Seattle, Washington, in 1959. First appearance in print. Reprinted by permission of KUOW Radio.

Gene Detro, "Patchen Interviewed," first appeared in *Outsider* 4/5 (1968). Copyright 1968 by *Outsider*. Reprinted with additional material in 1976 by Capra Press. Copyright 1976 by Capra Press, from *Patchen: The Last Interview*, 40, Capra Chapbook Series. Reprinted by permission of Capra Press.

Richard Bowman, "Notes from a Friend," first appeared in *Kenneth Patchen: Painter of Poems*, in 1969. Copyright 1969 by the Corcoran Gallery of Art. Reprinted by permission of the Corcoran Gallery of Art.

Richard Hack, "Memorial Reading for Kenneth Patchen," first appeared in *Chicago Review*, XXIV, 2 (1972). Copyright 1972 by *Chicago Review*. Reprinted by permission of Chicago Review.

James Schevill, "Kenneth Patchen: The Search for Wonder and Joy," first appeared in *American Poetry Review*, V, 1 (January-February 1976). Copyright 1976 by *American Poetry Review*. Reprinted by permission of James Schevill.

Amos N. Wilder, "Revolutionary and Proletarian Poetry: Kenneth Patchen," first appeared in *Spiritual Aspects of the New Poetry*, in 1940. Copyright by Harper & Row, Publishers, Inc. Reprinted by permission of Harper & Row.

Tom Ložar, "Before the Brave: Portrait of Man as a Young Artist," was originally presented before a Special Session on Kenneth Patchen at the 1976 meeting of the Modern Language Association of America. It appears in print here for the first time. Printed by permission of Tom Lozar.

Harvey Breit, "Kenneth Patchen and the Critical Blind Alley," first appeared in *Fantasy*, VI, 4 (1940). A search by the Library of Congress has disclosed no evidence of copyright registration.

David Gascoyne, "Introducing Kenneth Patchen," first appeared as the introduction to *Outlaw of the Lowest Planet* in 1946. Copyright 1946 by Grey Walls Press (U.K.). Reprinted by permission of David Gascoyne.

Richard Morgan, "*The Journal of Albion Moonlight:* Its Form and Meaning," first appeared as a chapbook in 1976, published by Black Cat Books. Copyright 1976 by Richard Morgan. Reprinted by permission of Black Cat Books.

Charles Glicksberg, "The World of Kenneth Patchen," first appeared in *Arizona Quarterly*, VII (Autumn 1951). Copyright 1951 by *Arizona Quarterly*. Reprinted by permission of Charles Glicksberg and *Arizona Quarterly*.

Peter Yates, "Patchen's Poetry and Jazz," first appeared as "Poetry and Jazz: III," in *Arts and Architecture*, May 1958. Copyright 1958 by *Arts and Architecture*. Reprinted by permission of Mrs. Peter Yates.

Carolyn See, "The Jazz Musician as Patchen's Hero," first appeared in *Arizona Quarterly*, XVII (Summer 1961). Copyright 1961 by *Arizona Quarterly*, Reprinted by permission of Carolyn See and *Arizona Quarterly*.

Ray Nelson, "The Moral Prose of Kenneth Patchen," first appeared in *Steppenwolf*, III (Summer 1969). Copyright 1969 by *Steppenwolf*. Reprinted by permission of Ray Nelson and *Steppenwolf*.

I

Reviews
and
Explication

William Carlos Williams

A Counsel of Madness

A REVIEW OF *THE JOURNAL OF ALBION MOONLIGHT*

White moonlight, penetrating, distorting the mind is a symbol of madness. It denotes, negatively, also an absence of the sun. The sun does not touch the pages of Kenneth Patchen's *The Journal of Albion Moonlight*. So that what virtues are to be found here may be taken for madness. Could we interpret them we should know the cure. That is, I think, Patchen's intention, so, in reverse, to make the cure not only apparent but, by the horror of his picture, imperative.

By such exhibitions the paterfamilias of fifty years or more ago, showing the horrible effects of syphilis, would seek to drive his sons to chastity. The age is syphilitic, cancerous, even leprous in Patchen's opinion — show it then, in itself and in its effects, upon the body and upon the mind — that we may know ourselves and be made whole thereby. And of it all, says Patchen, perhaps the only really normal and good thing remaining is the sexual kiss of two bodies, full fledged.

In criticising such a book one should pay Patchen at least the compliment of being as low down as he is himself — and as outspoken. If he has attempted drastic strictures upon his age may we not demand of him by what authority he does so? Is his picture a true one? And does he prove himself sufficiently powerful as a writer to portray it? To scream violently against vile practices does not dispose of them. Furthermore, though this book is full of violent statement, is it violent, really? Violence overthrows. Does this succeed in overthrowing anything at all or is it not, lacking full ability, no more than a sign of the author's and our own

3

defeat, hiding itself in noise? Shall not one say, finally, that this book is erotically and pornographically sound; if it lives at all it will be for no more than its lewdity that it does so? That is the danger.

Everything depends upon the writing, a dangerous genre: either to the minds of those who read it it will work toward the light or burrow in the mud. It can't be half good. It can't do both.

For myself I ask for no authorities, so likely to be gutted of any worth in our day, if not positively rotten. There is no authority evidenced in this but the man himself. If there are others like him, if we are not all somewhat as he is, provided he write truthfully and out of a gifted mind, he has a right to speak and needs no other authority. But if he belies himself and us, overpreens himself and makes use of devices that are shopworn and cheap, that's a different matter. We owe Patchen nothing as Patchen. But if he's a man and we feel a great fellowship with him, a deep sympathy, then we can tolerate his vagaries, his stupidities even, even his screaming. But if he shows that he en- joys that more than the cure. That would be bad.

For what we're after is a cure. That at its best is what the book's about. A man terribly bitten and seeking a cure, a cure for the bedeviled spirit of his day. Nor are we interested in a Punch and Judy morality with a lily-white soul wrapped in a sheet — or a fog, it doesn't matter which. We are ready and willing to accept a low down human spirit which if it didn't have a hip-joint we'd never be in a position to speak of it at all. We know and can feel for that raving reality, bedeviled by erotic dreams, which often enough is ourselves. This book is from the gutter.

The story is that oldest of all themes, the journey, evangelical in purpose, that is to say, with a purpose to save the world from impending doom. A message must be got through to Roivas, read the name backward.

May 2. It starts under a sky of stone, from the region about New York City, in a countryside where an angel lies in a "little thicket." "It couldn't have hurt much when they slit its throat."

There is a simple statement of faith at the beginning:

> *He was the Word that spake it;*
> *He took the bread and brake it;*
> *And what the Word did make it,*
> *I do believe and take it.*

He must get through a message to the people such as they are who have lost hope in the world.

It gets up to August 27. And that is all. It ends. It ends because it has never succeeded in starting. There is — after a hundred thousand words — nothing to be said.

Albion's heart is broken by the war in Europe. Surely his message has to do with that. That is the message. But it is not advice to go in or to stay out. It is order lost. For the war has been caused by humanity, thwarted not by lack of order but by too much. Murder is the desperate theme. Murder out of despair.

The chief defect of such a book lies in the very plan and method of it, one is locked up with the other.

Patchen slams his vivid impressions on the page and lets them go at that. He is investigating the deformities of truth which he perceives in and about him. Not idly. He is seeking, the book is seeking, if I am correct, a new order among the debris of a mind conditioned by old and persistent wreckage. Patchen is seeking a way through among the debris and, as he goes, seeks also to reveal his meaning by truthful statement — under conditions of white moonlight. From that to reorder the universe.

There can be no checks, taboos or revisions permitted to such a plan since the only chance it has of laying down positive values comes from first impressions, and they distorted. What else, in the writing, could a man do or say other than to put down the moonlight delineaments of the landscape he is witnessing? Could any traveller through a jungle do more? Or less? All that we demand of him is that he do not see and put down what is not there. Also that he do not fail to put down what is there. It is, in fact, one mind, his tortured own, that Patchen is travelling through and attempting to reveal to us by its observed attributes. In treating of that there can be no deleting, no pruning no matter how the initiative may wander.

Where does the journey take place did I say? In America? Why not? One place is like another. In the mind? How? What is the mind? You can't separate it from the body or the land any more than you can separate America from the world. We are all one, we are all guilty. No accusation is here permitted — Moonlight himself must, is forced to, take part in the murder no matter how he would escape it. All he can do is take part *willingly*.

The journey does traverse the mind. Therefore it gets to Chicago, Arizona, Galen. The dream which is more solid than the earth. And out of the cauldron of thought the earth itself is reborn and we walk on it into the small towns of Texas and Missouri.

There can be no graph except the map you pick up at a gas station — but as we hold it the graph becomes vertical also and takes us up into the tips of the mountains of Galen. People expand and shrink to the varying proportions of those in *Alice in Wonderland,* and every day but — desperately. We are at war, we are insane.

Reality? Do we think that America is not reality or that human beings are excluded from it? Death Valley appears. It is the mind itself, where Jackeen lies murdered. By Moonlight himself. It rots and stinks and is arrested and hung up — while one foot drops off on the gallows and a geranium sprouts from its left ear with roots in the heart of that corpse. Who is doing the hanging? It is again — Moonlight. Moonlight. He himself must be identified with the foulest crimes he imagines. He must. He cannot separate himself and be alone. Such is his journey.

Naturally everything observed will not be significant or new and it is the business of the writer to be careful of that. Yet, I shouldn't wish to advise him — at the edge of the thicket may lie a discovery, no matter how small it will seem at the time, which holds that quality of coming out of foulness faultlessly clean, a new order of thought shucking off the old which may justify a thousand redundancies. That's the chance taken by such a method. Tortured and perverted as we may think it, the book represents the same outlook over the world as did the Vita Nuova — reversed.

It is a book come of desperation, the desperation of the thwarted and the young. Write and discover. Go, move, waggle your legs in more terrible jungles than any primitive continent could ever afford, the present day shambles of the Mind. Tortured as you may be, seek cleanliness, seek vigor, unafraid. Seek love! Such is the New Life dimly perceivable through the mediaeval horrors of Patchen's hell. This is the order he is seeking.

Oh, we had a call to "order" some years ago, dead now or nearly dead now, fortunately. Its warts, like the hair of corpses, continue a separate existence, in the academies, and breed others of the sort from year to year; but the body has hygienically rotted away. This is not what Patchen is thinking of. Such an "order" consisted mainly in amputating all the extravagances, all the unimaginable off-shoots of the living thing to make it conform to — those very restrictions from which, at its best, the present day is an almost miraculous escape. What they attempted was like that Nazi "order" now familiar in Europe which already in order to maintain itself has found it necessary to commit three hundred and fifty thousand murders among the civilian population.

Whether or not this book is a good one (let's not talk prematurely of genius) I believe it to be a right one, a well directed one and a hopeful one. It is the sort of book that must be attempted from time to time, a book to violate all the taboos, a racial necessity as it is a paradisiacal one, a purge in the best sense — suggesting a return to health and to the craft itself after the little word-and-thought pansies have got through their nibbling. I don't say it's the best *sort* of book, as the world goes, but it is the sort of book some one should write in every generation, some one writer — let himself go! and drop it for at least twenty years thereafter.

Patchen lets himself go. Such a book will rest heavily on the character, ability and learning of the man who writes it. If it is a failure, not clear or powerful enough to deserve the concept of it I am suggesting, that is his hard luck. But the book should be written, a book that had better perhaps have been postponed to a maturer period of the man's career — but which had after all to be written *now*.

That's precisely it. Even though it acknowledge itself to be a foregone failure — the book must still have been made as it is, the work of a young man, a new man — finding himself unprepared, though vocal, in the world. He voices the world of the young — as he finds it, screaming against what we, older, have given him. This precisely is the book's prime validity.

Though Patchen is still young, still not ready, shall he be silent for that? That is the significance and reason for all his passion, that he is young, the seriousness and poignancy of it. And it does, whatever its failings, find a crack in the armament of the killing suppression which is driving the world to the only relief

it knows, murder! today. It is itself evidence, as a thing in itself, of
our perversity and failure.

We destroy because we cannot escape. Because we are confined. There is no opening for us from the desperate womb of our
times. We cannot get out. Everywhere we turn, to Christ himself,
we are met by a wall of "order," a murderous cross fire which is offered us by "learning" and the frightened conformists of our
world.

For once a writer insists on the maddening facts of our
plight in plain terms; we grow afraid, we dare not pretend that we
know or can know anything, straight out, in our own right. We
have to be "correctly" educated first. But here and there, confronting Christ with Hitler—you won't believe it can be done —
there are passages in this book where the mind threatens to open
and a vivid reality of the spirit to burst forth and bloom in
terrifying destructfulness—the destroying of all that we think we
know in our time. It threatens to break out through the writing into a fact of the spirit even though it may not often be quite powerful enough to do so. I cannot specify these knots of understanding,
of candor that—are the book's high places. The feeling that is experienced at those best moments is of an impending purity that
might be. This is the order that I speak of.

What might it not do to the world if ONCE a universal
truth, order, of the sort glimpsed here could be made free. It is
as if it were too bright and that that is the reason no one has yet
glimpsed it. Too bright! Van Gogh went mad staring at the sun
and the stars.

I say all this in approbation—but writing is also a craft and
we have to look well at that in this book. Florid and uncontrolled
as Patchen's imagination may be, his images foetid, the passions
of his Honeys and Claras funnelled into the socket of sex, compressed as a bomb to explode in colored lights—the writing must
not be florid in any loose sense. And I should say, tangential as the
thought may be, the writing is, in general well muscled, the word
often brilliantly clear.

Many devices are used at times successfully, but not always
so. There are lapses, disheartening lapses, and though I have said
that in this sort of writing a man cannot stop for corrections yet, as
readers, we have a right to object.

However we face it, one must still hold to the writing. Writing is not an instrument. The best writing happens on the page. It is the proof, with that stamp of the man upon it signifying it alive to live on independent of him, a thing in itself. The Word. We are responsible finally to that.

The book's defects are glaring, conjoined, as I have said, inextricably with its virtues. It must have been written haphazard to unearth the good. Whether or not there is enough good to carry off the method will remain the question. Many will doubt it, find the book to be no more a journey than that taken by a dog trying to catch his own tail.

One of the chief weaknesses of the book is its total lack of humor. Certainly the style is green and needs seasoning—but having said that, one has begged the entire question—nevertheless it must be said. The book would benefit by revisions and rather severe cutting. Sometimes the effect is fat and soft, even spotted, when Patchen confuses his subject matter with the workmanship to bad effect. These things make it at times difficult for the reader to plow ahead. But if, in spite of that, he is willing to face and cross these sapless spaces he will come to patches of really astonishing observation, profound feeling and a strongly imaginative and just use of the word which, to me, give the book a highly distinctive character.

Babette Deutsch

A Poet of the Steel Works

A REVIEW OF *BEFORE THE BRAVE*

Like much current poetry, Kenneth Patchen's work offers a challenge and a summons in terms that neither the challenged nor the summoned will find readily intelligible. Unqualified hatred of the existing order (granting that chaos is also a form of order) is companioned by unqualified faith that communism will establish permanently the values that English-speaking poets have cherished from the days of Langland to our own. But Patchen expresses this hatred and this faith in a quasi-private diction that is not intrinsic to his material, but derives in part from the symbolists and in part from the younger British school. It is seldom that he allows himself as direct a statement as his letter to a politician in Kansas City, which concludes:

> I'm not too starved to want food
> not too homeless to want a home not
>   too dumb
> to answer questions come to think of it
>   it'll take a hell
> of a lot more than you've got to stop
>   what's
> going on deep inside us when it starts
>   out
> when it starts wheels going worlds
>   growing
> and any man can live on earth when
>   we're through with it.

This cleavage between the simplicity of the poet's substance and the difficulty of his diction is less comprehensible in the case of Patchen than in that of men like Auden and Spender, both of whom have obviously influenced his technique. Aware of the obstacles to communication, they are often content to address their intimates only, and these are chiefly members of their own class, which they despise—so that a sardonic note of self-scorn is an almost inevitable element of their verse. But Patchen is not a middle-class British intellectual. He is a worker, the son of a worker. He knows the steel mills, the road gangs, the farms, as well as college football and Greek civilization (he spent a year in the Experimental College at Wisconsin). He knows America as only a migratory worker can know it, and at least one poem, Joe Hill Listens to the Praying, throbs with that knowledge. But too often he ignores the vocabulary and the imagery which are his birthright, and which would infuse freshness and vigor into his lines, for the images of warfare and disease that Auden has stereotyped, and not seldom he relies upon such radiant abstractions as Spender delights in. When he speaks of "Stalking gangs who fire at sight" or of "Sightless old men in cathedrals of decay," he seems as much bound by literary tradition, albeit it is one recently established, as if he dealt in metaphors "obsolete like poet's lark."

It is natural that the performance of a young poet—and Kenneth Patchen is only twenty-five—should show indebtedness to his predecessors. Patchen's verse reveals a study not only of Auden's compressed, alliterative, punning verse, and Spender's lyric line, but of Crane's kaleidoscopic symbolism, and Kenneth Fearing's jazzed ironic rhapsodies. Like these men, he is obsessed by horror of the contemporary scene—by the paradox of famine in the midst of plenty, and technological progress accompanied by utter neglect of all humane values, by the irretrievable waste, the ruthless crippling of body and spirit that our civilization compels, by the memory and the threat of war. Sharing their pain and their impatience, it is not strange that he should echo their cry; that, with Spender, he should claim "This end for all: long love and houseless honor"; that, with Auden, he should say to the tender-minded cowards in a poem only superficially ambiguous: "We leave you"; that, with Fearing, he should write cinematographic fantasias on contemporary themes, such as Leaflet (One) and Class of 1934; that, mimicking Crane, and scorning his way out, he should write his Farewell to the Bluewoman.

It is plain, however, that if Patchen is eager to employ the technique of these poets he is yet able occasionally to stand apart from them. In a Letter to the Liberals he mocks Spender's attitude in Spender's own words, this:

> Submit no more. They said the wind
> would polish names
> And thunder clear the quiet streets:
> I saw them smile
> I knew they lied
> Spies aware of danger grasp for guns
> Not straws: be noble and be true
> Your whiter cloaks provide a better
> sight on you.

In an Audenesque poem beginning: "Know government of gayety and mountain-love," he has a line that Auden never could have written:

> Be sure we know
> We miss a lot in rented-room and
> rented-life.

It is precisely because he is alert to technical innovation as well as agonizedly aware of the harsh immediate moment that one wishes he would free himself more completely from his teachers, and speak out of his own intimate experience with his own authentic voice. Exquisitely sensitive, passionately indignant, capable of true lyricism, Patchen may become one of the notable revolutionary poets in America. But he needs greater self-reliance and sterner self-criticism. These lines, though they too are reminiscent in their imagery, are eloquent of his hope and his power:

> Our task is not to clean the padded
> cells
> Or heal volcanic pity. We shall live
> In no cathedral: our country is the
> careless star in man.

Frajam Taylor

Puck in the Gardens of the Sun

A REVIEW OF *SELECTED POEMS*

A distinctively creative writer who would profit by the cultivation of the critical faculty, Kenneth Patchen requires editing in order to be fully appreciated and is therefore indebted to the editors and publishers of his *Selected Poems* for a chance to reach a wider public than any of his previous books of poetry may have accorded him.

For while he is a copious poet, Patchen is not always a good one. Eager and energetic, he is altogether too prone to abandon himself to his own abundance without regard to the quality of his forthgiving, so that too often, in earlier publications, such fine poems as *We Must be Slow* were buried under a mass of mediocrity which numbed the reader's sensibility and obscured the poet's undeniable ability.

Fortunately, that does not happen in this latest volume of his verse, in which—to borrow some phrases from Merezhkovski—something of the "measure of Apollo" has been added to the "super-exuberance of Dionysus" to produce a group of poems which explains, even if it does not entirely vindicate, the unidentified epigraph on its jacket's flyleaf to the effect that Patchen is the "most compelling force in American poetry since Whitman."

Whether Patchen reaches the stature of Whitman or not, there is no denying the compelling power of his poetry at its best—as it is here—nor the tremendous vitality of the personality from whence it flows. Moreover the coupling of his name with Whitman's is in a way inevitable, since the compulsion which drove Whitman to utter his "barbaric yawp" in non-metrical verse is the same as that which urges Patchen to the audacities of his own free technique; and what transpires from the poetry of both is the sense of a "fullness of being" too ebullient to be confined to the sophisticated and severely disciplined modalism of regular versification.

But while Whitman in spite of his "barbarism" achieved a kind of Olympian dignity, there is about Patchen a faint aura of darkness which betrays him as a sort of minor chthonian deity, at the same time a little above and a little below the merely human. Perhaps it was an awareness of this demonic aspect of his nature which caused him to adorn an earlier and self-designed volume of poems with sketches of a faun. At any rate, the poet who could write such lines as

> For whose adornment the mouths
> Of roses open in languorous speech;
> And from whose grace the trees of heaven
> Learn their white standing
>
> (I must go now to cash in the milk bottles
> So I can phone somebody
> For enough money for our supper.)

has an element of puckishness in his nature which is both delightful and a little exacerbating.

Sometimes he is more exacerbating than delightful as when, for instance, he writes the word "Wait" fourteen times in succession, appends the word "Now" and has the temerity to label his exercise in leg-pulling *The Murder of Two Men by a Young Kid Wearing Lemon-Colored Gloves*—a "poem" happily not included in these selected ones, but sharply reminiscent of another Puck who exclaimed with faint contempt at the foolishness of mortals!

This is not the sort of vagary one finds in Whitman who plucked every leaf of grass with equal seriousness; but then Whitman lived in an age when solemnities of utterance were more acceptable than they are today after two world wars and the incursions of the psycho-analysts into the sources of human activity. And much of the palpable cynicism which colors some of the finest of Patchen's poems, such as *I Don't Want to Startle You, Let Us Have Madness, We Leave You Pleasure, The Rites of Darkness,* and others, is attributable to the poet's disillusion with the dream which fortified Whitman and his contemporaries and

gave them that confidence in the future which is so lacking in our
own. In Patchen this disillusion takes many forms, expressing itself now in the violence of revolt and execration against the
established order of society, now in satire, and now in partial
escape through fantasy and the creation of a mythology free from
the exigencies of daily life in a world gone awry.

If, speaking for the men of his generation, Patchen could
write:

> we looked to find
> An open door, an utter deed of love,
> Transforming day's evil darkness;
> but
> We found extended hell and fog
> Upon the earth, and within the head
> A rotting bog of lean huge graves

it is not to be wondered at that he should be so much concerned
with darkness and impending doom. But this pre-occupation with
darkness and its complements, death, sleep and the subconscious,
which plays so large a part in his poetry, giving it at times a weird,
dreamlike and often nightmarish quality—as in the already mentioned *I Don't Want to Startle You*—while it is the natural consequence of the chthonian or demonic element in his character, is
also only the converse of a profound interest in life, light, and the
beautiful which illuminates and redeems all his dark brooding on
evil and ugliness—much as the therapeutic intentions of the
psycho-analyst justify his invasions of the forbidden areas in
private lives.

And it is this other side of Patchen—this Ariel as opposed
to the Caliban facet of his many-sided personality—which is
responsible for that love and faith in humanity which persists in
spite of all his knowledge of man's devious manueuverings and
which impels him to assert with joyous confidence that

> The hour of love and dignity and peace
> Is surely not dead.
> With more splendor than these sombre lives
> The gates within us
> Open on the brillant gardens of the sun.

Apropos of this continuing and unquenchable love for
mankind, it is not without significance that Patchen's poems in

celebration of man's love for woman such as *Fall of the Evening Star,* and the lines *Written after Reading an Item in the Paper etc.,* are among his best pieces. It was undoubtedly the joy and consolation he found in his own love for a woman that gave him that insight into the redemptive power of love upon which he bases his hope for the future of man and which gives to his own life and work that peculiar zest and abundance which is so characteristic. Actually he admits as much himself in *The Character of Love Seen as a Search for the Lost* when he writes:

> You, the woman; I, the man; this, the world;
> And each is the work of all.
>
> Then, not that man do more, or stop pity; but that he be
> Wider in living; that all his cities fly a clean flag. . .
> We have been alone too long, love; it is terribly late
> For the pierced feet on the water and we must not die now.

Incidentally, the attitude implicit in these last four lines is purely Dionysian: having through love experienced the breaking of the bonds of individuation by which man is separated from his fellows, Patchen utters the great "Yea" to Life which follows upon a vision of the eternal and essential unity of all men. As he tells us in *What Is the Beautiful?*—

> Because the white man and the black man,
> The Englishman and the German,
> Are not real things.
> They are only pictures of things.
> Their shapes, like the shapes of the tree
> And the flower, have no lives in names or signs;
>
> They are their lives, and the real is in them.
> And what is real shall have life always.

Reviewing the best of Patchen's work as it is set forth in his *Selected Poems* the feeling comes upon one that perhaps after all he does sometimes attain the eminence of Whitman. Certainly this carefully edited volume is an effective riposte to Gregory and Zaturenska for the disdainful brush-off given the poet in their *History of American Poetry.*

James T. Hall

Patchen's Angry Shoes

A REVIEW OF *RED WINE AND YELLOW HAIR*

If poetry had continued in the direction a segment was taking when Kenneth Patchen published his first book, a review of this latest volume would doubtless credit it with the combination of the shrill and the colloquial, the indignant and the tender, that Patchen's readers have learned to expect. But neither poetry nor events followed the pattern, other possibilities are being explored, and—a *therefore* would not be justified—*Red Wine and Yellow Hair* is not merely what Patchen's readers have learned to expect.

The new ingredient is uncertainty—and uncertainty, though not what might have been anticipated, is far from the least hopeful thing that might have happened. The resulting poems are of two kinds: tentative, ironic scenes whose titles (*Week-end Bathers, A Pile of Rusty Beer Cans, The Orange Bears, Old Man*) suggest the genre; and a more significant group juxtaposing symbols of greater complexity than Patchen has hitherto handled. The best, centering on the theme of "Pain is life's only reality,/ Greater than faith, or hatred even," show a more selective search for words and images, a wider concern with rhythm, a lessened reliance on challenging statement of the acceptable theme, and an increased determination to make the poem establish its symbols. The plastic nightingales have flown and Sweeney speaks less stridently. A new inclusiveness produces a new fluidity:

> Blood on the ancient water
> and darkness falling on the world.
> Down the beach
> The Marsden kids are torturing a snail

17

With a jagged stick.
(O star-led Caravans. . ."Master, master, I fear
this huge and surly fish!")
Sing correlay and correlemus
For all ladies, kids, and captains
                                    who're soon lost in
These coils of wet, gray hair.

Passages in the title poem have a similar force and movement—

O none save the fiery hunter would stay to mourn the tiger.
Dotellers told in the black dice of their cities. And I lie here
Removed from all sorrow. A withered heart and a rusted
dagger
The Laird of Emmet, my powerful hands they squeeze at the
dust.
Is life the meat that swings the falcon down from his highs?
Yes, a poisoned bait in the trap of a vicious fancier.

Patchen has apparently reached the middle-of-the-journey stage where a poet moves from a developed technique for rendering a limited kind of reality to one that, avoiding many weaknesses of the old, has not yet fully controlled its new devices. There are lapses in the volume—the faith in capital letters, the frequent preference for the easy word, the insensitivity to the devaluation of the shocking phrase. (Kenneth Rexroth, who considers himself in general intellectual agreement with Patchen and who has gone through a comparable, though quite distinct, transition, has a more consistent command of his new tone.) But the best of these poems fuse levels of meaning which the earlier work rarely touched.

The reasons behing this development are implied in a stanza on a pair of shoes left over from "those lousy winters of the 'recession' ":

Well, my cheap-shoe time is gone—
(For the moment anyway)—the rent
Is paid (clear to the first of the month),
And I smoke tailor-mades on the lawn.
Many of the books I wanted then
—And records, prints, and magazines—
I have. The work of 'our finest men'—
And every day I'm more amazed

> At how quickly I could choose
> Between the lot — and this pair of angry shoes.

Patchen's shoes are scarcely angry at all now. *Portrait of the Artist as an Interior Decorator* has the old manner, but a minute area of destruction. *The New Being* phrases a familiar complaint, but seems weary of its own diagnosis. Even *Wouldn't You Be After a Jaunt of 964,000,000,000,000 Million Miles* and *How Jimsy O'Roon and Peter Stack, Coal Miners, Came to be Put in the Ferbettville (Pa.) Jail Early one Saturday Night* seem more forced than their predecessors. Patchen has moved on to greater complexities without seeming wholly aware of — or wholly pleased with — the passage.

Kenneth Rexroth

Kenneth Patchen: Naturalist of the Public Nightmare

A REVIEW OF *HURRAH FOR ANYTHING* AND *WHEN WE WERE HERE TOGETHER*

Kenneth Patchen has recently published two books, *Hurrah for Anything*[1] and *When We Were Here Together*.[2] They are two big strides forward in his development as a poet. For my taste, there have always been two fields in which his stuff never quite came off: first, a peculiar topsy-turvy bitter whimsey; second, the sentimental love lyric. The little poems, each illustrated with one of Patchen's uniquely comic drawings, in *Hurrah for Anything* are free verse limericks. Patchen has gone back to the world of Edward Lear and interpreted it in terms of the modern sensibility of the disengaged, the modern comic horrors of *le monde concentrationaire*. It is as if, not a slick *New Yorker* correspondent, but the Owl and the Pussycat were writing up Hiroshima. In *When We Were Here Together*, the giggly coyness that defaced so much of Patchen's love poetry has vanished. These are grave, serious, immeasurably touching poems. They compare very favorably with the love poems of Paul Eluard of Rafael Alberti. In other words, they are amongst the very few poems of their kind written by an American, which can compete confidently in the international arena of contemporary "comparative literature."

Patchen is the only widely published poet of my generation in the United States who has not abandoned the international idiom of twentieth-century verse. He is the only one we have, to take these two books as examples, to compare with Henri Michaux or Paul Eluard. Twenty-five years ago no one would have prophesied such a comeuppance for what we then thought, and I still think, was the only significant tendency in American literature. What happened to the Revolution of the Word? Why is Patchen still there? Why did everybody else "sell out" or sink, like Louis Zukofsky, Parker Tyler, Walter Lowenfels, into undeserved obscurity? Why did American poetry, a part of world literature in 1920, become a pale, provincial imitation of British verse in 1957? We are back, two generations behind Australia.

Man thrives where angels die of ecstasy and pigs die of disgust. The contemporary situation is like a long-standing, fatal disease. It is impossible to recall what life was like without it. We seem always to have had cancer of the heart.

The first twenty-five years of the century were the years of revolutionary hope. Immediately after the First War, this hope became almost universal among educated people. There was a time when most men expected that soon, very soon, life was going to change; a new, splendid creature was going to emerge from its ancient chrysalis of ignorance, brutality, and exploitation. Everything was going to be different. Even the commonest, most accepted routines of life would be glorified. Education, art, sex, science, invention, everything from clothing to chess would be liberated. All the soilure and distortion of ages of slavery would fall away. Every detail of life would be harmoniously, functionally related in a whole which would be the realization of those absolutes of the philosophers, the Beloved Community wedded to the Idea of Beauty.

We who were born in the early years of the century accepted that hope implicitly. It was impossible that any feeble hands could halt the whole tendency of the universe. This was not the Idea of Progress, of indefinite human perfectibility, now the whipping boy of reactionary publicists and theologians. The nineteenth century had believed that the world was going to go on becoming more and more middle class until the suburbs of London stretched from Pole to Pole. We believed that man's constant potential for a decent, simple, graceful life was bound to realize itself within a very few years, that the forces of wealth, barbarism, and superstition were too weak to resist much longer.

On August 29, 1927, Sacco and Vanzetti were executed with the connivance of the leading descendants of the New England libertarians. A cheap politician and a judge with the mind of a debauched turnkey were able to carry through this public murder in the face of a world of protest of unbelievable intensity, mass, and duration. When the sirens of all the factories in the iron ring around Paris howled in the early dawn, and the myriad torches of the demonstrators were hurled through the midnight air in Buenos Aires, the generation of revolutionary hope was over. The conscience of mankind went to school to learn methods of compromising itself. The Moscow trials, the Kuo Min Tang street executions, the betrayal of Spain, the Hitler-Stalin Pact, the extermination of whole nations, Hiroshima, Algiers—no protest has stopped the monster jaws from closing. As the years go on, fewer and fewer protests are heard. The spokesmen, the intellects of the world, have blackmailed themselves and are silent. The common man dreams of security. Every day life grows more insecure, and, outside America, more nasty, brutish, and short. The lights that went out over Europe were never relit. Now the darkness is absolute. In the blackness, well-fed, cultured, carefully shaven gentlemen sit before microphones at mahogany tables and push the planet inch by inch towards extinction. We have come to the generation of revolutionary hopelessness. Men throw themselves under the wheels of the monsters, Russia and America, out of despair, for identical reasons.

With almost no exceptions, the silentiaries of American literature pretend that such a state of affairs does not exist. In fact, most of them do not need to pretend. They have ceased to be able to tell good from evil. One of the few exceptions is Kenneth Patchen. His voice is the voice of a conscience which is forgotten. He speaks from the moral viewpoint of the new century, the century of assured hope, before the dawn of the world-in-concentration-camp. But he speaks of the world as it is. Imagine if suddenly the men of 1900—H. G. Wells, Bernard Shaw, Peter Kropotkin, Romain Rolland, Martin Nexo, Maxim Gorky, Jack London—had been caught up, unprepared and uncompromised, fifty years into the terrible future. Patchen speaks as they would have spoken, in terms of unqualified horror and rejection. He speaks as Emile Zola spoke once—"A moment in the conscience of

mankind." Critics have said of him, "After all, you can't be
Jeremiah all the time." Indeed? Why not? As far as we know, all
Jeremiah ever wrote was *The Book of Jeremiah* and the world of
his day was a Chautauqua picnic in comparison with this.

It is not true, historically, that the poet is the unac-
knowledged legislator of mankind. On the contrary, poets seem to
flourish under despotism. It is difficult to say if the artist and the
prophet ever really merge. It is hard to find a common ground for
Isaiah and Richard Lovelace. Artist and prophet seem per-
petually at war in Blake and D. H. Lawrence. But there comes a
point when the minimum integrity necessary to the bare functioning of the artist is destroyed by social evil unless he arise and
denounce it. There is a subtle difference between the paintings of
Boucher and the cover girls of American magazines. It is almost
an abstract difference, like the difference between the North and
South Poles — all the difference in the world. If the conscience
remains awake, there comes a time when the practice of literature
is intolerable dishonesty, the artist is overridden by the human
being and is drafted into the role of Jeremiah.

Men in prison become obsessive. The prison itself is an objective obsession. Trotsky was paranoid, he saw assassins behind
every bush. They were real assassins, as it turned out. On the
other hand, men in madhouses console themselves by pretending
they are kings in palaces. Patchen, very likely, is obsessed. Popin-
jay, on the other hand, refines his sensibilities with the accents of
Donne and Hopkins. Writing this, sitting at my typewriter,
looking out the window, I find it hard to comprehend why every
human being doesn't run screaming into the streets of all the cities
of the world this instant. How can they let it go on? Patchen
doesn't. If no one cried, "Woe, woe to the bloody city of dam-
nation!" and nobody listened to the few who cry out, we would
know that the human race had finally gone hopelessly and forever
mad.

There is no place for a poet in American society. No place
at all for any kind of poet at all. Only two poets in my lifetime
have ever made a living from their poetry — Edna Millay and
Robert Frost. Neither of them would have done so if they had
started their careers in the last two decades. The majority of
American poets have acquiesced in the judgment of the predatory

society. They do not exist as far as it is concerned. They make
their living in a land of make-believe, as servants of a hoax for
children. They are employees of the fog factories—the universities. They help make the fog. Behind their screen the universities
fulfill their social purposes. They turn out bureaucrats, perpetuate the juridical lie, embroider the costumes of the delusion
of participation, and of late, in departments never penetrated by
the humanities staff, turn out atom, hydrogen, and cobalt bombers—genocidists is the word. Patchen fills these academicians
with panic. "Let us walk, not run," says one of the best in-
tentioned of them, "to the nearest exit. The bobbysoxers can have
him." Let me out of here. Somebody is doing something fright-
fully embarrassing to all concerned. Precisely.

The bobbysoxers do have him. Against a conspiracy of
silence of the whole of literary America, Patchen has become the
laureate of the doomed youth of the Third World War. He is the
most widely read younger poet in the country. Those who ignore
him, try to pass over him, hush up his scandalous writing, are read
hardly at all, unwillingly by their English students and
querulously by one another. Years ago Patchen marked out his
role. "I speak for a generation born in one war and doomed to die
in another." Some of his most ambitious books were published by
an obscure printer. Reviews of his work are almost all un-
favorable. He is never published in the highbrow quarterlies. In a
market where publishers spend millions to promote the mastur-
bation fantasies of feeble-minded mammals, his books have made
their way into the hands of youth, the hands that are being drafted to pull the triggers, the youth that is being driven to do the
dying—for the feeble-minded mammals and their pimping
publishers.

The official spokesmen of the Official Revolution have not
chosen to stand in the place Patchen stands. Read Upton Sin-
clair's anthology, *The Cry for Justice* and any anthology of
pseudo-proletarian literature of the Thirties. The contrast is
shocking. From Patrick Magill to the young Sandburg and Lind-
say, Oppenheim and Lola Ridge, the poets of the earlier day had
an integrity, a moral earnestness, which overrode their occasional
corniness and gave them a substance of things hoped for, an
evidence of things not seen, which has vanished from the work of

the approved poets of bureaucratic salvation. "Change the world" indeed, but from what to what?

It has been pointed out, time out of mind, that American literature has never been whole. It has always split into two antagonistic tendencies: the exhortative, expressive, responsible, sometimes prophetic utterance—Whitman; and the egocentric, constructive, irresponsible *machine*—Poe. Today, in the epigoni of Henry James and the Corn College Donnes, the constructive tendency has degenerated to a point where it is no longer only irresponsible, but socially invisible. For better or worse, Patchen belongs to the first tendency. He shares the faults of Whitman, Sandburg at his early best, and e. e. cummings. His contemporary literary antagonists are practically faultless.

In a nation where every second English Department assistant is a provincial litterateur, a past master of the seven types of ambiguity to be found in Barnaby Googe, Patchen is one of the few representatives (Miller is another) of a world movement—Anti-Literature. He is a descendant of Sade, Restif, Lautréamont, Rimbaud, Corbière, Jarry, Apollinaire, a contemporary of Artaud. It is significant that in his case this ideology of creation has become quite conscious, even "class conscious" in a special sense.

The Journal of Albion Moonlight can be compared very aptly with Apollinaire's *Poet Assassinated*. There is an important difference. The assassins of Croniamantal, the poet, are Boredom and Misery, and the vagueness of the figure of the enemy gives Apollinaire's work an air of naive imprecision which borders on frivolity. In Wyndham Lewis's *Childermass*, a similar book, the enemy is more carefully defined, but Lewis's impact is vitiated by the crankiness of his indictment. This is still more obvious if you compare Lewis's *The Apes of God* with Patchen's *Memoirs of a Shy Pornographer*. The *Apes* is certainly a great book, one of the monumental satires of our day, and it deals with events and issues of great importance. It also goes out of its way to pay off specific grudges against various denizens of Bloomsbury, Chelsea, and Charlotte Street. It ends with an extremely specific attack on the Sitwells. It is all very entertaining, but it is rather too monumental and you miss much of the fun if you don't know the people. The *Shy Pornographer* is not a *comédie à clef*. True, remarks like,

"Have you anything in view?" need a footnote already, but there aren't too many of them.

On the whole, all three of Patchen's prose works deal with the "great archetypes," the same figures who are found in Homer, *Gulliver*, Rabelais, or *Le Morte D'Arthur*. But these dramatis personae have undergone a change unlike anything they ever experienced before. The actors, the masks, who have always spoken, in all the classics, the words of humanist culture, in epic, satire, comedy, or tragedy, have been reduced to their simplest elements and then filtered through the screen of the commodity culture. Launcelot becomes the Thin Man, Ulysses is worked over by Mickey Spillane, the Poet is confused with Flash Gordon, love scenes slip in and out of the idiom of *Ranch Romances*, Tristan and Iseult are played by Elvis Presley and Kim Novak. The idiom of science fiction or the blood-on-the-scanties school of detective stories accurately but naïvely reflects the mass psychosis, however skillfully it may be rigged to augment that psychosis and sell commodities. Patchen turns it upon itself, dissociates its elements, and uses them to create a vast, controlled, social dream, a diagnostic symbol of the collapse of civilization.

Patchen's active interference, so different from the passive madness of Lautréamont, is continuous in the texture of the narrative. His sentences are saturated with the acid of undeluded judgment, a running clinical commentary on the periods of Henry James, the oratory of the United Nations, the velleities of the literary quarterlies. Beside the narrative—the picture of the universal disorder of values and death of the sensibility—there runs this obligato, the attack on literature, not out of any superficial épateism, but because the practice of literature today is the practice of acquiescence. This is a fundamental technique of all great comic writers; it is obvious in Erasmus, the *Letters of Obscure Men*, and Rabelais; but since that day humor has become a grimmer business. Characteristically, editors and critics cannot even comprehend the comic today, in this conspiracy of mutual guilt, mutual espionage, mutual silence. Imagine Gargantua, or Swift's savage indignation, or Nashe, or Lawrence's *Pansies*, or even *Absalom and Achitophel* in the pages of that refined quarterly which is devoted to perpetuating on a high-toned level the tradition of *Red Rock* and *The Birth of a Nation*.

The sort of thing Patchen does was written in France in the very brief period between the naïve revolt of Dada and the dissipation of all revolt in the deserts of Stalinist conformity or the swamps of neo-surrealist salon Freudianism. An example which occurs to me offhand is the early work of Aragon—which he, characteristically, no longer allows mentioned by his bibliographers. Was it he or Soupault who wrote a book of mockery called *The New Adventures of Nick Carter?* I no longer remember, but I do remember that it lacked Patchen's seriousness, his understanding of the real causes of the contemporary Black Death, his organized system of values, his solid vantage point of judgment. When Aragon deserted this medium, he said, "The newspapers present us daily with infinitely more horrible nightmares than we can manufacture in our studios." Patchen is well aware of this. *Albion Moonlight* and *Sleepers Awake,* not *Les Cloches de Basle,* are realistic portrayals of the modern world. Similarly, Patchen must be distinguished from the later, orthodox Surrealists. This stuff was largely a dreamy rehash of the troubles of rich women and their favorites of the literary, artistic, and pathic international. Rare, unhappy schoolboys here and there around the world may have read Breton once with excitement, but it takes modistes, comtesses, and American heiresses to read him with understanding. The nightmares of Patchen's narratives are the daily visions of millions.

Anti-literature is, of course, largely the real literature of certain epochs. Dynamite is one of the most powerful instruments of construction. One would think that any critic with a high school education would recognize the genre of *Don Quixote.* It is amazing to read the few reviews of Patchen's books that have ever been printed in the fashionable quarterlies. These little academic bunnies cannot even guess what he is about. Haven't they ever read *Don Quixote,* or *Tristam Shandy,* or *Gulliver?* The answer is no. They read one another in the fashionable quarterlies.

The other day one of the subalterns of the Bronx edition of *PMLA,* otherwise known as the *Vaticide Review,* said to me, "Patchen is no good, he has no feeling for the weight of words and no sense of literary responsibility." When I told him I was doing this piece he warned me, "Don't get tied up with Patchen. He'll destroy your reputation, just when you are getting recognition in

the right circles." Un hunh. I have been around since the Twen-
ties and have always had the recognition of my—or Patchen's—"right circles." I'll take a chance. To paraphrase old Stef-
fie, I have seen the future and in some cases it wears bobby sox, at
least for now.

Notes

[1]Jonathan Williams, Highlands, N.C., 1957.
[2]New Directions, N.Y.C., 1958.

John Ciardi

Kenneth Patchen: Poetry, and Poetry with Jazz

My good friend Kenneth Patchen came to town to read his poetry to jazz at The Five Spot, and though I did my best, within my ignorance, to pump him on the theory of such readings, I found myself as confused at the end as I had been at the beginning. There was, for example, a Chinese poem in translation that "had a sort of circular rhythm," and naturally, as Patchen put it, that wanted to be read with Dixieland behind it. Another poem had a long, smooth line and that one wanted to be read against a jump-rhythm. Still another poem had "a sort of jump rhythm in the line" and that one wanted to be read against a long, smooth, swinging line.

Whatever the merits of the theory—and I confess they escape me—the performance itself managed to be two things going on at the same time with no convincing sense that one was related to the other. The combo, working under only the most general instructions, with no real rehearsal, and with no sense of what the poems were, followed itself into itself; while Patchen recited the poems, guessing as best he could what the combo would do next. Worst of all the music kept drowning the words. I ended up knowing neither what was being played nor what was being read.

Kenneth Patchen claims to have been the first to read his poetry to jazz and certainly "Kenneth Patchen Reads His Poetry with the Chamber Jazz Sextet" (Cadence CLP 3004) is a serious effort to eliminate all haphazard from the performance.

Patchen's poetry is in many ways a natural for jazz accompaniment. Its subjects and its tone are close to those of jazz.

29

And most of it is written not metrically, but in phrase groups that adapt naturally to jazz rhythms. For this particular recording, moreover, the poems were first taped, then underscored for the accompaniment, and then re-recorded to the nicely mental phrasings and fine woodwindy sound of the Chamber Jazz Sextet.

It is a careful effort. As a general formula, each number starts with a spoken phrase . . . pause . . . sextet enters with a longish series of introductory phrases . . . fades or pauses . . . then the voice again . . . and then the sextet coming up over (rather than under) the voice, with the result that one begins to lose the words. Had a printed text been supplied (and the omission of such a text, I must insist, is always a mistake) the listener might better have followed the reading, but as a partisan of the word (and confessedly no jazz enthusiast) I can only resent having the word drowned out by its accompaniment.

I rather like the effect that can be achieved when voice and music alternate, but I find it merely distracting when the two are coming on together, especially when the music comes on loud enough to drown the reading.

For that reason I much prefer the earlier Folkways release (FL 9717) of "Selected Poems of Kenneth Patchen. Read by the Poet," in which Patchen reads his poems without musical accompaniment, as straightforward and admirable — exercises in the word itself. Patchen has grand powers as a reader. His voice is casual, almost matter of fact, yet sensitive, resonant, and immediately engaging. A gentle and easy voice, always deeply concerned for the natural rhythms of speech, yet kept exciting by small modulations and by a superb sense of timing. Patchen with sextet is a good recording and an interesting one, but Patchen by himself is one of the really grand readings.

II

Biographical
and
Personal

Henry Miller

Patchen: Man of Anger and Light

The first thing one would remark on meeting Kenneth Patchen is that he is the living symbol of protest. I remember distinctly my first impression of him when we met in New York: it was
that of a powerful, sensitive being who moved on velvet pads. A
sort of sincere assassin, I thought to myself, as we shook hands.
This impression has never left me. True or not, I feel that it would
give him supreme joy to destroy with his own hands all the tyrants
and sadists of this earth together with the art, the institutions and
all the machinery of everyday life which sustain and glorify them.
He is a fizzing human bomb ever threatening to explode in our
midst. Tender and ruthless at the same time, he has the faculty
of estranging the very ones who wish to help him. He is inexorable: he has no manners, no tact, no grace. He gives no quarter.
Like the gangster, he follows a code of his own. He gives you the
chance to put up your hands before shooting you down. Most
people however, are too terrified to throw up their hands. They
get mowed down.

This is the monstrous side of him, which makes him appear ruthless and rapacious. Within the snorting dragon,
however, there is a gentle prince who suffers at the mention of the
slightest cruelty or injustice. A tender soul, who soon learned to
envelope himself in a mantle of fire in order to protect his sensitive
skin. No American poet is as merciless in his invective as Patchen.
There is almost an insanity to his fury and rebellion.

Like Gorky, Patchen began his career in the university of
life early. The hours he sacrificed in the steel mills of Ohio, where
he was born, served to fan his hatred for a society in which

33

inequality, injustice and intolerance form the foundation of life. His years as a wanderer, during which he scattered his manuscripts like seed, corroborated the impressions gained at home, school and mill. Today he is practically an invalid, thanks to the system which puts the life of a machine above that of a human being. Suffering from arthritis of the spine, he is confined to bed most of the time. He lies on a huge bed in a doll's house near the river named after Henry Hudson, a sick giant consumed by the poisonous indifference of a world which has more use for mousetraps than for poets. He writes book after book, prose as well as poetry, never certain when "they" will come and dump him (with the bed) into the street. This has been going on now for over seven years, if I am not mistaken. If Patchen were to become well, able to use his hands and feet freely, it is just possible that he would celebrate the occasion by pulling the house down about the ears of some unsuspecting victim of his scorn and contempt. He would do it slowly, deliberately, thoroughly. And in utter silence.

That is another quality of Patchen's which inspires dread on first meeting — his awesome silence. It seems to spring from his flesh, as though he had silenced the flesh. It is uncanny. Here is a man with the gift of tongues and he speaks not. Here is a man who drips words but he refuses to open his mouth. Here is a man dying to communicate, but instead of conversing with you he hands you a book or a manuscript to read. The silence which emanates from him is black. He puts one on tenterhooks. It breeds hysteria. Of course he is shy. And no matter how long he lives he will never become urbane. He is American through and through, and Americans, despite their talkiness, are fundamentally silent creatures. They talk in order to conceal their innate reticence. It is only in moments of deep intimacy that they break loose. Patchen is typical. When finally he does open his mouth it is to release a hot flood of words. His emotion tears loose in clots.

A voracious reader, he exposes himself to every influence, even the worst. Like Picasso, he makes use of everything. The innovator and initiator are strong in him. Rather than accept the collaboration of a second-rate artist, he will do the covers for a book himself, a different one for each copy. And how beautiful and original are these individual cover designs[1] from the hand of a writer who makes no pretense of being a painter or illustrator! How interesting, too, are the typographical arrangements which he dictates for his books! How competent he can be when he has to be his own publisher! (See *The Journal of Albion Moonlight.*) From a sickbed the poet defies and surmounts all obstacles. He has only to pick up the telephone to throw an editorial staff into a panic. He has the will of a tyrant, the persistence of a bull. "This is the way I want it done!" he bellows. And by God it gets done that way.

Let me quote a few passages from his answers to certain questions of mine:

> The pain is almost a natural part of me now — only the fits of depression, common to this disease, really sap my energies and distort my native spirit. I could speak quite morbidly in this last connection. The sickness of the world probably didn't cause mine, but it certainly conditions my handling of it. Actually, the worst part is that I feel that I would be something else if I weren't rigid inside with the constant pressure of illness; I would be purer, less inclined to write, say, for the sake of being able to show my sick part that it can never become all powerful; I could experience more in other artists if I didn't have to be concerned so closely with happenings inside myself; I would have less need to be pure in the presence of the things I love, and therefore, probably, would have a more personal view of myself. . . . I think the more articulate an artist becomes the less he will know about himself to say, for usually one's greatest sense of love is inseparable from a sense of creature foreboding. . .it is hard to imagine why God should "think," yet this "thinking" is the material of the greatest art. . .we don't wish to know ourselves, we wish to be lost in knowing, as a seed in a gust of wind.

> I think that if I ever got near an assured income I'd write books along the order of great canvases, including everything in them — huge symphonies that would handle poetry and prose as they present themselves from day to day and from one aspect of my life and interests to another. But that's all over, I think. They're going to blow everything up next time — and I don't believe we have long. Always men have talked about THE END OF THE WORLD — it's nearly here. A few more straws in the wall. . .a loose brick or two replaced. . .then no stone left standing on another — and the long silence; really forever. What is there to struggle against? Nobody can put the stars back together again.

There isn't much time at all. I can't say it doesn't matter; it
matters more than anything — but we are helpless to stop it
now.

It's very hard for me to answer your questions. Some
were Rebels out of choice; I had none — I wish they'd give me
just one speck of proof that this "world of theirs" couldn't
have been set up and handled better by a half-dozen
drugged idiots bound hand and foot at the bottom of a ten-
mile well. It's always because we love that we are rebellious;
it takes a great deal of love to give a damn one way or
another what happens from now on: I still do. The situation
for human beings is hopeless. For the while that's left,
though, we can remember the Great and the gods."

The mixture of hope and despair, of love and resignation,
of courage and the sense of futility, which emanates from these excerpts is revelatory. Setting himself apart from the world, as poet,
as man of vision, Patchen nevertheless identifies himself with the
world in the malady which has become universal. He has the
humility to acknowledge that his genius, that all genius, springs
from the divine source. He is also innocent enough to think that
the creature world should recognize God's voice and give it its due.
He has the clarity to realize that his suffering is not important,
that it distorts his native spirit, as he puts it, but does he admit to
himself, can he admit to himself, that the suffering of the world
also distorts the world's true spirit? If he could believe in his own
cure might he not believe in a universal cure? "The situation for
human beings is hopeless," he says. But he is a human being himself, and he is not at all convinced that his case is hopeless. With a
bit of security he imagines that he will be able to give profounder
expression to his powers. The whole world now cries for security.
It cries for peace, too, but makes no real effort to stop the forces
which are working for war. In his agony each sincere soul doubtless refers to the world as "their world." No one in his senses
wishes to admit being a voluntary part of this world, so thoroughly
inhuman, so intolerable has it become. We are all, whether we
admit it or not, waiting for the end of the world, as though it were
not a world of our own making but a hell into which we had been
thrust by a malevolent fate.

Patchen uses the language of revolt. There is no other
language left to use. There is no time, when you are holding up a

bank, to explain to the directors the sinister injustice of the present economic system. Explanations have been given time and again; warnings have been posted everywhere. They have gone unheeded. Time to act. "Stick up your hands! Deliver the goods!"

It is in his prose works that Patchen uses this language most effectively. With *The Journal of Albion Moonlight,* Patchen opened up a vein unique in English literature. These prose works, of which the latest to appear is *Sleepers Awake,* defy classification. Like the Wonder Books of old, every page contains some new marvel. Behind the surface chaos and madness one quickly detects the logic and the will of a daring creator. One thinks of Blake, of Lautréamont, of Picasso—and of Jakob Boehme. Strange predecessors! But one thinks also of Savonarola, of Grünewald, of John of Patmos, of Hieronymous Bosch—and of times, events and scenes recognizable only in the waiting room of sleep. Each new volume is an increasingly astonishing feat of legerdemain, not only in the protean variety of the text but in design, composition and format. One is no longer looking at a dead, printed book but at something alive and breathing, something which looks back at you with equal astonishment. Novelty is employed not as seduction but like the stern fist of the Zen master—to awaken and arouse the consciousness of the reader. THE WAY MEN LIVE IS A LIE! — that is the reality which screams from the pages of these books. Once again we have the revolt of the angels.

This is not the place to discuss the merits or defects of the author's work. What concerns me at the moment is the fact that, despite everything, he is a poet. I am vitally interested in the man who today has the misfortune of being an artist and a human being. By the same token I am as much interested in the maneuvers of the gangster as I am in those of the financier or the military man. They are all part and parcel of society; some are lauded for their efforts, some reviled, some persecuted and hunted like beasts. In our society the artist is not encouraged, not lauded, not rewarded, unless he makes use of a weapon more powerful than those employed by his adversaries. Such a weapon is not to be found in shops or arsenals: it has to be forged by the artist himself out of his own tissue. When he releases it he also destroys himself. It is the only method he has found to preserve his own kind. From the outset his life is mortgaged. He is a martyr

whether he chooses to be or not. He no longer seeks to generate
warmth, he seeks for a virus with which society must allow itself to
be injected or perish. It does not matter whether he preaches love
or hate, freedom or slavery; he must create room to be heard, ears
that will hear. He must create, by the sacrifice of his own being,
the awareness of a value and a dignity which the word *human*
once connoted. This is not the time to analyze and criticize works
of art. This is not the time to select the flowers of genius, differentiate between them, label and categorize. This is the time to accept what is offered and be thankful that something other than
mass intolerance, mass suicide, can preoccupy the human intellect.

If through indifference and inertia we can create human as
well as atomic bombs, then it seems to me that the poet has the
right to explode in his own fashion at his own appointed time. If
all is hopelessly given over to destruction, why should the poet not
lead the way? Why should he remain amid the ruins like a crazed
beast? If we deny our Maker, why should we preserve the maker of
words and images? Are the forms and symbols he spins to be put
above Creation itself?

When men deliberately create instruments of destruction
to be used against the innocent as well as the guilty, against babes
in arms as well as against the aged, the sick, the halt, the
maimed, the blind, the insane, when their targets embrace whole
populations, when they are immune to every appeal, then we
know that the heart and the imagination of man are no longer
capable of being stirred. If the powerful ones of this earth are in
the grip of fear and trembling, what hope is there for the weaker
ones? What does it matter to those monsters now in control what
becomes of the poet, the sculptor, the musician?

In the richest and the most powerful country in the world
there is no means of insuring an invalid poet such as Kenneth Patchen against starvation or eviction. Neither is there a band of
loyal fellow artists who will unite to defend him against the unnecessary attacks of shallow, spiteful critics. Every day ushers in
some fresh blow, some fresh insults, some fresh punishment. In
spite of it all he continues to create. He works on two or three
books at once. He labors in a state of almost unremitting pain. He
lives in a room just about big enough to hold his carcass, a rented

coffin you might call it, and a most insecure one at that. Would he not be better off dead? What is there for him to look forward to — as a man, as an artist, as a member of society?

I am writing these lines for an English and a French edition of his work. It is hardly the orthodox preface to a man's work. But my hope is that in these distant countries Patchen (and other now unknown American writers) will find friends, find support and encouragement to go on living and working. America is immune to all appeals. Her people do not understand the language of the poet. They do not wish to recognize suffering — it is too embarrassing. They do not greet Beauty with open arms — her presence is disturbing to heartless automatons. Their fear of violence drives them to commit insane cruelites. They have no reverence for form or image: they are bent on destroying whatever does not conform to their pattern, which is chaos. They are not even concerned with their own disintegration, because they are already putrescent. A vast congeries of rotting sepulchres, America holds for yet a little while, awaiting the opportune moment to blow itself to smithereens.

The one thing which Patchen cannot understand, will not tolerate, indeed, is the refusal to act. In this he is adamant. Confronted with excuses and explanations, he becomes a raging lion.

It is the well-off who especially draw his ire. Now and then he is thrown a bone. Instead of quieting him, he growls more ferociously. We know, of course, what patronage means. Usually it is hush money. "What is one to do with a man like that?" exclaim the poor rich. Yes, a man like Patchen puts them in a dilemma. Either he increases his demands or he uses what is given to voice his scorn and contempt. He needs money for food and rent, money for the doctor, money for operations, money for medicines — yet he goes on turning out beautiful books. Books of violence clothed in outward elegance. The man has uncommon taste, no gainsaying it. But what right has he to a cultivated appetite? Tomorrow he will be asking for a seaside cottage perhaps, or for a Rouault, whose work he reveres. Perhaps for a Capehart, since he loves music. How can one satisfy a monster such as that?

That is the way rich people think about the starving artist. Poor people too, sometimes. Why doesn't he get himself a job? Why doesn't he make his wife support him? Does he have to live in a house with two rooms? Must he have all those books and records? When the man happens also to be an invalid, they become even more resentful, more malicious. They will accuse him of permitting his illness to distort his vision. "The work of a sick man," they say, shrugging their shoulders. If he bellows, then it is "the work of an impotent man." If he begs and entreats, then "he has lost all sense of dignity." But if he roars? Then he is hopelessly insane. No matter what attitude he adopts he is condemned beforehand. When he is buried they praise him as another *"poète maudit."* What beautiful crocodile tears are shed over our dead and accursed poets! What a galaxy of them we have already in the short span of our history!

   In 1909 Charles Péguy penned a *morceau* for his *Cahiers de la Quinzaine* which described the then imminent debacle of the modern world. "We are defeated," it begins. "We are defeated to such an extent, so completely, that I doubt whether history will ever have to record an instance of defeat such as the one we furnish. . . . To be defeated, that is nothing. It would be nothing. On the contrary, it can be a great thing. It can be all: the final consummation. To be defeated is nothing: [but] we have been beaten. We have even been given a good drubbing. In a few years society, this modern society, before we have even had the time to sketch the critique of it, has fallen into a state of decomposition, into a dissolution, such, that I believe, that I am assured history had never seen anything comparable. . . . That great historical decomposition, that great dissolution, that great precedent which in a literary manner we call the decay of the Roman decadence, the dissolution of the Roman Empire, and which it suffices to call, with Sorel, the ruin of the ancient world, was nothing by comparison with the dissolution of present society, by comparison with the dissolution and degradation of this society, of the present modern society. Doubtless, at that time there were far more crimes and still more vice[s]. But there were also infinitely more resources. This putrefaction was full of seeds. People at that time did not have this sort of promise of sterility which we have today, if one may say so, if these two words can be used together."[2]

   After two annihilating wars, in one of which Péguy gave his life, this "promise of sterility" appears anything but empty. The condition of society which was then manifest to the poet and thinker, and of course more so today (even the man in the street is aware of it), Péguy described as "a real disorder of impotence and sterility." It is well to remember these words when the hired critics of the press (both of the right and the left) direct their fulminations against the poets of the day. It is precisely the artists with the vital spark whom they set out to attack most viciously. It is the creative individual (*sic*) whom they accuse of undermining the social structure. A persecutory mania manifests itself the moment an honest word is spoken. The atmosphere of the whole modern world, from Communist Russia to capitalist America, is heavy with guilt. We are in the Time of the Assassins. The order of the day is: liquidate! The enemy, the archenemy, is the man who speaks the truth. Every realm of society is permeated with falsity and falsification. What survives, what is upheld, what is defended to the last ditch, is the lie.

"It is perhaps this condition of confusion and distress," wrote Péguy, "which, more imperiously than ever, makes it our duty not to surrender. One must never surrender. All the less since the position is so important and so isolated and so menaced, and that precisely the country is in the hands of the enemy."

Those who know Kenneth Patchen will realize that I am identifying his stand with Péguy's. Perhaps there could not be two individuals more different one from another. Perhaps there is nothing at all in common between them except this refusal to swallow the lie, this refusal to surrender even in the blackest hour. I know of no American who has as vigorously insisted that the enemy is within. If he refuses to play the game it is not because he has been defeated; it is because he has never recognized those phantoms created out of fear and confusion which men call "the enemy." He knows that the enemy of man is man. He rebels out of love, not out of hate. Given his temperament, his love of honesty, his adherence to truth, is he not justified in saying that "he had no choice" but to rebel? Do we find him aligned with those rebels who wish merely to depose those on top, in order that they may hold the whip hand? No, we find him alone, in a tiny garret, riveted to a sickbed, turning frantically from side to side as if imprisoned in an iron cage. And it is a very real cage indeed. He has only to open his eyes each day to be aware of his helplessness. He could not surrender even if he wished to: there is no one to surrender to except death. He lies on the edge of the precipice with eyes wide open. The world which condemns him to imprisonment is fast asleep. He is furiously aware that his release does not depend on acceptance by the multitude but on the dissolution of the world which is strangling him.

"The situation for human beings is hopeless," did he say? In *Albion Moonlight* this desperation is expressed artistically: "I want to be a carpet in a cat-house." Thus, to use the title from one of his own poems, "The Furious Crown Conceals Its Throne." Thus, to paraphrase Miró, persons magnetized by the stars may walk in comfort on the music of a furrowed landscape. Thus we take leave of our atavistic friend, the poet, doomed to inhabit a world that never was, never will be, the world of "flowers born in shining wombs." For flowers will always be born and wombs will always be radiant, particularly when the poet is accursed. For him the beast is always number, the landscape stars, the time and the place of creation now and here. He moves in a "circle of apparent fates," ruler of the dark kingdom, maligned, persecuted and forsaken in the light of the day.

Once again the night approaches. And once again "the dark kingdom" will reveal to us its splendors. In the middle of this twentieth century we have all of us, none excepted, crossed a river made of human tears. We have no fathers, no mothers, no brothers, no sisters. We are returned to the creature state.

"I have put language to sleep," said Joyce. Aye, and now conscience too is being put to sleep.

Notes

[1]So far Patchen has done paintings for limited editions of *The Dark Kingdom* and *Sleepers Awake,* one hundred and fifty covers in all. To date he has turned a deaf ear to suggestions that these remarkable productions be exhibited—I, for one, hope he changes his mind. It would be a feather in the hat of any gallery to show these wonderful paintings!

[2]See *Men and Saints,* Charles Péguy, Pantheon Books, New York.

Holly Beye

and

William McCleery

The Most Mysterious People in the Village

On a stroll through the Village a few weeks ago, we noticed that bookshops were displaying a strangely-titled book, *The Journal of Albion Moonlight*, by Kenneth Patchen, with whose name we were only vaguely familiar. And at a cocktail party a few days later we heard a couple of NYU students arguing over whether or not this same Patchen was the greatest American poet of this generation. So we asked one our girls, Holly Beye, to look him up, which she did on a recent Saturday afternoon.

Patchen lives in the Village, our girl says, over toward the river end of West 12th Street, in a little two-room house, one room on top of the other. The house was built in a back yard. The entrance is a metal-grill gateway that opens into a long, narrow passage between two brick buildings; this opens into a tiny court.

I crossed the cobbled court to the small wooden door of the small building and was greeted by Miriam Patchen, the poet's wife, a chubby, girlish little person with long brownish hair, and friendly blue eyes.

She hustled me into the ground-floor room. It had a fireplace and lots of bookcases and was bright with flower-painted dishes on shelves and on the walls.

"Kenneth isn't up yet," she said, "I'll go fix the room." She hurried lightly up the wooden stairway at one end of the room and I could hear her bustling around up there. Then, suddenly, I heard a man cry, "Miriam! Miriam! Cut that out!"

Miriam's head bobbed out of the doorway at the head of the stairs and she called cheerily to me to come on up, "I'm just pinching his toes," she said. "Every day I pinch his toes just to make sure he's on them."

I had been told that Patchen had suffered a back injury that kept him in bed for long stretches at a time. When we got into the upstairs room, which was tinier than the one below, he was lying on top of the bed covers, his head and shoulders propped up on a pillow.

Coffee all day

The bed was massive and so was the man. He wore a faded gray sweatshirt with washed-out blue cuffs and pocket. The shirt was tucked into the waistband of black woolen trousers that were frayed at the cuffs. Patchen wore blue, maroon and tan Argyle socks, but no shoes. His body seemed muscular and powerful; his face was delicate and sensitive. His skin was white and his eyes were a deep blue-gray.

The bed took up most of the room, but there was a dresser against one wall. Beside the bed, there was a small bookcase on which rested a lamp with a delicate gold inlaid base.

As Patchen, who looked about 30, was welcoming me with a strong handclasp, his wife reappeared at the head of the stairs, carrying a huge pot of coffee.

"Kenneth loves coffee," she said, pouring a cupful for him and one for me. "He's absolutely impossible until he's had a whole pot of coffee in the morning—and I make him coffee all day long."

I looked questioningly at him. "I have a terrible temper," he said. "But I finally learned to control it. That is, I can prevent myself from blowing up out loud."

"But when he suppresses his temper," his wife put in, "he looks absolutely black. He's that way about everything—violent." She went out again. I asked him if he had black dreams.

"Oh, terrible," he said. "Nightmares, sickness, and the actual work of writing all have about the same effect on me. From a psychologist's angle, I suppose you might explain the nightmares by my childhood. I used to get teased a lot. My family thought it was awfully funny to see a little kid get fighting mad over something.

"You see, I'm a proletarian. My family are steel workers. I'm the only one who ever finished high school and went to college."

He reached painfully for a cigaret that was on the bookcase at his left. "My father's a roller," he went on, after he had lighted up. "That's a very responsible job for a steel man. He's the most famous roller in the Mahoning Valley, and in Niles, Ohio, where I was born."

Mrs. Patchen, who had been dusting the stairs, reached the top just then and, from her position on her hands and knees in the doorway she broke into the conversation.

"You should see his father's back. The muscles look like a relief map of the Appalachian Mountains."

"My brother and I both worked in the steel mill at one time or another," Patchen went on. "He started out as a doubler—that's a man who jumps on the hot steel with cleated shoes, to flatten it. I worked as an extra man during the summer, before I went to college.

"They need an extra man to take the place of those who go out on account of mill cramps. Working in that mill," he said with deep feeling, "was my idea of hell on earth."

Patchen had been an honor student in high school. In addition, he had been the star of the track team, end on the football team, bassoonist in the school orchestra and saxophonist in the school band. "My family respected me," he said, "but they did not understand me.

"Once my father showed what he called my *poultry* to the minister. The minister told him, 'Your son must be a very deep young man; this poetry is too deep for me.'"

How he writes

I asked Patchen what he had meant when he had said earlier that sickness had a strange effect on him.

"I used to get pneumonia regularly every year," he said with a sigh. "Even now, injustice and cruelty upset me to the point of becoming really sick."

Mrs. Patchen, who now was emptying the ashtrays, remarked with childlike incredulity, "He gets delirious at the slightest illness. And he raves something terrible!"

Patchen was gazing absently out the window, flicking his cigaret impatiently. I asked him if writing came easily.

"Writing exhausts me," he said. "I have a real sense of being attacked by the conditions under which I write. When I start to work on something, I work 12 or 13 hours at a stretch. Right now I'm working on two prose works and some poetry simultaneously."

"Don't forget, Kenneth," said Mrs. Patchen, "to tell her you've got a book coming out soon by New Directions."

Oh, yes, he said. It would be called *Memoirs of a Shy Pornographer;* it was a funny book. I wanted to know how he set out to write. He handed me a manuscript from the bookcase, "I outline my books in my head," he explained, "but the outline only serves as a point of departure. If something doesn't satisfy me, I start again, and attack it from another angle."

I glanced through the manuscript. It was written in ink, in a hand that was large, round and clear. I noticed that although the book began with Chapter I, the introduction was somewhere in the middle. Why was that, I asked.

The artist's job

"An introduction is supposed to summarize for the reader what the book is about," he said, raising his eyebrows. "It should be put in when the reader has had a chance to gather the threads of the story together for himself."

What did he think the purpose of art was, and what should be the artist's place in society? He looked toward his wife, who was sitting on the top stair, and waved his hand impatiently.

"The primary aim of the creative artist," he began slowly, looking at me steadily, "is to protest. Out of that protest will come whatever validity there is in art. It's not just going on record against something — that's journalism. It must be more than an intellectual thing; it must affect the artist's whole being."

What should the artist protest against?

"The artist must protest against evil. He must point at the specific evil in society and write against it." He banged his fist on the hard surface of the bed for emphasis.

Then, I asked, what made an artist different from a reformer?

"The hallmark of a reformer is to compromise his means to achieve his ends. But the hallmark of the artist is to make no compromise for any reasons."

I asked Patchen if he was a romanticist or a realist.

He looked annoyed. "Art itself is an attack on labels," he snapped. "I can't be classified. No real artist can be. One of the most dangerous labels of today is that of *Americanism,* for instance."

Americanism, he said, was characterized by vulgarity, and cheapness. "And the vulgarity of American life and culture is predicated on the fact that the artist never has taken his proper place in America.

In Arkansas and Boston

"Writers like Poe and Herman Melville are real creative artists, but Henry James belongs in the bathroom. His work was an attempt to glorify the asininity of the middle class life to the public and to himself."

He called Walt Whitman a bad writer, although Patchen felt that certain passages in *Democratic Vistas,* where Whitman said liberty was non-existent for any people unless all the people enjoyed it, were worth while.

I asked how Patchen had come to be a writer.

He said he had gone to Alexander Meikeljohn Experimental School, in Wisconsin, after leaving high school, but had suffered a heart injury playing football during his freshman year. The next year he went to Commonwealth Labor College, in Arkansas, but he soon left, he said, to follow a girl to New York, where he stayed for four months.

"I object. Don't put that in," called Mrs. Patchen from the stairway, where she was now darning socks. Her husband laughed and pretended to throw something at her. I asked him when he had met Mrs. Patchen.

"We met," Mrs. Patchen answered, "at a party in Boston. He was very rude and unsociable. He looked very sad and thin. I was a student at Massachusetts State College, and I was very impressed with him. Five months later we got married."

"I had been hoboing around the country for four years," explained Patchen. "It was during the depression years. I was writing all the time, but I left hundreds of manuscripts all over the country because I forgot them."

Opinion of publishers

After he brought out his first book, *Before the Brave* (which he has no use for today) they went to Hollywood in 1936, with the idea of making some quick money.. Hollywood was "a sordid small town with the psychology of a big city," they agreed.

In Hollywood, Patchen did some ghostwriting, and it was there that he met William Saroyan, with whom he has sometimes been compared. But before long the Patchens returned to New York and settled in the Village.

At this point in the interview, Patchen gave out with some opinions about publishers. He doesn't like them. They are, he says, unbusinesslike.

"They never respond to questions pertaining to work, they delay their schedules, they don't live up to their contracts. But the worst thing about them, after all, is that they have no interest in culture; they are businessmen — commercial."

I asked if there were any country where that wouldn't be true. "In Europe," he said emphatically. "In Europe, there were centuries of culture to bring about a cultural tradition in the publishing business. Publishers brought out books for purely esthetic and literary reasons — books they knew they couldn't sell."

Patchen published his first novel, *The Journal of Albion Moonlight*, himself; no publisher would take it. It sold out — 300 copies at $10 each — within the first month. It is being reprinted at $3 now by the United Book Guild.

The titles of Patchen's books all have romantic flavor: *First Will and Testament, Teeth of the Lion, Cloth of the Tempest, The Dark Kingdom*. And all of them carry this dedication: *To Miriam*.

"And Miriam," her husband announced, "is the best spaghetti-maker in the Village."

What did he like besides spaghetti?

Red wine, cats, football. And boogie-woogie, only he and his wife could not agree on who was the best boogie-woogie player. She favored Albert Ammons, he liked Pete Johnson. They did agree on painters, though — George Rouault was their man. They have a print of his *Head of a Clown* in the bedroom, a second print of the same picture in their living room.

I was getting ready to leave when poet E. E. Cummings arrived from his home in Patchin Place to have dinner with poet Kenneth Patchen and his wife. Patchen introduced me as being from PM and Cummings exclaimed, "So they have found you out! And I thought you were the most mysterious people in the Village."

(Facing page) Posters advertising Patchen's poetry-and-jazz performances. (Above) Patchen reading in "Stars of Jazz" performance on KABC-TV (Los Angeles), June 11, 1958.

Alan Neil

Kenneth Patchen Reads with Jazz in Canada

We got to the studio expecting to wail. Behind us we had a good half dozen performances with Patchen—at colleges, couple of nightclubs, and on television; and today we could count on three hours rehearsal before doing the radio show. The band was in a mood to groove.

When Kenneth arrived he told us that in an hour he was due at a dental surgeon's to have a broken tooth attended to—maybe an infection, he didn't go into detail, he was quite calm about it. We ran over some numbers but nothing much happened; no acts of love, no fires starting. It was all right, and it was nothing. At the end of the hour we broke off and, while the guys went for a beer, I walked over to the surgeon's office with Kenneth. Robert Patchell, who was in charge of the program for the C. B. C., looked pretty worried as we left. Bob is a fine, quiet, hip type of guy, and he had gone to a lot of trouble arranging the session—without him there wouldn't have been any session. And right now, right in the middle of rehearsal here we were off on an emergency trip to the dentist!

Well, Patchen had a major tooth surgery right on the spot as I waited. It was much more serious than any of us could have imagined. His jaw had to be chiselled away at, literally gouged out in an excruciatingly painful operation that took almost an hour. Finally he emerged into the waiting room, his face drained of color, and those great tired eyes more tired than I had ever seen them. His mouth was bleeding through big cotton plugs—still he smiled, and when the girl at the desk asked for his occupation he mumbled "Writer, self employed."

The guys were waiting for us at a cafeteria and we munched at hamburgers while Patchen chewed slowly on rare steak. In maybe ten minutes his face stopped being gray, and his eyes got back their straight look of seeing right through everything and everybody. Ordinarily this is a scary thing, but it wasn't for us just then! A strange and amazing man. Somehow—but how?—he had pulled out of it, was ready to get going. (In fact, Patchen did a midnight show with us at The Cellar that same night! Talk about separating the men from the boys—well, that's not the only reason he'll get our votes!)

We went back to the station and got set up again. Kenneth sat at a little table maybe ten feet from us; his cheek was getting puffed and he kept dabbing at his mouth with the cotton. Time to time in that run through I could see he was having trouble with his numbed lips on some syllables, so I guess it was lucky we had our own problem—and a large one. Since he was speaking into the recording mike, we could't hear him; and we *had* to listen to that lead horn or we would just be going through the motions—without the lead horn we were spooked.

Then somebody (Kenneth, I think) hit on the idea of each of us having earphones. We put them on—and we had a scene! It was extremely exciting! Now we could aim our language, our feeling, at Patchen's—the thing had come to life! The time we could stay in the studio was getting short—who cared! We could make it, we could maybe blow a little! In a couple of minutes I waved to the engineer to tape away.

We went through the numbers with one break (maybe 2 or 3 minutes) just before "Glory, Glory"—Kenneth drew on a cigarette, stretched his legs, refused coffee, and nodded that he was set. And during that last number I don't think he looked down at the paper once. We had all been caught up in the reading from the start—we knew that something was happening, that this was "something else"—but now he really went out for it, he wailed! With our nerves, our hearts, we heard him coming on, ringing the changes, threading and pulling us in and out of the light — the King Cat making his scene! And on his face we could see that what we had to say back to him was making the same kind of "heart-sense." It was *there*.

Every jazz guy going on the stand wants it to happen — call it wailing, swinging, what you like—every night he goes on he

wants it — but it can't be made to happen. The jazz guy has to get
in his own trance, feeling his feeling, really *feeling* it — contacting
the guy who lives inside him — call it getting up his own blues, his
own peace, his own anguish. And this is the ONE mystery of jazz.
A mystery nobody, critic or musician, can explain; and which
musicians usually have too much care about to try.

We had it that afternoon. The thing was there, it happened. But if you think I am talking about playing good — or
about anything like that — well, I said it couldn't be explained. It
is a mystery — it *really* is.

As for my own notion of poetry reading with jazz, it's
something I have been kicking around ever since I heard tapes
brought up here in the summer of 1956 — and by the way, this was
long before the big picture magazines "discovered" it down in the
Frisco area. These were tapes of Patchen reading to jazz records;
and Bob Patchell got them programmed on the C. B. C. network
that autumn. Anyway, one of the ideas I have about it is that the
band has to be free to play jazz; it must be spontaneous or where is
the jazz? It can't be muddied up by literal or arty "interpretations"
of verbal meanings — that would do for musical comedy numbers.
The feeling the poet releases through his reading must be met by
the jazz guys with some type of honest *paralleling* in their own
speech, in the idiom of jazz — the thing has to be honest: then even
when it isn't very good (and God knows most of the attempts have
been pretty awful), nobody will get hurt. But when the attempts
are both dishonest — on both sides — and bad, it's not just a cheap
scene; it's a vicious, hurtful farce. Which brings me to the fact
that most jazz musicians don't dig poetry anyway; and this type of
thing will really close the book on it. The jazz guys are bugged by
what they read and see of the "beat" — *this is false, weird:* it's not a
real scene, it only pretends to be. And behind all the trappings of
the "beat," behind the falseface, there is something real: the
world of the jazz guy. The world the critics are pretending doesn't
exist — the critics who are trying to "elevate" jazz from its place at
the foot of the social ladder, who would forget all that unpleasant
"early" history and get it all safely settled in the university
classrooms and concert halls.

Hallowed or not, jazz has its own bordellos and twist-gut
dives; and it goes on, much as the bad, money-whoring novels

about jazz musicians paint it, and no amount of lecturing before women's clubs and critics' forums at the new jazz music colleges will blur the real picture—the real, guts-level world of jazz where pot and heroin and casual sex are not just easy words in a fast-buck book.

To the jazz guy the "beat" thing goes right along with the job of fouling up, of falsification, that the high pressure, Johnny-Come-Never critics have been doing. He knows the score—and it isn't "All's right with the world" either. But I better get back to what I was saying.

Patchen was the one exception. I've heard of many jazz-men who have been digging him all along. Myself, it's been ten years. (On this, I should say that it pleased me a lot when Dale Hillary and Bill Boyle went round quoting big hunks of his poetry for weeks after Kenneth left here. They probably dug him more as a man than as a poet, but they did dig him. And these two would never know they were on a desert island if they had their instruments and a good supply of records along.)

Patchen has called the "beat" business a lot of harsh names. "A freakshow worth every Madison Ave. penny of the three-dollar-bill admission," is one of the things he said about it. Yet it couldn't miss that the biggest name on the scene—and the one all the "beats" tried to imitate—would get swept into it.

And from this distance it all seems pretty unimportant. The sow's ear purses don't hold up for long, and the people who like spending bad money won't lose much time finding new ones to carry it in. Anybody who cared enough to look at the thing could see that what Patchen didn't like about the "beat" was the same faking of the genuine article that the jazz guys saw in it. For Patchen is a real rebel, a nonconformist from far back, all the way to FIRST WILL & TESTAMENT (1939); he's been genuinely beatific and all the rest of it claimed for the "beats"—if you can scare up a copy, read his ALBION MOONLIGHT, published in 1941; SLEEPERS AWAKE, 1946—these are *real swingers,* books which Henry Miller called "works of genius"—(prose books). Why aren't these books around? Why do the critics pretend they never existed? I don't know—maybe for the same reason Lester Young died without rent money. "It's dark out, Jack."

But with all this, with this type of scene, I still think nobody who listens to Patchen read will give a hoot about what has been said or not said about "poetry and jazz" — I think the experience of hearing this man read will just wash all that out! This is *something else*. So you haven't and you likely won't dig other poets reading with jazz — what does that prove?

Well, for one big thing it should prove that you can't lump someone like Patchen with other people just because there's a handy tag for what they are doing — right here these general tags make no sense. (Like pepper and salt are both tagged condiments, we don't get mixed up about knowing that they are pretty different). Any given time you can figure about one to a customer — they had Whitman, we have Patchen. I say that little stuff, the confusions, they aren't important.

Anyway, on this session we all felt a special kind of identity and love for him. For the reasons I described at the beginning, and also because somehow Kenneth's dignity — so easy and *natural* — his bigness and deep honesty, these things came through to us with added force that day. As I said, something happened.

I am happy too about this record because a lot of people will be able to hear Dale Hillary at the start of a career that with any type of break should take him all the way. Dale, from a little town in the backwoods section of Canada, was eighteen at the time of the session; and he's now taken his alto and his talent down to the States — and along with them the best loving wishes of the jazz guys up here!

Now a last thing. The other day I learned that Charlie Parker, the originator of modern jazz, used to carry Patchen's books about with him, and knew many of his poems by heart, and would often be saying the poems when he was working up something for his music. So I'm happy, *very happy*, though it was just a coincidence, that the opening blues on this record was written by the late, great Charlie Parker.

Jonathan Williams

Out of Sight, Out of Conscience

"There is no place for a poet in American society. No place at all for any kind of poet at all. . . The majority of American poets have acquiesced in the judgment of the predatory society. They do not exist as far as it is concerned. They make their living in a land of make-believe, as servants of a hoax for children. They are employees of the fog factories — the universities. They help make the fog. . . They turn out bureaucrats, perpetuate the juridical lie, embroider the costumes of the delusion of participation, and of late, in departments never penetrated by the humanities staff, turn out the atom, hydrogen, and cobalt bombers — genocidists is the word. Patchen fills these academicians with panic. . ." Which is Kenneth Rexroth pegging the scene, inimitably, in the essay, *Kenneth Patchen. Naturalist of the Public Nightmare.*

Before I talk about Patchen as a man, let me quote the only piece of *literary* criticism worth reading about his recent work. Oddly enough it appeared in one of those highbrow quarterlies Rexroth likes to consign to nowhere: *Sewanee Review* (Spring 1958). The critic is James Dickey, the poet from Atlanta. Dickey is a conservative, fond of that faultless breed of stale literary poet. But, he is also very perceptive.". . . Patchen is still, despite having produced a genuinely impassible mountain of tiresome, obvious, self-important, sprawling, sentimental, witless, preachy, tasteless, useless poems and books, the best poet American literary expressionism can show. Occasionally, in fragments and odds and ends nobody wants to seek out any more, he is a writer of superb daring and invention, the author of a few passages which are, so far as I can tell, comparable to the most intuitively beautiful writing ever done. . . . If there is such a thing

59

as pure or crude imagination, Patchen has it, or has had it. With it he has made twenty-five years of notes, in the form of scrappy, unsatisfactory, fragmentarily brilliant poems, for a single, unwritten cosmic Work, which bears, at least in some of its parts, analogies to the prophetic books of Blake. . . . He has made and peopled a place that would never have had existence without him: the realm of the 'Dark Kingdom,' where all who have opposed in secret are. . .provided with green crowns,' and where the vague, powerful figures of fantasmagoric limbo, the dream people, and, above all, the mythic animals that only he sees, are sometimes as inconsolably troubling as the hallucinations of the madman or the alcoholic, and are occasionally, as if by accident, rendered in language that accords them the only kind of value possible to this kind of writing: makes them obsessive, unpardonable, and magnificent. It is wrong of us to wish that Patchen would 'pull himself together.' He has never been together. . . ." Despite what Mr. Dickey perhaps does not see (i.e., what I see), he sees a great deal I might not have, and I thank him accordingly, and I admit that I buy the *Sewanee Review* if nobody's looking.

So, the 'problem of Patchen,' as some piss-ant journal like the *Saturday Review* once put it, continues. One knows of other poets with grave problems (Raymond Larsson, Merle Hoyleman, Lorine Niedecker)—it is a *discredited* profession because, it seems, almost no one is interested in present developments leading towards any appreciable improvement in a pejorative public taste. Pound (1933): "The effects of capitalism on art and letters, apart from all questions of the relations of either capitalism, art, or letters, to the general public or the mass, have been: (1) the nonemployment of the best artists and writers; (2) the erection of an enormous and horrible bureaucracy of letters, supposed to act as curators, etc., which bureaucracy has almost uninterruptedly sabotaged intellectual life, obscuring the memory of the best work of the poet and doing its villainous utmost to impede the work of contemporary creators. . . . The stupidity of great and much-advertised efforts and donations and endowments is now blatant and visible to anyone who has had the patience to look at the facts. The 'patron' must be a live and knowledgeable patron, the entrusting of patronage to a group of bone-headed professors ignorant of art and writing, is and has been a most manifest failure." It is not difficult to identify the gentlemen in question who grace the universities and foundations but it is considered impolite to unmask or deface these ivied columns in academic groves. People whose culture is 'storeboughten' have a taste for style that is silk off a spool. It is provided by those who are not traitors to their class, etc., at Wesleyan or Iowa or Connecticut College or the Woman's College of the University of North Carolina. Charles Ives preferred associates from the world of insurance and perhaps so did Wallace Stevens.

Thoreau's mouth watered at a woodchuck next to the pond not because he was hungry but because he longed to inhabit the wildness of the creature. We read him for that 10% genuine native ferocity, not for the Elbert Hubbard parts. There are many other American writers who work more or less instinctively and we read them for what they can give us of themselves and the wilderness. (Man is symbiotic and the 'wilderness' is a multiple metaphor. In our agora there is savagery, filthy lucre, despoiled nature and dead spirit in abundance—enough to defeat any creator.) As stylists these writers are often amateurs or, let's put it, Yankee inventors. I mean Crevecoeur, Bartram, Audubon, Thoreau, Dickinson, Anderson, Patchen; and such commentators on the American 'thing' as Lawrence, Williams, Dahlberg, and Olson. Visionaries, prophets, moralists—particularly men who live in terms of a frontier. Such writing tells us how to live in that peculiar American knowledge.

I heard from Patchen yesterday, an exhausted letter but one full of anger that his wife is having to clerk in a store in Palo Alto, despite the fact that she suffers from multiple sclerosis. It provides what income there is. The letter also brings news that the last of the terrific surgical procedures to correct his spine (July 13, 1959) apparently has damaged his back (a plexus of nerves and another disintegrated disc) to the point that further surgery is too dangerous, i.e., only drugs can be expected to control the steady pain. God knows, Patchen's case is a pure and simple horror story—one thing after ten others: fourteen years in which he was largely incapacitated, 1937-51. The operation paid for by public support (1951) at Yale which did not take; the partially successful spinal fusion of 1956 which held up until 1959. Yet, I have heard one or two of the Literary Gentlemen suggest that Patchen must

need the pain—it keeps the public alert. That's the genus of com-
patriot one is likely to have these days. "90% of the worst human
beings I know are writers," to quote Rexroth.

But, what to do? I see nothing to appeal to but conscience.
One cannot 'demand' that society support anyone, particularly a
man like Patchen whose life is lived in defiance of society's official
literature of filth, money and religion. It is precisely such a poet
whose best work functions "to incite humanity to continue living"
(EP) who stands the greatest chance of destruction. Once, when I
had some money, before publishing books I believed in (a
vocation proven tenable only on Mars), I gladly gave a portion of
it to Patchen. That is still the one thing most of us could do in this
present emergency. I noticed in the *Times'* obituary of Boris
Pasternak that the Pen Women of America sent him a wreath.
Swinging! Keep it up girls, Oscar Williams will touch you with his
wand. . . . What else to do? Maybe we should picket the *New
York Times Book Review*? Demand the scalp of Francis Brown
and J. Donald Duck? Implant new adrenaline glands in the two
hundred paid keepers of the Literary Kudos? Feed the maenads of
the Academy of American Poets and the Poetry Society of
America the proper mushrooms and ivy beer at the next meeting?
I don't know what to do. I do know that one of the very damn few
poets in America who deserves the name is a very sick man and
that the foundations and awards committee should be constantly
reminded, cajoled and embarrassed until they render some
assistance. It has been twenty-five years and twenty-five books
since Patchen's one Guggenheim. It has not been renewed. One
can think of a couple of cornfed bards who have had three or four.
If this is not so, it seems so.

An Interview with Kenneth Patchen

INTERVIEWER: Kenneth Patchen is one of America's major poets and authors and he is in Seattle right now [1959], and with us on Front Row Center and will be appearing this evening on a program at the music auditorium at Third and Cedar in a program of poetry and jazz, in which he will be reading his poetry backed by The New Bed of Roses chamber jazz group. We'd like to welcome to Front Row Center and say what a great pleasure it is to have Kenneth Patchen with us. You've done, both on record and in person, I know, a number of performances working in front of a jazz group. Do you particularly like this type of performance, do you think that your work is especially adaptable to performance with a jazz group?

KENNETH PATCHEN: Yes, I think so in that for many years the interest I've had in jazz has not been a one way street. I'm aware more and more that a lot of jazz players have found something in my work which was meaningful to them, and I feel that it is possible through this as yet undeveloped medium to reach a new audience, an audience of people who have accepted jazz as America's great contribution to world culture, something I think

---

Editor's Note: This interview took place in 1959 at Station KUOW (University of Washington, Seattle). It began with Patchen reciting "In Order To," and closed with a reading by him of "A Sigh is a little altered," and "Lonesome Boy Blues," none of which have been included in this version of the transcript, which I edited from the original tape. No records exist which identify the interviewer. — RGM

it is, and also are receptive to the idea that poetry is something a little more meaningful to people's lives than so many black marks on a paper in a college textbook.

INTERVIEWER: But you feel, this nature of performance is valid apart from the attractiveness in the fact that it may draw people who would not ordinarily come to poetry or this poetry, the combination for you is artistically valid?

KENNETH PATCHEN: It has a validity in that you mentioned that I had done this a number of times. I've done it literally hundreds of times, and no time in my memory has it not been a living experience, a creative thing, an exploration of the evening of a living substance, of things going on between human beings at a level, it seems to me, removed from the ordinary one of entertainment. It's possible, I think, to bring the immediacy of jazz to bear on the spoken word. An electric switch is thrown. I've had many people tell me that they had had this experience and it was a new experience.

INTERVIEWER: Digressing from this topic, to a question that probably is a chronic one, and one that you may not enjoy answering, but is one that I've heard asked over and over, we know that you are active in the San Francisco area, and so I suppose anyone who is, and is a contemporary author and poet, must make some comment as to his position in relation to the North Beach Beat Movement. I know that your position is not one similar to many of the active poets and authors there.

KENNETH PATCHEN: Well, I live and have lived for some time about thirty-five miles from San Francisco on the map, but I think further from San Francisco than is imaginable almost in every other way. I think in the first place that there is no such thing as a San Francisco "scene" outside of the inkpots of certain Madison Avenue soap vendors, who were selling something and found people who were willing to demean themselves in public in a synthetic bohemian spectacle, a sort of a freak show, and I have no sympathy whatever with either the instigators of it or the people who are willing to dehumanize themselves and to cast a dark shadow over the plight of the American artist. This to me is a real thing despite all the nonsense in *Time* Magazine about the new audience for poetry. What has been demonstrated by these people is that there is an audience for people who are willing to strip in public, dance about, put on ladies' hats and the whole nonsensical pseudo-bohemian bit, and this is not my dish and it's not the dish of any artist I know of, or any writer I admire.

INTERVIEWER: Which is in one regard perhaps, a comment that would not be expected by many, particularly considering the fact that you share the same publisher with many representatives of this group. But that's as far as the relationship extends, you would say then.

KENNETH PATCHEN: I breathe the same air as Liberace.

INTERVIEWER: Jazz has reached a tremendous audience and so many people like jazz, almost everybody does, but poetry in a way is still considered effete. Poetry is a pretty neglected art right now, don't you think?

KENNETH PATCHEN: Yes and no, I feel that there is too much emphasis placed on the obscurity of modern poetry; I think it's obscure because people don't read it, that's true, but the so-called "older poetry" is also obscure for the same reason. People don't read it or they read it through the clouded, fogged-over glasses of professors and so on. It must be remembered that poetry is not Johnny-Come-Lately on the scene, that it preceded everything which people nowadays seem to think of as literature. The novel is a baby in swaddling clothes and the reading of poetry in public, which some bedazzled subscribers to *Time* Magazine think of as a new thing, is perhaps the oldest communication, cultural communication, mankind knows about. Most of the legends and sagas of the human race were handed down in just this way. And not in people's living rooms either, but in cafés and gathering places and so on, and often the saga poets accompanied themselves on instruments or had with them people who played instruments, and the rhythms of the verse were determined pretty much by the capacity of the particular instrument being used. And there was a very close affinity between the reading and the instrument accompaniment to that reading, and I think most of the "prosody" patterns of poetry are to be traced to this very thing. Little is known; it's a long, involved, subject—Greek verse and how it was influenced by dancing and music. In fact, almost nothing is known about early Greek music, but it would seem that there was a notation which had to do with the scoring for instruments as it had to do with the voice accompaniment to these instruments, so that before man sang to a musical line he spoke to a musical line which was carried out by instruments.

INTERVIEWER: You spoke with rhythm.

KENNETH PATCHEN: That's right, yes. And of course it's something which man can feel quite proud about, and humble about at the same time, because it would seem judging from the instinctive feeling children have for rhythm, and animals have, that it is a rhythm present in the universe itself.

INTERVIEWER: Do you, are you consciously aware of, and does it concern you greatly, the acceptance or lack of public acceptance and popularity of your work, or does the reason for your work lie outside real communication? What I am asking is, how introverted is your approach to your work?

KENNETH PATCHEN: I think this is a personal thing. I think it is very difficult for any writer or artist to talk about his own feelings about audience and so on, but my own feeling when I think of it, which is never, is something that just doesn't come into it at all. I think the moment any artist thinks in terms of what fate the work under his hand will have in the minds and emotions and sensibilities of others, he is off in left field somewhere, he is not on the side of the angels any more. He is on the side of people who are trying to sell books or paintings or prints or what-have-you, and that is none of the artist's business.

INTERVIEWER: Can we to some extent conclude that in *First Will and Testament,* the fat poet in the corner is somewhat representative of an attitude toward your audience?

KENNETH PATCHEN: I haven't the slighest idea what my audience is. I, once again, don't think about it, but I might say just to stress what I have in mind that I don't usually think of it in terms of people I know or people who are reading reviews, or buying books, or what-have-you. I'd like to just say that I hope my audience includes somehow, I don't know exactly how, but I hope it includes the spirits of some of the men now dead who have worked in poetry and in the other arts and I don't feel that they're dead at all. This is perhaps a sentimental way of putting it, but it's a very real thing for me. I'm often consoled thinking about some of the poets and artists who have had no "audience," as people think of audience, someone like William Blake for instance, who in reality have a vastly greater audience than a thousand Ernest Hemingways or William Faulkners, or anybody else you can think of in that catagory. These men who were read by no one, known by no one in their time, yet command a hearing by men of spirit, and all artists have anyway, is this one little pinpoint of light in the darkness, the fact that out of all the morass of mediocrity and conformity there is this small current of communication, not with an audience limited or confined to a period of time, but an audience which resides solely in terms of the human spirit, and if anything lasts on earth, it is this, a small thing, but a thing which, until now at least, has shown more endurance than anything else that man has advanced before him, this small light, this small desire to be true, not so much to art, no man knows anything about that, but true to the best instincts and feelings in himself in regard to what he does. This thing to me is all of it; the rest of it is just talk, hot air.

INTERVIEWER: Why then do you travel thousands of miles and take hundreds of hours away from productive writing for public performances to your contemporaries?

KENNETH PATCHEN: That's a question which I would like to ask or have you ask one of the innumerable foundations which are almost everyday giving huge sums of money to writers in this country and who, for reasons I might say known quite well to me, never quite turn the golden flow in my direction. I'm trying to make a living. Put it as simply as that.

INTERVIEWER: It hurts because of the comment that it is on American letters.

KENNETH PATCHEN: Well, once again I'd like to repeat that I am trying to make a living, but I certainly don't want Hemingway's vast audience; in fact I don't think that Hemingway has any audience, but that again is a big story in itself.

INTERVIEWER: We certainly heartily recommend to those of you who are not familiar with Kenneth Patchen to go hear him. If you are familiar with Kenneth Patchen, you are already in line outside the musicians union and aren't listening anyway.

KENNETH PATCHEN: If we're about to say goodnight, I'd like to just say that in Seattle lives a very great poet, Theodore Roethke, and I am here and I would like to just say that.

Gene Detro

Patchen Interviewed

DETRO: Your wife has told me you've been writing daily since about the age of twelve. Is there a point you can identify at which you became a poet, or have you always been of that sensibility?

PATCHEN: That's a difficult question, and therefore a good one. I'd say that I had a consciousness of being a poet when I first realized that the medium of writing had something in it more than just communication—the kind one has with friends or family, that one is very fortunate—something happens, and I suppose it has to do with you know with being a poet and writing poetry.

DETRO: The thing that's always grabbed me with your works is the very high and highly refined degree of magic. Would you attempt to identify how that gets in, or do you work for it—or does it just happen?

PATCHEN: It's interesting you should say that, because that which is called a sense of magic is to me the great strain which separates versifiers and writers of poetry. Now I'm not talking about my own work or making any assessment of it—I'm simply talking about magic as I think of it, and this is associated too with the only possible reason I can think of as a cause for my beginning to write. That is, my grandfather who was a Scot and who had a wonderful sense of humor, and a tradition going back to the time of Burns, whose poetry he knew thoroughly, whose poetry he read to me when I was a little boy, had this bardic strain very definitely; and in the stories he told me, in the sense I had about him, there was what you call magic.

DETRO: And the old druidic thing, poet as priest?

PATCHEN: Exactly.

DETRO: I was rereading some of your work the other night, and which poem is it that refers to—I take it to mean levels of being and where we are now must always attempt in honesty to match up with another version of ourselves. What do you mean in that poem?

PATCHEN: You have me stumped. I don't offhand know which of the poems you have in mind. I would think that almost any poem of length of mine would have something of that theme, the ascendency of person out of chaos and non-being through feeling, through love.

DETRO: Here we are—*Cloth of the Tempest.* 'The one life must be attempted with the other, that we may embark upon the fiery work for which we were certainly made.' That seems to me to be an extremely priestly statement, in the sense where using the word priest—

PATCHEN: You are hitting close to home with almost everything you say— in that, for instance, what you've said just now reminds me that my mother had the thought and the hope that I would become a priest. I was raised a Catholic, and Mother is a very devout Catholic. And the poem you mention and the levels of being in it, I think refers primarily to the miraculous which is in the commonplace.

DETRO: But there was no strict reference to another level of being that's concurrent with what we're doing right now, here and now on the temporal level.

PATCHEN: No, there is always of course, between words and the meanings of words, an area which is not to be penetrated. I think this is, once again, the region of magic, the place of the priestly interpreter of nature, the man who identifies himself with all things and with all beings, and who suffers and exhalts with all of these.

DETRO: You certainly do hit the extremes of feeling in your work. I'm wondering, as you are a major influence upon me and many other poets of my age, what are your own influences?

PATCHEN: They are as varied, I imagine, as your own, and as difficult to pin down. I would be hard put to say whether I was more influenced by poets or by people in general. I have found that oftentimes a poet's work has meant something more to me as it is revealed by association with a person.

DETRO: I don't quite—

PATCHEN: I mean that in many cases the poem misses its mark with me, but very rarely do people miss the mark.

DETRO: Back to the magic thing, many poets are concerning themselves more and more with legitimate theatre and films. I have always been of the opinion your *Journal of Albion Moonlight* would make a magnificent film. Have you done anything in this area yet, or script thing?

PATCHEN: Not in any fashion satisfactory to me. I wrote a play which was performed but which was never satisfactorily developed. I mean, as it happened during the performance of the play things beyond my control made it impossible for me to make certain corrections from the performance on the stage which I thought necessary.

DETRO: Are you speaking of your physical ailments?

PATCHEN: Yes and no. But in any case, the play you refer to has not been published. I've never felt that it was in publishable form.

DETRO: Are you working on the play now?

PATCHEN: I would hedge on that by saying that should an opportunity arise where I could work with a dramatic group in close association, I probably would complete the revisions. In other words, the play which was produced is very far from being the play which I now envision—or envisioned. It's the sort of thing that happens I guess to poets, probably more often to poets than to playwrights. I don't know too much about playwrights, but revision seems to be sort of the order of the animal.

DETRO: They're not written to be rewritten.

PATCHEN: That's exactly right.

DETRO: Do you still write daily?

PATCHEN: I have in the last—oh fifteen years, as you know—done a great deal of graphic work, and it happens that very often my writing with pen is interrupted by my writing with brush—but I think of both as writing. In other words, I don't consider myself to be a painter. I think of myself as someone who has used the medium of painting in an attempt to extend—gives an extra dimension to the medium of words.

DETRO: Who was it—Margaret Rigg?—wrote that your work with paintbrush and words reminded her of the Keltic Illuminated Manuscripts. I think it's really much more basic than that—in fact, I've seen many of your paintings and they seemed to be original in the strictest sense; that is, they incorporate people, and what a person is is to a high degree what you'll see in the painting. Is this conscious effort on your part?

PATCHEN: What I say now will probably sound like false modesty. I don't mean it to be, but what you have been kind enough to call originality in the painting is from my point of view the result of ignorance. In other words, were I a painter I feel that this particular aspect of my work would not stand out as it does. This is to devalue it, of course.

DETRO: Then your poetry and prose will never take a back seat to your painting, as it has with Henry Miller and some of the others.

PATCHEN: No. This does not mean that I value one medium over the other. It's just that I feel my own nature, temperament, talents or whatever, are more verbal than visual. And I would also think that in the cases of the greatest painters there is once again, and this will refute what I have just said, a quality of searching, of clumsiness in the craft almost—like Van Gogh, for example, whose breaking with tradition seems almost as though he didn't know what to do next, and I think this is the stance of the creator.

DETRO: I think he was pretty much controlled by things, forces that he could neither understand nor control.

PATCHEN: This is true. I would withdraw his name. You are probably thinking of the difficulties which let him to the miserable years in the asylum, and so on. I would withdraw his name and insert in its stead the name of almost any creative artist, and say once again I feel that in the act of creation there is always a losing of contact with the medium; and when this happens to a marked degree, as happened in the case of someone like Picasso at a certain point, it leads to a breakthrough. In other words, what the artist has no thought of becomes what other artists are full of—that is, if the creation is successful.

DETRO: Then if you're true to your own medium you will communicate. Or are you talking about a gestalt kind of thing?

PATCHEN: No, I'm talking about a type of creative person who

is closer to me than some others. For instance, a man like Paul
Klee. I feel that every time he approached a new canvas it was
with a feeling that 'well, here I am, I know nothing about painting, let's learn something, let's feel something'—and this is what
distinguishes the artist of the first rank, the innovator, the man
who destroys, from the man who walks in the footsteps of another.
You cannot express yourself without admitting, it seems to me,
that no true self-expression is possible. It'll have to be left until
tomorrow, you'll have to try it again. Another man will have to try
it tomorrow.

DETRO: It seems to me that you're saying—well, despite the huge
amount of work you've done, are you saying that nothing is ever
enough, that somebody else will have to finish the job?

PATCHEN: Of course your own job is one thing. The moment
the artist is asked about his influences he of necessity flounders, I
believe. Because it is not the nature of the artist to know what his
true influences are, or what they have been, and I'm not by this
statement saying that it remains for a third party to know. I think
that the mystery of life will ring in the work, and when it rings
most strongly, truly and honestly, it will ring with a sense of
mystery.

DETRO: Wonder—

PATCHEN: Of wonder, childlike wonder. I think of someone like
Kelderly who, like Van Gogh, ended his life in an asylum. He had
a sense of wonder, a sense of identification with everything that
lived, with everything that had its being around him, much in the
way that to take an extremely different personality. Immanuel
Kant—

DETRO: This country still hasn't got over his seemingly native
distrust of the poet, capital P. I know you've been through some
rough times, and it is hard for any poet to keep a roof over his
head through poetry alone—how have you managed to retain
your sense of wonder and have such a nice environment around
you?

PATCHEN: My only answer to that is to say that I cannot conceive of any way in which I could lose the sense of wonder. To me
that would be death.

DETRO: Then it's obviously the reason why you don't use
painkilling drugs despite your back injury.

PATCHEN: That is the reason.

DETRO: Are you in pain now?

PATCHEN: Yes.

DETRO: Your collection, when is it coming out?

PATCHEN: The selected poems, my first, is scheduled for publication with New Directions. It's been a sad task for me to make the choices and to assemble this first collection because it meant choosing one of three poems from my published works—in other words, I had to exclude two of every three.

DETRO: Was it commercially impossible to bring together all of your published poems?

PATCHEN: I think the answer lies in the fact that this will be a volume which is not of a size usually attempted today by/for commercial reasons—it will run upwards of 500 pages, and will represent roughly a third of my published works. I emphasize the published works, because I have a great volume of work which is unpublished as yet.

DETRO: At this point in your career do you submit for publication, or is whatever you approve acceptable to your publisher?

PATCHEN: Yes, everything I do finds ready publication. I would put it that way because at the moment I have, and this has been true now for some ten years, I have three publishers.

DETRO: I didn't know that.

PATCHEN: Yes, the problem of publishing is one I have never had.

DETRO: Who did the Padell books—They were of beautiful design.

PATCHEN: I have, as much as I could manage, had a hand in the design of all my books. More in the case of the Padell books which were done when I lived in New York City than the books which were done when I lived at a distance—such as books that are appearing now from New York

DETRO: Standard type of question: what, besides how to get a good job—what advice would you give to younger poets?

PATCHEN: I would advise the young poet in no way at all. I would offer no one advice. This again seems, I suppose, an evasion of your question—but I have consistently refused to comment on the work sent to me, not that I'm not concerned, and vitally concerned, with the work of young poets, but I believe it is no service to them to have someone they may have a special feeling about make a black and white statement about their work. I think this is not helpful—it is again a personal thing with me. It was not something helpful to me when I was a young poet. I think of the tragic case of Hart Crane who not only asked for advice but accepted it. And he accepted advice from poets who were diametrically opposed to him temperamentally—in a craft sense, and in every possible way. Of course I feel too, as a footnote to that, that every true poet is one who cannot be successfully imitated, and those who fall into the error of such imitations usually end with a product of their own only after struggling to throw off influences. In other words, it's very natural for the young poet to admire older members of his craft and to consciously and unconsciously imitate them—but as he gains confidence in his ability to express what he wants to say and as he finds what I'd call his own voice, all of this sort of falls away, and it becomes then a question of the poet saying: yes, I admire, I very much admire the work of such-and-such a poet — but the discerning listener or critic will understand that this does not by any means imply that he is imitative of that poet.

DETRO: Your effect on my work, I'd say, is not technical, but more of a conceptual thing opening up areas of consideration, and this happened many years ago. Something that has bothered me is your political poetry — It's a stuffy idea of mine that poets are simply apolitical, or should be.

PATCHEN: I would react to that by saying that I have never written political poetry. I know what you have in mind, the fact that when I started to work in the field of poetry, strictly when I started to get books published, there was a kind of great depression in this country. No one had jobs, no one had hope, no one had anything, and particularly was this true for the young. There seemed no way out at all, and this was reflected in the work of the times, and as time passed much of the work acquired the label of proletarian literature, or political writing, or what have you. But in the midst of this, I think those who were sincerely reacting to the world in which they found themselves did not think of the work as having any unusual coloring—it simply reflected the world that they knew.

DETRO: I'm glad to contradict myself, because hearing what you say it seems to me that these poets who go beyond their social condition in time and place because they're still applicable—now, nothing seems dated or antique as in the work of some other writers. I didn't—

PATCHEN: Of course in terms of poets and poetry, the length of time that has elapsed between my first book and my last book is very, very slight. I mean if one is to think of the great poets as one contemporary, as I'm sure you do, you know that poetry is, in a very real sense, a handing on from one man to another—perhaps through the span of years, perhaps not. Some consciousness, that you called an opening into consciousness, something that would enable him to see the world and himself with less distortion than other people do perhaps. I think of William Blake who has been called a man without a mask. I think that is a very apt description of him. I'm sure that had it been said to him, he would have rejected it—because he felt of himself that he was many many men. This is the primary expression of his work—his identification of himself with so many poets and so many ideas of people from the past—Milton, Shakespeare, Dante, and with many people whose names have fallen into disrepute—Swedenborg, a shining glowing name for William Blake, for us a curiosity perhaps, not one of the vitalizers. But how is one to take this away from Swedenborg, when it found a place and a polish and is reflected in the mirror of a wonderful mind, a wonderful man such as William Blake was.

DETRO: Who are the vitalizers in your highly educated view?

PATCHEN: I would find that hard to answer in the time we have today, because as I said earlier: often people who are in the lexicon of the popular press called ordinary people will say and do and be things which have tremendous significance for the poet—you know this yourself.

DETRO: Incredible things happening—

PATCHEN: That's very true. Particularly associated with reaction to my work or its reception, or whatever you might say, the simple fact is that we are this moment in a world of the paperbacks. The paperback is cheap relative to books you and I had to buy when we started to hunt around for the books we wanted. And being relatively cheap they have a much wider distribution, much wider sales, and often a shorter life. Fortunately this hasn't been true of my books. I have never had a book remaindered. Quite a number of my books are out of print. But I believe that it is the intention of the publisher to bring them all back into print. And I also understand, this in answer to your question, that all of the books are alive in that people are searching for them and anxious to acquire them.

DETRO: Are you familiar with William Carlos Williams little book *I Wanted to Write a Poem*?

PATCHEN: Not familiar enough with it to discuss it.

DETRO: Well, in this he talks about each book that he has written, describing the where and how and what he was doing, and how different ideas came to him, and what he was attempting to do, which is in conversation much as we're doing right now. Do you ever think you'd get around to something like that?

PATCHEN: No, I wouldn't. I think the reason that I'm not able to discuss the book with you, it's one of the few books by Williams I didn't finish reading. Because it seemed to me that Williams was attempting to relive his life, and this is something no one can do. No one in my opinion can write a good poem twice. No one can remember, can possibly remember, how a good poem came into being — and from what I know of that book of Williams, he made a manful effort to do the impossible, to recreate his own feelings, the feelings he had when he was in the act of creating.

DETRO: Do you think that's wasted effort?

PATCHEN: I can only speak out of my own mouth and experience — to me it is an impossible thing to do.

DETRO: Yes, many poets—Dylan Thomas was the last most notable example—seemed to run scared regarding the possibility of drying up, or burning out, whatever poets do when they go downhill. Apparently you have none of these fears.

PATCHEN: I think poets can be great going down the damnedest hill anybody can imagine. I have no such fears. Earlier you said that the poet in America is not looked upon as one of the people—that isn't exactly what you said, that's what you meant. In other words, behind your thought was that the poet is looked upon as being somewhat of a freak.

DETRO: I'd say rather the vague suspicion attached to poets would resemble the pre-Hollywood attitude toward actors.

PATCHEN: That's exactly true, and a very good point. The old notion people had about theatrical people, that they were always *on* — and that people have now about so many people: that they are in show biz. I think certain poets have — I don't condemn them for this particularly — have given way to this popular notion that the only person worthwhile is the person who is being something outlandish, or different, or something they wouldn't do, *they* being the great mass of people. Certain poets have played this role.

DETRO: Crane?

PATCHEN: Not so much Crane. I'd prefer not to name names in this connection, but they did play a role which the public expected of them. And it's all right if they do not believe it. The moment they believe it the show's over, because the show is all inside. It's not something the people can see, or that the people can be told about.

DETRO: Well, difficult question, difficult to formulate: you've seen the word wild in a complimentary way — you certainly have one of the wildest minds I've ever encountered. What is the difference between you and other people? Is it a kind of perceptual chemistry, or — you actually see things?

PATCHEN: I couldn't answer the question since I am — I'm limited to one — to one phase of —

DETRO: But you have read other people and talked to other people. Are there any apparent differences between you and your makeup, and —

PATCHEN: I don't know. I would answer you in this way: as is commonly thought no one has a true picture of himself, so in my opinion people never have a true picture of their fellows, so that there is always the difficulty of not only communication with one another but having the vocabulary, the substance to communicate to another mind. It's a very difficult thing. I think for instance of someone like William Shakespeare as the prime example of a man who was capable of being the most secret and creative and personal being — at the same time he had the capacity to understand and to feel what other people were, what they were thinking, what they were experiencing. This to me is a miraculous thing. It has

happened very few times in the arts. I think someone similar to
Shakespeare, although it would be difficult to make a very sound
case, but similar in the way I'm attributing to Shakespeare, what
Blake felt — the universal in the grain of sand, all humanity in one
person. And that one person being all people. Shakespeare
demonstrated this, this is what Shakespeare does. Shakespeare
shows in his plays that this is true, that all people are one person,
and they are all understood, they are all. . .

*EDITOR'S NOTE: Abruptly, the interview was over. Patchen,
exhausted, and in pain, was unable to go on. In the last dozen or
so sentences his voice expressed it, and there was anguish in them,
in the struggle to go on, and in the last three words uttered in the
interview there was agony, of a man crucified to a bed; hordes of
youths rampaging the streets crying out for freedom; the brain of
a genius imprisoned in this huge masculine body crucified to a
bed, not struggling to get up out of it, just to go on talking,
without pain, without exhaustion; an hour later (wrote Miriam)
he was painting, grimacing, a picture poem.*

Richard Bowman

Notes from a Friend

Kenneth Patchen is a brave man. He is a loner in his field. I first met Kenneth in 1955 when he and his wife, Miriam, lived in a small cottage in Palo Alto. Our mutual friend, publisher Bern Porter, had told me that Kenneth was about to undergo an operation on his spine. I had had the same and successful operation in 1951, and Porter suggested that I might reassure Kenneth that he could again be mobile. Out of that rather clinical meeting our friendship began.

As an artist, I feel honored to write about Patchen, his creative work and personality. Often he has remarked to me that he is not an "artist" (making "paintings"): however, Kenneth Patchen is truly an *artist-poet* and a *poet-artist*. Was not William Blake equally gifted in drawing and painting as he was in composing his mysterious poems? And like Patchen, Blake's "illustrations" fitted his poems like a glove on a hand. The paintings-drawings-illustrations of Patchen's poems are absolutely unique in their conception; they have the same wry, magnificent and natural humor that flows from him when he writes, or even in conversation with friends. Also, they have the stark power that is found in his poems. In his graphic works one sees the meeting and happy marriage of apparently dichotomous images, just as in the best Surrealist works. His sense of color, too, is very personal—sometimes extremely subtle, sometimes trenchantly powerful. Just as Patchen creates new forms of poetry, so does he often create some oddly pungent but successful combinations of color and form.

I have never before met anyone who has the balance of gentleness and anger that Patchen has. Both of us deeply feel the wonder of nature, animals, love and the positive acts of humans.

This duality of spirit is certainly evident in his LOVE poems and in his WAR poems. Everything Patchen does has the gentility or fierceness of the creative act at its best. This *crying out to be heard* is a very natural human phenomenon, from the greatest man to the least — all want to be recognized for their own human (or inhuman) message, even be it in death.

We equally despise the "operators," the Judases in the art world, business and government. The *Establishment* of either art, industry or government usually is blind to (or neglects) the independent, honest, inventive individual. Perhaps soon there will be a change.

It is timely and rewarding that thousands of the bright and frustrated younger generation have discovered and are really attuned to Kenneth Patchen's message and art. This is perhaps his proudest moment. Kenneth Patchen is a creator who is destined to take his place with Walt Whitman, Albert Pinkham Ryder and Charles Ives as inventor and hero in the history of American arts.

Richard Hack

Memorial Poetry Reading for Kenneth Patchen

I was living in that city at the time, my first time, and heard about the reading a few hours before it was to take place, thanks to a chance phone call to some friends in Oakland who were thinking of going. They didn't, so I went alone. Walking up Mason St. from Market St. past glittering restaurants, liquor stores, and expensive dives, I thought the big line of people was going to "King Lear" playing at a movie house next door. But no, by God, they were all heading into the poets' theater. Afraid I wouldn't get a seat, I decided not to wait in the outdoor box office line, and barged right in like I had a ticket, over a corner of the carpeted foyer and down the carpeted stairs to the actual theater entrance, where I waited and wondered what to do, until one of the ticket takers, beleaguered by the pressing crowd, said, "We'll take cash if you have it."

Tickets were $1.50. A woman next to me said, "How are we going to do this? I don't have any change."

I didn't either. I wasn't working then. I pulled out a buck as offering to a pot. She looked at me and didn't know what to do. Well, neither did I.

Then her people materialized, a man and another woman. I kept offering my dollar and suggested we fiddle through together; but they couldn't figure it out. They said nothing to me, and then could say nothing to each other. I had to give up, then, since I was unwilling to lead, to take them and say, "Come on!" I figured it was time to talk, and said to the guy as I offered my dollar, "I don't have any change," in a sort of apologetic tone.

He frowned but indicated silently that I could pass.

81

I did. Now I was in art's inner sanctum, eh? One of the 5% of the audience who looked like a low class element (which I was, there), and proud of it. Walked around the place, sides & back, through well-dressed arty folk, poetry lovers, and poets & writers, stuffy and spirited people, and finally chose a seat.

It was a fine little theater, which on other nights was housing a crazy play (I saw on a free night, quite by accident) called "Revolt of the Good People." On still other nights, imagined ones stretching back somewhere into my pre-adolescent past, or practically, I could imagine the then half-imaginary Kerouac & Ginsberg reading their crazy poems, spinning their legends that turned on thousands across the continent. And yet San Francisco was only a forum of fame for Kerouac, et. al.; the substance of the all-American free road legend grew in the soil of New England, New York, and other cities, not to mention the wildernesses—it's all around here—certain stories can be everywhere true. The function of City Lights, with its links to other media, was to spur the great popularization of writing, to distribute the songs & insights of the avant-garde, to give meaning & hope to the burgeoning population of poets and prosists, old and ever-regenerated, groping for articulation of themselves and this most materialistic of nations. Till every neighbourhood has its writer and its magazine, furthering the cultural promise of past masters...to create something really new in the tiresome wash of novelty, of boredom, imitation, abstraction, and journalistic literature. To fertilize the breeding and seeding ground of literary ambitions, till the new great and lasting works are created in this center of international crisis—based on the contradictions of freedom & slavery, good & evil, cooperation & animosity—abstract contradictions which are so complex in their worldly reality. Through the mask of decadence, dogma, play-acting, & false consciousness will emerge, finally, the high art which reflects and inspires a striving, not so confused world.

Such the dream. And in that theater many dreamers, there below the street level carpeted foyer small as an afterthought, its marquee too small to show more than the first word in the title of the play appearing there. The theater with its established bohemian hipness, seen in a detached moment as only another mediator between audience & reality, like a poem or a poet, yet a melting pot of heads and words, hopefully true to its rebellious origins, by now something of a success, with the danger of becoming frozen in time, and with the promise of fostering literature in the 70's as it (or at least its publishing parent, City Lights Press) did in the 50's and 60's.

The bare black theater slowly got jammed to the gills, audience on the few rows of chairs in back, spilled over onto the floor in front, seated also in back of the lectern, and standing up against the four walls. There was a quiet, but highly charged expectancy: Who was going to read? The center was empty. Those who occupied it would have to face spotlights in front of them — yellow, white, red, pale blue — as well as hundreds of ears, eyes, and minds coming from all directions — and a few tongues, too, as it turned out.

Eventually the man showed — Al Young, the poet who organized the reading. Afterward on the street he gave full credit to Nancy Phillips of the City Lights group, who says that she only handled the technical details from the theater's end of it, that he thought up the idea, spoke to Mrs. Patchen, and invited the readers. Such modesty in a poet! He knew that the reading was not just his own, as Patchen knew that in one open, honest, compassionate, and critical human mind resides the whole human race, and practically everything else.

Al Young, sitting on a phone book on top of a wooden stool in front of the lectern, spoke of how at the age of 15 or 16 he discovered Patchen in the Detroit Public Library; and by this revelation learned that the best contemporary poetry could be natural and real, more than just a "code" taught in a "civilized" way in the classroom.

Young then gave some biographical data about the poet being honored. I think it useful to digress from the journalism a while to list some of the facts here (as well as others later related to me by Mark Linenthal, a teacher at San Francisco State). They can help provide a better understanding of both the poet and the reading given in his memory.

Patchen was born Dec. 3, 1911 in Niles, Ohio. Died Jan. 8, 1972 after living many years in the magic region around the San Francisco Bay, to which he moved in 1951.

At age 10 he published two sonnets in *The New York Times* and started his first diary. At age 17 he started a short stint as a steelworker in Ohio.

An athlete and scholar, he attended Alexander
Meiklejohn's experimental college at the University of Wisconsin
in Madison. He traveled. Met his wife, married in his early twen-
ties, and dedicated his books to her.

It was in his young manhood that he suffered his first back
injury. In 1937, a slipped disc was erroneously diagnosed as arthritis, and the bad back plagued him most of his life. His first
spine operation, in 1950, paid for thanks to benefits by poets like
Auden, Sitwell, and Eliot, brought no relief. In 1956 a spinal
fusion succeeded; but he was injured again during another
operation in 1959. From then right up to 1972, it is said, he left
his house in Palo Alto perhaps no more than twice a year.

Through all the suffering — and high joy — he remained
a dynamic, principled, avant garde writer. In 1950 he made his
first recording of poetry read to jazz. In 1957 he appeared with
Chambers' Jazz Quartet and with Charles Mingus in New York.
He knew where the fires of culture were burning. And if anybody
had a "built-in, foolproof, shock-proof shit detector," it was Patchen.

In his life he wrote many books, drew pictures, put some of
the books together with his own hands. He was the only writer invited to the Brussels Worlds Fair. While he was a major figure in
contemporary literature, he never made a hill of dollars (though
he did have the good fortune of being consistently published). His
main windfall seems to have been a $10,000 grant from the
National Endowment for the Arts—one of five grants bestowed in
1967 on "senior American writers." The U.S. government has
always been a cultural tightwad, and usually misguided as well as
reluctant. But that time, at least, they did a right thing. When he
was 56.

Now while his loved ones and friends have their memories,
the rest of us have his books. What he had, frequently realized in
literary work of his own hand, may be indescribable. Here's how
the eulogizing poets served him in San Francisco that night:

Robert Duncan led off, deep-voiced, mature, emotional,
with a poem from Patchen's *First Will and Testament* (New
Directions: 1939): "Scream, curse, sing! O wind of a people's
wrath!/Soar in a million tongues. Flay all hate from the earth."

Duncan departed. The name of the next reader was an-

nounced, and he advanced to the lectern from a side aisle. This
was the procedure. It was a long reading that went fast.

Harold Norse: "He was a part of youth, revolutionary
feeling, independence, the far-out." He was like "a Renaissance
master, a Welsh bard, a Hebrew prophet."

Yes, this was high tribute. Maybe a little exaggerated at
times. Things went smoothly, and the audience was almost
stiflingly quiet. Somebody's shit detector started ticking, or
thought it did. A young writer in the audience, Jerry Kamstra,
quite understandably & quite entertainingly, began making loud
interjections, sometimes interrupting a poet, sometimes riling
members of the audience with his bellowing comments from the
pit. Drunk on feeling, and probably alcohol (there was more than
a little jug-heading that night), he took part in some stormy ex-
changes, claiming he was a bastard son of Patchen (many are, I
suppose) and that he also represented the spirit of poetry. He said
that he anticipated being thrown out, but warned that he was
bigger than most persons present. Al Young let him read a poem
(it was one of Patchen's) just before the intermission.

Some were angry, but in fact the heckler fit in with the
spirit of things. Except for him, the reading might have been only
a genteel wake, or not a wake at all, but totally engulfed in its
other aspect, that of an almost still and silent churchly rite. He
quite clearly, if sometimes crudely, reaffirmed Patchen's faith in
man's animal and in his role as incorrigible renegade. Why put up
with someone else's preordained program of remembrance (loving
as its motives may be), & stay quiet and politely clap at the end
with all the be-sweatered and be-suited folkies, like a mental invalid? There are many moods that fit a memorial, and every death
should give birth to new life. Didn't Patchen write, "How like to
Power is our nature slain"? Well, it's a minor point of exegesis.
Through all the small storms, the high-feelinged ceremony went
on:

George Keathly read. Then George Hitchcock: "Have you
seen the homeless in the open grave of the hand of God?" Followed
by enthusiastic applause.

Lawrence Ferlinghetti, father of City Lights, read an elegy
he wrote. You might say an older, ever-beautiful Ferlinghetti, still
the angry man, impeccably dressed and groomed, always ap-

proachable, his look hard, rosy fires burning under his pale skin:

> Even the agents of death should take note
> and shake the shit from their wings
> in Air Force 1!
> but they do not
> and the shit still flies.

Toward the end, a warmer, more personal note:

> He is gone under the scattered undersea
> and knows what time it is but won't be back to tell it
> and would be too proud to anyway
> and too full of strange laughter to speak to us any-
> more anyway.

Morton Marcus began with a rap on Kundalini and the Philosophy of Essence, trying to articulate a symbolic interpretation of Patchen's back injury (energy is centered in the lower spine and rises, to the mind). "When a poet dies," said Marcus, "it is fitting that other poets gather & chant. Words must be spoken so that others hear again."

Then David Henderson read. A fine poet with a dramatic presence. Wore a little brown hat of some old-fashioned high style, and a khaki bag over his shoulder. In his introductory remarks, he praised Patchen's mixing of poetry and jazz, noting that he represented a multicultural force that is often lacking in contemporary art. Then he read his own poem, written a couple of years ago, called "Death of the Ice Queen." It is a very tight poem challenging the oppressive sterility of our civilization's power structure, transferred, in a sense, from Germany to the U.S.:

> doctor frankenstein
> and his family of golems ghouls and zombies
> lost the war
> and won the west

It is a poem that draws on various cultural forces — Afro-American, Yiddish, European — but especially it is a poem of youth, a revolutionary not a despairing poem, that believes in the concrete reality of a "showdown in the land of the dead," and victory for the forces of life.

David Meltzer read an emotional-discursive poem, one perhaps too obsessed with an abstract, monolithic concept of Love that wraps all rich and poor alike in one matrix of sentiment.

Then came another reader, Cecil Brown, against whom I still have a personal grudge deriving from what happened during a month he spent in one of my old apartments in Chicago. His faults and ambitious evilness could be expanded *ad nauseam,* but it's hardly worth the trouble. One needn't feel at all competitive toward other writers, but it will always be necessary to separate the chaff from the wheat. I booed when he finished his "poem."

Ishmael Reed, strong-looking, casually dressed, read an easy folksy poem—about a certain Railroad Bill—that pleased many listeners.

Sotère Torregian, one of the three members of the *French* (get that right) surrealist group in the U.S. (the other two are Lamantia and Nicolla), read a contemplative, as yet unpublished poem entitled "The Planet at 1:00 A.M."

Then Al Young read two absentee statements eulogizing Patchen sent from poets Allen Ginsberg and Barbara Payne. Followed by brief readings by Mary Norbert Korte, Eugene Ruggles, and Tom Parkinson.

During the intermission that followed, I spoke briefly with Ruggles, a spirited and friendly poet who looked like one—that is, dressed cheaply. He carried a book of Patchen's work and said that more readers should be choosing Patchen's own poems. I agreed—I guess automatically—threw in quick remarks on egotists using the ceremony for themselves, at which he nodded, and then started to explain my dislike for one of the persons invited. Ruggles interrupted with a sudden, nervous, perhaps pained laugh—indicating to me that this was not the time for that—and clapped me on the shoulder as he moved on.

I saw Torregian, too, speaking with some folks by the wall. He seemed almost contemplatively possessed by a light silliness. "Are you press?" he asked. "Hopefully," I replied.

"Hopefully," he repeated. Then laughed, almost moaning, "Oh, what can I *tell* you?"

Plenty, but I didn't know how to condense it. I asked him a few factual questions, asked him for the titles of his published volumes of poetry, and wished him well. He did likewise, asked my

name, was very friendly—waiting for questions rather than just
tolerating them.

Ah, me—I walked around—so many hearts and brains
remembering Kenneth Patchen. And still more to come. For me it
was an introduction to the man. Only later did I read any of his
books cover to cover. Here at the poets' theater I was finding out
just how broad and deep Patchen's influence was, how many
generations it spanned.

After the intermission came short readings by Gail
Chiarello and Robert Creeley. Shirley Kaufman read one of Patchen's, then one of her own, a feeling and piercing poem about
rock.

Then Gary Snyder. A poet who's been a forest ranger and
studied in a Japanese Zen monastery. Of medium height, erect,
short brown & silver hair tied in back, cleanly dressed,
psychically integrated, empathic & compassionate, his har-
monious presence expressing perfect physical & mental control. A
light smile. He recited his poem, pausing after each thought. His
clear lines and images spoke of six types of poets—Earth, Air,
Water, Fire, Space, & Mind—and celebrated universal communication:

> The earth poet who writes small earth poems needs help
> from
>   no man.
> ....
> The mind poet stays in the house
> The house is empty, but there are no walls
> And the poem is seen from all directions by everyone.

When he finished, a gasp, applause, a happy force
released from the audience.

Last on the program, a denouement to Snyder's easy yet
transcendent spiritual harmony, was a rather academic statement
of praise for Patchen read by Peter Winslow (member of an
American surrealist group).

Al Young closed with a few more facts and quoted from
Patchen's *First Will and Testament:* "there are so many little
dyings what does it matter which of them is death." Remarked
that Patchen's body was cremated and his ashes scattered over the
Pacific.

We filtered out slowly, some leaving immediately, some hanging around to talk and listen to a beat sidewalk guitarist strumming some downhome rag. It was happy and sad. Here we were again in that garish outside world which demanded perception, poetry, and change. Walking down again to Market St., I passed a topless joint giving forth the mournful music of Jim Morrison's last big hit, "Riders on the Storm."

Too high to wait for a streetcar, I walked home, my mind and spirit more alive than they had been, feeling that this night and Patchen's work had to be remembered. Now, I may have made a couple mistakes here—the reading was fast, and not blessed with a photographic memory, I have only my notes to go on. Radio Station KPFA in the Bay Area has a tape, but it was inaccessible; and as of late March, neither City Lights Press nor anyone else was making plans to create a permanent record of the reading by publishing it. However, from what I've seen, this is the most complete and accurate report yet to appear.

And so to Patchen on the printed page ...

Poets, the measure and measurers of civilization, make music with the silence of print and over the airwaves of the voice. With word, line, stanza, image, and idea, they sing love, vitality, freedom, and the community of persons. The best of them are the Permanent Loyal Human Opposition who sell out to no establishment. By being in opposition, by seeing well what is, and like prophets and visionaries seeing, feeling, & knowing what is potentially, they sometimes scare or disgust people with their disillusionment, their wounds, their morbidity, and their egocentrism. At other times they are like transcendent religious heroes, political martyrs, great sympathizers with and comforters of all human suffering. Kenneth Patchen? He fought with God, especially over the matter of who was responsible for the world's suffering, and concluded, in bold display type near the end of his novel, *The Journal of Albion Moonlight,* that the guilt belongs to God. We often say that the guilt is society's, and in this way we are able to analyze our great problems more or less objectively, with the aim of finding systematic solutions, instead of impotently beating our breasts and declaring our guilt, as some do in times of crisis. Pollution, for example, is mostly not a matter of individual carelessness; it is an industrial problem. War is not caused by the

violence in human nature, but rather by the greed of power-
mongers, the clash of their desires, and the clash of systems.
Naturally the objectification of guilt can also be too extreme, and
become merely a way of evading a responsibility in the struggle for
change.

Patchen did not protect himself from the world's evil
doings — to do so would have been to draw away, to isolate and
eventually sterilize himself and deny his human links. Through
travel and other forms of communication, he knew people's and
government's filth, stupidity, and meanness. Sometimes he
wallowed in it like a pig; or transcended it like a Buddha or a
saint; or preached his word like a Christ. His identity was rich and
of infinite extension. A left-wing, nonsectarian, religious poet.
Not exactly *engagé,* but certainly an honest reporter of the universe and highly inflammatory. One of his many self-conscious
statements of purpose in *The Journal of Albion Moonlight* runs:

> I shall want above all other things to see at that
> awful moment. I shall never deny my deepest instinct:
> which is to face all things with open eyes.

This is the attitude of the consummate literary artist of
these times. But it is not the only one expressed in Patchen's work.
He was Christ, Gandhi, and Marat; but also a hip Joyce, a
gamester, a fantasist, and a wild wit. One of his earlier books,
First Will and Testament, is a collection of poems, dialogues, and
short narratives. In "Poem Written After Reading Certain Poems
Sired by the English School and Bitched by the C.P.," he condemns the corruption of literature by dogmatic (and wretched)
party politics, seeing

> The originating brow of poetry
> Made to squat like an epilogue at the beginning
> of a fool's play.

As usual, the political situation was a mess. In "The
Hangman's Great Hands," written in 1937, he concludes:

> We have a parent called the earth.
> To be these buds and trees; this tameless bird
> Within the ground; this season's act upon the fields of Man.
> To be equal to the littlest thing alive,
> While all the swarming stars move silent through
> The merest flower...but the fog of guns...

The face with all the draining future left blank...
Those smug saints, whether of church or Stalin,
Can get off the back of my people and stay off.
Somebody is supposed to be fighting for somebody...
And Lenin is terribly silent, terribly silent and dead.

For Patchen as an artist, the despair and menace and
fragile hope of that era of Depression and War came to a colossal
head in *The Journal of Albion Moonlight,* published in 1941. In it
he saw that German fascism might be defeated, and that
something still worse might then be born in the U.S. As a con-
scientious objector during World War II interned by the government, as a free-thinking lefty, and as a poet, he saw through
patriotism and the false, obstructing glitter of any of the existing
systems. One of his first person male characters says, in a moment
of bitter denunciation of a female (often a symbol for the
established world in all its beauty and pride, while the male often
symbolizes the citizen):

> "You're so dead right now, you stink; the whole God-
> damn thing you come out of is—America? Who said
> America? America is the biggest cemetery that was ever on
> the face of the earth. *Everybody is dead here.* Everybody!
> Rot and stench—a stinking slop pail—every least thing that
> could be crapped-up for the sake of a nickel has been buried
> under in filth—did I say death? Well, I was wrong...there's
> no death here—only a dying; no disaster—only a crew of
> overgrown punks messing their pants."

The Journal of Albion Moonlight, still an avant garde
novel 30 years later, is written as a man's journal of the war,
beginning on May 2, 1940, shortly before the fall of France.
("FRANCE FALL? WHERE TO?") Albion Moonlight and his
friends move on a mysterious path through unknown territory
near a battlefield, guided by an unknown leader with whom they
hope to rendezvous. But strange things happen. The leader is
never encountered for more than a few instants. Their purpose is
splintered in a million directions. They begin to plot against each
other; later to kill each other, over and over again. Albion is alone
and hunted. Time stands still, the journal's dates never moving
out of that summer in 1940; Albion crawls through August only to
start May or June over again, each time with a new twist of the

knife. The war foams out of Europe and across the entire world. All humans are at war with each other, and packs of carnivorous animals join them. Albion Moonlight, the courageous prophet in this wilderness of blood, meets constant defeat and participates himself in the most hideous crimes.

To say what was on his mind, Patchen used a wild formless form that includes five or six little novels (often just tables of contents) within the larger novel; plus random notes and maxims, among the shifting scenery, a thousand fragments of plot, prayers, screams, mad speeches, prose poetry of the kind that Joyce made famous, socialist theory, endless bedroom and battlefield tableaux, a parody of the love talk in *Lady Chatterley's Lover*, pages with two and three columns of text running simultaneously, etc., etc. Everything a writer ever dreamed of putting into a book—all the products of his inspired mind—but usually left out because familiar notions of structure and mistaken definitions of realism and beauty demanded that he do so. Not for Patchen—he put it all in. *The Journal of Albion Moonlight* is a spontaneous novel. "I wanted to make a book that I could read for the first time *after I had written it...* This novel is being written as it happens."

This technique, though rare, is not unique. But what is more difficult to find is the ability and richness to do it well. It works here because the work is honest and basically realistic; mere craftsmen and experimenters are a dime a dozen. Yet Patchen was a craftsman, too. He not only expands the language, stretches concepts of what is art, and throws down a heavy challenge to literary criticism, but he also expresses a tremendous variety of human attitudes and feelings, including a gamut of ecstatic states (love, hate, fear, flying, falling, giving birth, dying, killing, madness, revelation, living in another world, etc.). The fact that many of these attitudes & feelings are, or seem, contradictory only emphasizes the richness of Patchen's personal universe; he was energetic and open enough to plunge and soar in the larger psychic life that most individuals are too unaware of or too afraid to unlock, even in times of crisis. There is really only one character in *The Journal of Albion Moonlight*, but this character is everyone, goes everywhere, sees, feels, and does practically everything.

But while the character finds all the best and worst within himself, he also sets himself apart from the world and from people. "I have risen from the land of the living," he says. And more arrogantly, a chapter heading from one of the internal tables of contents reads: "Albion Moonlight receives a charter from God and declares himself to be the eighth continent." Another one goes: "One star defies the heavens." He is a renegade with a purpose. On a cosmic level he fights God and depicts a bitter, disillusioned Christ. He sees that there must be change of a fundamental and total nature. The maker has fouled-up, and the world is at war, full of ignorant plundering humans directed by less than human leaders. A completely new universe is needed, one that will be born from the activity of the man-god, which is the potential, flickeringly realized, nature of the lowliest people on earth. Here Patchen is fulfilling a prophetic role, like Blake and a few other literary figures. A religious and social prophet. With this in mind, he leveled literary conventions along with others; and says that his purpose in the novel is not to *write* (though he does, very well), but to *speak*.

> This is what I am getting at: a new Christ is needed.
> My hands are empty.
> I spit on literature.
> The inexhaustible vision of despair...

As one who not immodestly realizes that he sees better than most others, he also recognizes that the great change can only come from the world itself, not from outside it. His life, then, is spent in trying to become an influential member of the race, not in trying to obtain a more peaceful but sterile life apart from society. So, in the world, he naturally falls frequently victim to despair, becomes a murderer himself, and a tyrant over others. Albion Moonlight knows how illusory "morality" is...and how much morality needs to be revitalized if we are not to wallow endlessly in this crisis.

Symbolically (and sometimes very tangentially), Albion Moonlight's murderousness emphasizes the need for destruction — in the service of change to a higher state of social existence, not for the base purposes already motivating societies. As I have said, his female characters sometimes represent the state; often they are whores. His maltreatment of them can be understood not

only as a counterweight to his desire to be better than the world,
which he is not, but also as a drive to master and destroy the old
order. It is not a promising, and often a perverting, task: he stabs
a woman to death and "in each bone of hers I split open I find a
photograph of an old man in a green trench-coat buggering a
windmill." Of course, there is another side to this gruesome symbology: the recurrent death of a young woman is the recurrent
death of hope and the death of love, perpetrated by Albion's own
hands.

As a committed of the world, Albion Moonlight is a victim
of vulgar, brutish impulse and mental despair. However, hope,
while fragile, does persistently exist, along several distinct lines.
Most important is love. This is an uplifting emotion, the basis of
comradeship, a source of happiness. It is a silent circle of security
among the screams of war. Love between the sexes has been perverted by role playing, competition, inequality, brutality, and
disloyalty. "Pleasure is a lonely thing," Albion recognizes. And
constant love too rare. But: "Give a man enough and he won't
want to conquer any (there are two ways to spell it) countries."

But give him what? Not what lots of people think they
want, according to the ideas and values of their masters:

> Are you heavy laden? Throw off your load. Do you un-
> derstand this? Your backs are bent under the junk of proper-
> ty, which you came by because of your fear. You were afraid
> to possess your soul, so you went by the wayside & acquired
> property.

Just as chauvinism, competition, and greed must be overcome in order for there to be love between the sexes, so they must
be overcome if there is to be a real death of the old social order
and birth of a really new one. Hope for society lies in an end to
mastery—of people by other people, of people by property, and of
all life by the death culture (oppressive pseudo-traditions, worn-
out ideas, the desire for plunder, profit, and blood, etc.). This
will probably mean class war, as Albion Moonlight says a number
of times. Class war is society's mechanism of hope. But it must be
carried out by englightened warriors, not by elites and not corrupted by dogmatic party allegiance.

Now reality intrudes itself most violently: the obstruction
to social rebirth lies not only in the power of the masters, but also

in the ignorance, fear, blood-lust, and allegiance to dominant values that exist among the complicatedly oppressed people. To dispel ignorance and foster enlightenment was one of the primary tasks Patchen set for his art. The artist should offer head food—criticism, vision, and commitment. He must be heard, must be both a utopianist and one who will work to achieve utopia.

The beauty the artist creates is not sterile—it can be fantastic, ecstatic, or visionary—but beauty usually expresses some kind of love, unity, and balance. It also provides hope; but in order for it to survive, the reality of social existence must be different. Beauty is a concept that must be carried to the world-at-large—to the infidels, if you will. And if it is seen and valued, its adherents will also see that the earth it is rooted in must be made conducive to its further growth. This is why a literature of despair, or of mere prettiness, is a dead end. This is a basic feature—often ignored—of the relation between art and civilization. But as things are now, and were in 1940, art is also in need of some vital energy and moral backbone:

> In art there is ever the demand for the distorted, for an indefinable thing termed 'magic.' But for the artist, there can be only one distortion: that which is not art. To say it in another way, the world is in a mess precisely because a bunch of stuffy fools insist that there is no mess. Everyman his own Marx! Let's have some honest-to-God fun—smear everything up and down and sideways. To hell with Liberty, Fraternity, Equality, and all the rest; let's make one whopping, beautiful botch of it—do I hear a second? (I was only kidding, you blasted lick-ass.)

In Patchen's work an awareness of the indestructible links between art and society are everpresent. While acknowledging the need for occasional "escape'" relaxation, simple fun, he is still committed to seeing, speaking, and changing (and to uniting these "opposites," now unfortunately at war with each other). Let us see again a direct expression of his purpose, from poet to reader:

> I told you not to slink away from me. Since you have not done so, I am moved to confide in you again. This time concerning my central, all-important problem: you see, it

was necessary for me to go out of my way entirely in order to write *that which I did not want to write.* To put it simply: I had to become a person I was not; indeed to *become* a person it would kill me to be. Thin ice, eh? I was determined to show you precisely what the world is. I had no intention of writing about it, or at it — by Jesus! — I would be that world!

The Journal of Albion Moonlight is a vile part, an inspired product, and a raging offspring of that world — Western society, the U.S. in particular, of 1940. For anyone who *knew* things as Patchen did, the hope remaining in that bloody world must have been fragile indeed. We have experienced worse shocks since 1940, and enjoyed brief stretches of peace; but in numerous ways the present world is still that of World War II. The threats have grown more menacing, the trickery and self-trickery more widespread, the will to work, to be an artist, to create beauty, and to talk sense even more difficult to maintain.

Clearly Patchen can easily excite us now for his being a forerunner and nourisher of the "life culture" striven for by an articulate minority in contemporary U.S. society, who see the value of nature, of work, of brotherhood. He believed in the organic unity of all life and saw how it was threatened by perverted pretensions. Says Albion Moonlight:

> I believe that the revolutions of the future will be concerned with altering the minds of men, with vomiting out all that is insane for his animal.

Always confronted with the lower, primary, more difficult desire to see humanity make itself into a true child of the earth. The promise of social revolution is great; but its greatest changes can only come about when the human being sees itself, and lives, in responsible greatness. The internal and external battle of the human being is still the person vs. the pig. The pressures to distort the person are great; the rewards of living right sometimes seem strange and insignificant in comparison with the illusory rewards of piggishness. But we must not go under to the malaise and decadence:

> There is a plague from which there is no escape for anyone. *The great gray plague*—the plague of universal madness.

It is everywhere. We—animals, organic life—are everywhere. Even Patchen's natural imagery takes on the duality of human impulse:

> The wind sniffed at the trees' scented hair. A great paw
> of sun played with the million blue tits of the sea.

That versus:

> The little green bushes of gorse rushed by us like prairie
> chickens dead from ptomaine.

The book is history itself, on a local and eternal scale. Its author was a keeper of the flame, an educated spark of the divine commoner. He knew that mere writing was garbage (though he tried it), that phantoms oppress us and possess us, that articulation of the real is all. For this, his good work is universal and lasting.

James Schevill

Kenneth Patchen: The Search for Wonder and Joy

1

The search for wonder and joy radiates from Kenneth Patchen's work. In a cynical, specialized time his poems and paintings have an essential unity of spirit that restores one's faith in
the concept of wholeness. When I first met Patchen I asked him
why he didn't exhibit his art in galleries. "I like the atmosphere of
bookstores better," he said with a smile. "In bookstores I feel my
art is part of my poetry. Things don't get separated so much."
Patchen was a true exponent of the root meaning of poetry — the
art of making. A physical *maker* he refused to be restricted in his
search for artistic connections.

Traditionally poetry and art have been closely related even
if the connections have become relatively invisible. Leonardo, as
André Malraux reminds us in *Museum Without Walls,* wrote:
"Painting is poetry that can be seen." In this age of increasing
technological specialization, art and poetry have sacrificed often a
sense of universal subject matter to an exploration of new
techniques. Painting became the frequent subject of painting and
poetry the subject of poetry. What was gained was a range of
brilliant, fresh, subjective techniques. What was lost was the complex relationship between man and society, man and nature.

In Kenneth Patchen's paintings, the poetry is in the
restoration of these relationships. The means that he uses are
almost always curious figures that stand out with unique poetic
characterization — half-animal, half-man beings that express
their delight and horror at a mysterious world. One on my study
wall has enormous black eyes staring out of a saucer-shaped head

98

set upon two spindly legs. A man? No... An animal? No... It's a
Patchen. The red, pink, and black colors possess you — the work
of a marvelous colorist. As for the draftmanship, some call Patchen's vision "primitive" or "naive," trying to pigeonhole him with
other self-taught, isolated painters. These are totally inadequate
terms that critics use desperately to differentiate complex,
sophisticated techniques from self-taught, self-contained
techniques. A man of Patchen's reading, wide-scale experience,
and extraordinary endurance of physical pain, cannot be
classified.

Another Patchen painting that I love shows a blue-green
elephant facing a yellow moon. Wait — it's a kind of elephant
because it has a long trunk ready, maybe, to spray the moon. Yet
the elephant's head is a jagged crown and he's shaped somewhat
like a teapot with a tail, a *human* elephant on *two* legs. Another
singular Patchen being radiating laughter and joy... Patchen's
genius never lets us forget our animal connections in the universe.
His sense of man-animal kinship is the source of his poetic con-
tributions to art.

A more demonic figure — half-dog, half-man — ravished
by the knowledge of pain, glares under a turbulent, jagged sky. A
furious, red, angular head, without ears or hair, encloses two blue
eyes with deepset, lost, white pupils. A red teardrop of a nose
floats above a stark, white-gashed mouth. He has only two legs on
a yellow pedestal-body, yet he's not really a man. Well, he's a Patchen beast-man, a mysterious, hell-fire creature, maddened
perhaps in a universe at war. The technique of these paintings is
almost always a two-dimensional, flat surface, used without any
attempt at perspective: a self-taught vision if you will, but certainly not naive in its range and variety of subjects, comical and
serious.

Alas, Patchen's paintings are little-known. His one
national exhibit was at the Corcoran Gallery in Washington,
D.C., in 1971. Due to his long illness he never worked on large-
scale paintings. Without a "studio" he painted usually in his
bedroom in Palo Alto. Generally he used watercolors on Japanese
papers that he loved, standard watercolor-size papers that stress
the poetic, illustrative side of his art. In an age of large-scale painting Patchen's work might at first seem of limited scope. Yet,

when the range of his art is finally revealed, he will be recognized
as an artist of rare poetic compassion — a compassion that transforms a Patchen Poem-Scape: "Above all I wish you joy in the
things which are fashioned for joy, and an honest sorrow in what is
of its nature sorrowful." Dignity, joy, compassion, honest sorrow
— these qualities dominate the strange Patchen beings in his
paintings. They teach us how to view humanity again in a
corrupt, cynical time dominated by the visual power of advertising and television.

2

The clearest connections between Patchen's poetry and art
are in his Poem-Paintings, Poem-Drawings, and in the
remarkable series of painted covers that he created for special
copies of his books. In *Motive*, 1964, Margaret Rigg wrote of Patchen's art: "They are beings from the same stream of imagination
and realization as the ones which inhabit the worlds of Thurber,
Chagall, Edward Lear, Grandeville, Klee, William Blake." To
this list one could add many other artists from the medieval monks
with their illuminated manuscripts to Steinberg, who with Patchen is the contemporary master of visual poetry. Still there are
distinct differences between these artists and writers and Patchen.
Klee and Chagall inhabit worlds of the eye, where, as in Klee's
marvelous titles, poetic language is subordinate to visual
mysteries. Lear and Thurber are primarily writers who illustrated
their work. Even Blake is mainly a great illustrator for the printed
page. As S. Foster Damon, the great Blake critic, said: "William
Blake was exceedingly precise when he illustrated." Blake wrote:
"As Poetry admits not a Letter that is Insignificant, so Painting
admits not a Grain of Sand or a Blade of Grass Insignificant —
much less an Insignificant Blur or Mark."

As opposed to Steinberg, who dissects society with a
brilliant scalpel, Patchen's world is fanciful and romantic. Patchen is a lover willing to fall into the trap of sentimentality that
sometimes haunts his work with simple expressions of benediction
— like the final picture-poem in *Hallelujah Anyway* which shows
a face speaking over an animal form with the inscription: "A
feeling of passionate mercy — the rest doesn't matter a damn."

A
feeling
of
passionate
mercy
the rest
doesn't
matter
a damn!
Patchen

There is a level in Patchen's work that operates with this kind of direct sentiment which offends sophisticated intellects who prefer the more Swiftian-Kafkaesque tone of a Steinberg.

Despite his many publications the range of Patchen's work is complex and still hidden. Although several of his New Directions books contain many valuable examples of Patchen's picture-poems, the one book that really reveals the possibilities of Patchen's work in this field is a limited edition of silkscreened reproductions published in 1955 under Patchen's personal supervision called *The Moment.* The difference, of course, is in the brilliant color so essential to Patchen's nature. This instinct for color is eliminated in the New Directions books because of printing costs.

The Moment opens with a dedication poem to his wife, Miriam, a handwriting poem without any drawing. In a black script the poem is repeated later in the book in a more precisely drawn, red handwriting:

THE MOMENT

before the girl picking field daisies
becomes the girl picking field daisies

there is a moment of some complexity

In black and white type and print this becomes merely rigid instead of fluid. In Patchen's handwritten drawing conception, "the moment" becomes a mysterious event of transformation — the girl becoming the action of love, the flowing moment when life is transformed by the magical recognition of love. It should be added that Patchen's distinctive handwriting adds to the effect of his work. A round, rolling scrawl, it is a kind of American anticalligraphy, calling attention to its demerits as classical penmanship, voicing its humorous desire to wander around in words and encounter laughing mysteries. It is the handwriting of a man who has endured a lifetime of pain, who has transformed that pain into a singular joy. A joy that surmounts pain as in Yeats's famous line, "Their ancient glittering eyes are gay." After closer inspection what may seem to be crude penmanship becomes a large, wide-eyed scroll of wonder. Beware again of calling it naive. The shape of a painful will, doggedly enduring, searching, is everywhere evident.

A unique, whimsical humor is the ingredient in Patchen's work that marks him off from related poet-artists such as Steinberg and Blake. Blake never tries to be funny and his rare instances of humor come as a surprise. Steinberg's humor is the wit of an international razorblade cutting the fat from the nationalistic social pretentions. One often laughs painfully at Steinberg. With Patchen there is more crackerbarrel humor, a Twain-like, mid western story teller inventing folk-tales with Patchen twists for endings. Over a bleary portrait in purple of a man in a broad, western hat runs the legend of:

GARRITY

The Gambling
Man
......grown old

Once Memphis Grandee of the Quick-
Chill Deck
Now at rainy 3 a.m. out of Dallas T
And all the pretty queens have long
since gone hagging
All the brave jack-o-knights have
been shunted down slack's lane
O Garrity — once the best of all
the river's best —
This is what it comes to then
A sick old man in a smelly daycoach
Riding nowhere through the night
Without a lousy dime to his name

It's a Patchen-western with the "Quick-Chill Deck" and a sad sense of the end of the Mississippi riverboat gamblers. You have to see it as a poem-print to get its real force. You have to know the lure of the Mississippi to a midwesterner as even T.S. Eliot knew it.

Another example of Patchen's unique humor is "The Little Bug Angel," a title lettered in red over a sly-looking, almost weasel-headed being who stands on two stick-like legs before a table flapping his un-angelic wings in clouds of red and black colors:

He bangs his wings on the table!
Still no service!
What's the matter that waiter!
Wow! Smell that roast biff!
Ah! He takes out a stick of dynamite —
Brr-uump! That *should teach them!*
But nothing happens!
Of course, obviously, the dynamite of an
        angel that size
Does not (unfortunately) pack very
        much of a wallop.

No caution about exclamation marks with Patchen! When a Bug Angel uses dynamite don't hold back. Alas, the Bug Angel's instinctive American tendency to violence on a grand scale doesn't "pack very much of a wallop" in the end. He's not big enough. This Bug Angel desires only to be a grand-scale Angel in his search for "roast biff" (another characteristic of Patchen's is his leap for the pun, good, bad, or indifferent). Visually the Little Bug Angel is an entrancing being as he bangs his wings on the table above the words. He reminds us of a unity among the Patchen beings — a hierarchy of outcasts who endure despite the lack of physical and mental equipment to triumph. Suddenly one catches a vision of their place in the tradition of American outsiders from, say, Huck Finn, through the humorous and sad grotesques in Anderson's *Winesburg, Ohio,* to Chaplin's Tramp. The vision vanishes. With his restless, mystical nature ("The epic begins when a man leaves his home, not when he is throwing the boards of it together" as Moonlight notes in Patchen's *Journal of Albion Moonlight*), Patchen embarks on another journey to escape from attempts to classify his work. Every commentator on Patchen should pause to look at his poem-painting which shows a man-like creature with red wings (a critic-devil?) confronting a fanciful, dancing, penguin-shaped being between an inscription that says:

It is somehow
        reassuring
to contemplate
        (even in a
purely representational
work
like this)

TIGERS
IN THE ABSTRACT

As it were (and/or — fortunately — is!)

3

When I listen to the recording and look at the pictures of
Patchen reading with the Chamber Jazz Sextet in the 1950s, I feel
a surge of loss because I never knew this relatively healthy man at
this time when he was the only poet to make a success out of the
Poetry and Jazz movement. Somehow other poets were unable to
work with jazz musicians and shape words and music into a
unified web of sound. Only Patchen achieved this effect. Fortunately it's there to hear on the record — a marvelous voice
balanced between a grave, compassionate tone and a defiant,
satirical attack. A spinal fusion in the 1950s helped to repair his
disc problems and he was able to travel. For the first time in his
life, through his readings, he was on the verge of earning a sizable
income. Then, in the early 1960s in San Francisco, his back was
re-injured, and he remained a house-bound invalid enduring
daily agony in his Palo Alto home until the end of his life. Patchen
claimed that the new injury to his back happened during a minor
surgical procedure that he underwent in San Francisco. In 1963
he sued the surgeon for malpractice. I was then Director of the
Poetry Center in San Francisco and Patchen's lawyer asked me to
testify about Patchen's literary reputation. Naturally I could not
testify about the medical nature of Patchen's illness, only the
financial loss he had suffered because of his newly crippled condition. Patchen himself was physically unable to testify at the
trial. The day of my testimony was revealing as to the power of
American medicine. With the help of the American Medical
Association, a battery of defense lawyers had been mobilized for
the surgeon. Two of them, one geared to mild pleasantries and
the other deliberately sardonic and cruel — a Mr. High and Mr.
Low of deliberate contrasts to break down the witness and impress
the jury — started to bait me with questions designed to impugn
poetry. Mr. High would ask a few, pleasant, trivial questions to
show that there wasn't much importance in my opinion of Patchen's work. Then Mr. Low would start in with a sneer: "So you're

the Director of the Poetry Center at San Francisco State College. Why should the taxpayers finance poetry?" As though the Poetry Center, and, by implication, Patchen and I, were involved in some poetic conspiracy to swindle honest American taxpayers. Although the Poetry Center was located at San Francisco State College, it was also part of the community and its pathetically small budget was financed mainly by private donations and subscriptions.

Patchen's wife, Miriam, testified movingly that since the exploratory operation he had become an invalid, unable to leave the house. Despite his condition there was no conceivable way that Patchen could summon medical testimony in his behalf. The weight of power in the courtroom was almost wholly on the side of medicine. Finally the Judge dismissed the case for lack of sufficient evidence and entered judgment for the defendant doctors and hospital. I left the courtroom feeling shocked — not just by the verdict. Perhaps it was inevitable that in a man of Patchen's size and strength, his back would break down again. Consequently it was difficult to prove medical blame. Nevertheless it seemed clear that American society and, particularly the medical profession, should feel responsibility for such a case rather than indulging in this vengeful, irresponsible charade.

This feeling of shock was bolstered when, as a result of this malpractice suit, Patchen began to experience difficulty in receiving medical treatment. Clinics refused to supervise his case and doctors even refused to visit his home on house calls. Patchen needed constant medication for his pain and the medication needed to be carefully prescribed as he was allergic to various drugs. Finally a Regent of the University of California interceded in Patchen's behalf and this enabled him to be examined and to receive drugs through prescriptions from doctors at the University of California Medical Center. After several hospital stays and a long series of excruciating tests, the doctors decided that another operation would be too risky and that he might lose the little mobility that he had. The result of this final decision that nothing could be done to improve Patchen's condition was to leave him in a cruel medical limbo. As many other invalids have learned in the United States, you have to have a certain potential for health to be treated by doctors. If you're considered incurable and have also sued a doctor — watch out. American society is designed for health, not for incurable illness and death. Furthermore the institutionalism of American medicine has proceeded apace with the growth of American bureaucracy. Consider the following two experiences that I witnessed.

On July 25, 1963, alarmed at Patchen's condition, I drew up a petition to the two medical societies that cover the area in which Patchen lived and had been treated. Many well-known educators and writers such as Alexander Meiklejohn, Mark Schorer, and Josephine Miles signed this petition. The end of the petition read:

> We should like to request that an investigation be made of Mr. Patchen's case by impartial officers of the San Francisco County and the Santa Clara County Medical Societies, with a view to helping him in whatever ways possible. Despite the difficulties of Mr. Patchen's medical history, we hope that the fairness and idealism of American medicine can find a new approach to Mr. Patchen's case that will permit him to write again and to continue his contributions to American culture.

Nothing ever came of this petition. As far as I know it disappeared into a tunnel of darkness and no action was ever considered by these Medical Societies. If this happens in the case of someone as well-known as Patchen, what chance is there for some impoverished unknown to receive medical treatment and medical justice?

Even at the University of California Medical Center, an institution noted for its extraordinary research and treatment facilities, Patchen's experience was largely a saga of agony. On Monday, September 12, 1966, I drove him to this hospital. We arrived around 4:15 P.M. Despite prearrangements it took three hours to get him admitted. Without food he lay in pain on a gurney until almost 8 P.M. while frantic phone calls were made by an apologetic supervisor of admissions. First there was a room, then a ward bed, then finally, a room again. Meanwhile, as Patchen waited in these dismal circumstances, patients were wheeled by constantly. Despite his pain Patchen made wry comments to me about the Marx Brothers atmosphere of hospital bureaucracy.

The next day, September 13, I visited him in the afternoon. Because of a battery of impending X-rays he had had no
food all day. In the morning technicians had taken two and a half
hours of back X-rays. His afternoon schedule called for barium X-
rays for a possible ulcer. Somehow these X-rays never took place
because word came that "the X-ray room was too busy." Finally
late in the afternoon he received some food and pain-relieving
medicine. When I saw him the following day after another series
of painful tests he told me: "I feel as though I were adrift on a raft
and the sharks were attacking me."

As I've mentioned the result of all this agony was a decision
that nothing could be done to improve Patchen's condition.
During the last decade of his life he struggled to endure in a
surrealistic isolation. Only the remarkable devotion of his wife,
Miriam, sustained him during this final period. Many times he
told me that he worried about her future and hated the way his
illness confined her to the house. Yet there was no choice. She was
sentenced to be his loving nurse. Her reward was a love that transcended illness and is evident in all of the dedications of Patchen's
books and, particularly, of course, in the moving range of love
poems. To save his strength for the short periods when he could
work, she handled all of his correspondence in addition to the
household business. She made possible the work that he still
managed to produce through a drugged world of isolation and
pain.

4

My usual sight of Patchen was of a once-handsome man —
his face now deeply lined by pain and his body overweight from
enforced inactivity — dressed in pajamas, lying in bed or on a sofa
in the living room. Often our conversation centered on his illness
and his financial insecurity. Doggedly, courageously, he was
always searching for some way to escape from his plight. But there
was no escape. His financial insecurity was eased a little by a grant
of $10,000 from the National Endowment of the Arts that he
received in 1967. This was the only major award that Patchen
received during the last part of his life when he most needed help.

His medical expenses were staggering and outrageous. In 1966 alone he told me he had to use over $1500 worth of medical drugs.

Yet it would be wrong to give the impression that pain had become his only world. While illness had moved in to shadow and change his life, his creative spirit was too great to be conquered. It moved jaggedly to adjust itself to pain. This often caused his conversation to swing backwards and forwards in time abruptly. Sometimes he talked about his start as a writer and how certain events in his family background influenced him. He grew up in a small mill town in Warren, Ohio, although he was born not far away in Niles. His father, Patchen said, was "a very practical man who invested all his salary in real estate. Still he was musical — he learned to play the zither by numbers, also the violin. My grandmother came over from France when she was about seventeen and met my Scotch grandfather in Liverpool. Even though they couldn't speak to each other they married. When they emigrated to this country they lived in a grim Pennsylvania mining town. They lived an incredible life on the edge of a cliff where night rushed in. In that town she bore nine children and died in childbirth of the ninth. It was this Scotch grandfather whose knowledge of Scots poetry and ballads set me off. When I was a boy and my grandfather came to live with us, we shared a bed. He'd tell me poems before I went to sleep."

Patchen started writing early in strict, conventional forms. At the age of fourteen he published a sonnet in the *New York Times.* A good athlete in high school, particularly in football (it was a football injury that started his back torments), he went on to the University of Wisconsin. There, after a battery of tests, he was selected for Alexander Meiklejohn's famous new experimental college. Meiklejohn was testing his theory that a broad education focusing in detail on a particular, great period of history would enable a student to learn more about the unity and possibilities of a society than he could in the usual academic curriculum of specialized courses. When Patchen was a student, the subject was Athens in the Fifth century B.C., an exposure to a civilization that Patchen never forgot and which influenced his work decisively in terms of social viewpoints. After a year in this program Patchen transferred to another experimental college in Arkansas in which Meiklejohn's son had interested him. These years were the extent of Patchen's formal education. He felt the need of a different kind of education and spent the early depression years in the 1930s wandering about the United States, working at any odd jobs he could find. In 1934 in Boston he married Miriam Oikemus, of Finnish background, who gave him the stability he needed. From these events that shaped his imagination, it is clear that Patchen took poetry mainly from life, not from aesthetic stance. At the end, in what should have been his major working years, he triumphed over his world of pain by shaping his poetry into visual art. After one visit, my wife, Margot, said, "Patchen seems more like his paintings and less like his poems that I've read." Undoubtedly the daily battle that he was fighting with pain and drugs contributed to his increasing preoccupation with a hallucinatory, visual world.

In 1964 I drove Alexander Meiklejohn and his wife from their Berkeley home to visit the Patchens. It was a pleasant, nostalgic visit. Over eighty Meiklejohn was still working hard on his investigations into the constitutional defenses of free speech that have meant so much to freedom in the United States. Although retired he was still vitally concerned with educational matters and had played a key role in the defense of the faculty members at the University of California who in 1960-61 had refused to sign the loyalty oath. He and Patchen talked about their experiences at the experimental college in Wisconsin and how education seemed to be growing more conservative and bureaucratic again. As usual Miriam's hospitality was warm and generous. Particularly the Meiklejohns enjoyed the opportunity to see Kenneth's paintings which they had not seen before. The possibilities of Kenneth becoming associated with some university as a Writer-In-Residence were discussed. Meiklejohn was enthusiastic about this (it was Meiklejohn who hired Robert Frost to be the first Poet-In-Residence at Amherst), but, since he was retired and removed from academic life, he had no means to bring this about. On the way home Meiklejohn expressed his deep concern over Kenneth's plight, but there was little he could do to help. He and Patchen never met again.

It was painful to see how the Patchens were forced to live in deeper and deeper isolation. Whenever they sought help there was little, real help to be given. The agonizing combination of circumstances — the seeming incurability of Patchen's illness, the medical profession's indifference, the traditional isolation of the poet in American society, the disaster of the Viet Nam War which drained the entire country — all combined to weave a net of tragic circumstances around him. A visitor was likely to see barbs in the net and turn away with a shrug of hopelessness. Then hurt, in their battle for life and Kenneth's creativity, the Patchens would withdraw a little more into the sanctuary of their home, their cats, their garden where Miriam fed the birds and the squirrels that gathered.

One who understood the problems and appreciated the Patchens was the painter, Richard Bowman, who drew the portrait of Patchen in 1966 that is reproduced on the jacket of the picture-poems, *Hallelujah Anyway*. Bowman, an important west coast painter, was one of the few artists to admire and encourage Patchen's attempts to bridge the frontier between art and poetry. After Patchen's death, when an exhibit of his art was presented in 1973 at the San Francisco Art Institute (the only previous exhibits in San Francisco as far as I know were ones that I arranged at San Francisco State College and that Lawrence Ferlinghetti arranged at his City Lights Bookstore), Miriam quoted Bowman in a broadside for the exhibit: "Just as Patchen creates new forms of poetry, so does he often create some oddly pungent but successful combinations of color and form...Kenneth Patchen is a creator who is destined to take his place with Walt Whitman, Albert Pinkham Ryder and Charles Ives as inventor and hero in the history of American Arts."

Another frustration occurred when I drove the Patchens to San Francisco for a consultation with the well-known surgeon, Dr. Lindstrom, the former husband of the actress, Ingrid Bergman. Dr. Lindstrom was wary and noncommittal about the possibility of doing anything for Patchen. He wanted to get him into the hospital for further observation and tests. Patchen was bitter and sceptical about this "runaround." He had endured too many hospitals, tests, consultations, and he was increasingly suspicious and sarcastic about the institutional medical world.

A final sense of Patchen's solitude, and the isolation of American poetry, came when Carolyn Kizer visited and I took her to see the Patchens and Yvor Winters. Carolyn was then the literary consultant for The National Endowment of the Arts and was the key person in arranging for the award of $10,000 that Patchen was given in 1967. What struck me was not just that Patchen and Winters had been living in the same town for years and had never met, but that it was literally impossible for them to meet. Here were two aging, sick eagles of the art — Winters had already had one operation and was doomed from cancer at the time — whose ideas of poetry were fiercely and totally opposed. Once, in a rare reading at the San Francisco Museum of Art, I heard Winters read his poems in the dark, regular monotone that he considered appropriate for the rhythm and tone of his work. After the reading I overheard a dazed woman comment: "It was like hearing someone read underwater." Winters was notorious for the intellectual and moral rigor of his approach to poetry. In his last book, *Forms of Discovery,* he wrote: "Five hundred years from now the subjects which will appear to have been most important to our time will be the subjects treated by the surviving poets who have written the most intelligently. The best poets have the best minds; ultimately they are the standard." In a way this is a revelation of the American split between mind and eye. If Winters claimed the mind, Patchen might well have claimed the eye and the ear. Yet it would be too simple to claim that a mere separation of ideas stood between Patchen and Winters. Physically they were both formidable men who had survived severe illness and isolation and developed their own totally different styles and beliefs. Their wives — sensitive, compassionate ladies both — if they had been able to meet would have been great friends. But Winters withdrew to the sanctuary of his student-poets with whom he could shape poetry according to his intellectual, classical standards. Never in any of his books does he even mention Patchen. To him the free-forms of a Patchen were merely intellectual laxity. As for Patchen he never spoke or thought much of Winters except to mutter once to me about "all those student-genius poets of Winters" — a sardonic reference to the loyal, if hazardous habit of Winters including many of his students in his books as modern masters.

Perhaps it makes little difference. Yet it struck me forcefully that the isolation of Patchen and Winters was another example of American extremes, an inability to exchange ideas of which they were both victims even though living a few miles apart.

What we give the artist in America is the torment of endurance. It makes for a stringent, savage art that will dare the extremes of form and formlessness, but it has failed completely to create a civilization, an audience that nourishes the arts and the artist.

5

It is too soon for any authoritative statement about Patchen's poetic range. Too much of his poetry is concealed. When he was working on *The Collected Poems,* Patchen told me that he was having difficulty cutting the manuscript and that it represented "less than half" of his work. He was always a prolific, hardworking writer who scorned increasingly any boundaries between poetry, prose and art. This tendency to focus on new, unified dimensions of art, combined with his illness and inability to give readings, caused his reputation to suffer during the 1960s. Various critics tended either to ignore his poetry or dismiss it too easily. When they did discuss Patchen's work they were apt to take lines out of context — such as "Boo! You well-fed bastards" or "There is a beautiful work for all men to do,/And we shall at last wake into the sun" — and call these too literal or too sentimental. In a time when poetry has often limited itself to the search for novelty in every line (Pound's dictum: *Make it new*), Patchen always sought the complete expression. This makes it relatively easy for apolitical, formalist critics to object to Patchen's poetry and to criticize individual lines.

The term "every line tried and tempered" does not apply to Patchen because he is concerned with the creation of his own unique, visionary world. It is an unclassifiable world, a "Dark Kingdom" where machines meet strange mishaps, where "The Joiners of Everything" get their just reward, where "The Little Green Blackbird" presides satirically over the eternal imagination, where the compassionate seeker is the one who always perceives "The Character of Love Seen as a Search for the Lost." This last, of course, is the title of Patchen's fine love poem which begins with a superb, grave rhythm:

> *You, the woman; I, the man; this, the*
> *world:*

> *And each is the work of all.*
> *There is the muffled step in the snow;*
> > *the stranger;*
> *The crippled wren; the nun; the dancer;*
> > *the Jesus-wing*
> *Over the walkers in the village; and*
> > *there are*
> *Many beautiful arms about us and the*
> > *things we know...*

"Beautiful" is a word that is almost taboo in poetry today — perhaps rightly so in a society that has sentimentalized beauty into commerce — but it is characteristic of Patchen that he often presents a desperate, personal plea for the real mystery of "beauty" in a world that mocks or sentimentalizes "the beauty of reality."

Another aspect of his poetry that is controversial is his prophetic tone. Many readers don't like to be warned and Patchen, his antennae alert to disasters, warns constantly. Although a social stance in poetry has strong historical connections — from the Bible through Blake and Whitman — Patchen's sense of prophesy often has a singularly ironic political religious tone:

> *No honor may be had*
> *Except the Highest see it*
> *And mix it well in the dirt between his*
> > *toes.*

If prophetic and lyric describe key aspects of Patchen's poetry, they do not describe the variety and range of his poems. For the sake of future exploration, these might be divided into the following groups:

1) *The Love Lyric* — These poems, all dedicated to Miriam, are perhaps his best-known work. The fact that they have been set to music by many composers indicates their essential mastery of intricate lyrical textures. To appreciate their sound they must be read aloud. Often the theme is the quest for the simplicity of wonder and beauty that are central to his concept of love:

> *Do I not deal with angels*
> *When her lips I touch*

So gentle, so warm and sweet — *falsity*
Has no sight of her
O the world is a place of veils and roses
When she is there

I am come to her wonder
Like a boy finding a star in a haymow
And there is nothing cruel or mad or evil
Anywhere

2) *The Social Satire* — Born to workingclass conflicts, Patchen knows the materialistic contradictions of American life as few poets do. His industrial Ohio background and his ability to portray the poverty, filth and insanity of much of our so-called "affluent society" are revealed in such poems as "May I Ask You A Question, Mr. Youngstown Sheet & Tube?"

Mean, grimy houses, shades drawn
Against the yellow-brown smoke
That blows in
Every minute of every day. And
Every minute of every night. To bake a
*   cake or have a baby,*
With the taste of tar in your mouth. To
*   wash clothes, or fix supper,*
With the taste of tar in your mouth. Ah,
*   but the grand funerals...*
Rain hitting down
On the shiny hearses. "And it's a fine
*   man he was, such a comfort*
To his old ma. — Struck cold in the
*   flower of his youth."*
Bedrooms
Gray — dim with the rumor of old sweat
*   and urine. Pot roasts*
And boiled spuds; Ranch Romances
*   and The Bleeding Heart*
Of Our Dear Lord...

Unfortunately, because of his illness and isolation during his last years, this kind of perceptive, concrete description of American environments is less prevalent in the later poems which tend to stress more abstract social and metaphysical themes.

3) *The Portrait* — Usually Patchen is not regarded as a portrayer of character. In an age that has focused increasingly on subjective poetry, the sense of Patchen's relationship to the kind of characters that Sherwood Anderson called "grotesques" in *Winesburg, Ohio* has gone almost unnoticed. Yet in poems like *Ohio River Blues* there are marvelous descriptions of midwestern eccentrics:

> *Now not every man has the makings of*
> *a barber*
> *Or even a tuner of one of those classy*
> *white-wood pianos*
> *Like they used to have in most of the*
> *river towns hereabouts*
> *But when you stop to think of it up real*
> *close*
> *It takes something special to be*
> *something special*
> *Clint Burrows, now, his kind don't just*
> *happen*
> *Sure, there was something to start with*
> *But you might say a man like him*
> *Shook the hand of all his chances*
> *One Sunday, for example, he comes*
> *walking into church*
> *Naked as a jaybird and says in that soft*
> *deep voice of his*
> *Thanks, Lord, for making me like I am*
> *— thought I'd just drop in*
> *And let you know I'm not ashamed of it*
> *either...*

The humorous, yet terrifying isolation, so similar to that in characters in such diverse writers as Mark Twain, Anderson, Masters, and Robinson, reveals Patchen's connections with a mainstream of American literature. Another fine example of his compassionate insight into character, more formally written in ten line stanzas is the elegiac voice of "Old Man." Here are the first and last stanzas:

> *I'm now tending a son's hearth,*
> *And the hours of my life seem as flies*
> *Rasping at the closed screen doors*

Of a house where a world lies dead.
There's no rest there's a grumbling
          wound;
And as I toss on this narrow cellar cot,
A young woman dances through the
          stains,
As real now as ever then — but, ah, I'm
          not.
These gray furnace ashes are as lively
As her husband is now, and as warm...

******

By life wasted and by death denied —
O a sour breath breathes on the rose;
And what I have left I would hide —
Gray hairs in a shrunken nose.
Rude are the words of old men,
But far ruder this talking flesh
That would speak to its Maker again —
And I think not about fire
Or prints of a hand on stone,
But of a grave being gone.

4) *The Fantastic Narrative* — Like Blake, Patchen often creates
his own legendary world of terror, fear and wonder with fan-
tastically named beings and places, a modern realm of absurdity,
of vast technological warfare that leads to irrational and
anonymous death. Yet this place of Kafkaesque absurdity (the
work of Kafka was conspicuous in Patchen's bookshelves) is also a
source of beauty and love. "The world Kenneth Patchen lives in is
wild with surprise, complete with its own fantastic system" wrote
John Holmes in 1958 in *The New York Times Book Review*. To
enter this surprising world with its "fantastic system," an unusual
narrative journey is almost always involved, as in "The Permanent
Migrations":

A suitable entrance to this village
Is made by walking down three white
          steps
That lead past a table

Upon which the continents are green-
         ing.
Apparently what is suspended
From the overhighest throne
Is not an object to throw cathedrals
         at;
For here, beneath it, having an infinite
         perfection,
Stand the beautiful horsemen of death,
Their plumes unstirred by what is com-
         manded on earth...

This epic thrust to create extraordinary, fantastic worlds is evident from his second book, *First Will and Testament,* where he began to project a "life-work," a seven-volume poem to be called *The Hunted City.* This was conceived as nothing less than "an attempt to write the history, spiritual and real, of these times and this country." When I asked Patchen what happened to this project he merely shrugged and said, "Things changed." But the epic thrust remained. Instead of focusing on language it shifted to the visionary beings of his drawings and paintings, which are a unified body of work. Future writers about Patchen must investigate and praise his remarkable, final work in this field.

5) *Poem-Paintings and Poem-Drawings* — Here, in Patchen's late pioneer work on the borderlines of art and poetry, is the clearest way to perceive his real originality. Perhaps the best place for the unfamiliar reader to begin is the poem-drawings in *Hurrah For Anything.* The poetry is simple and direct, the drawings wild with grotesque humor. Patchen's touching, comic treatment of people and animals take on uncanny forms of man's absurd, joyous ways. The drawings are counterpointed, not fused with the poems as in the poem-paintings. Beneath a profile drawing of a large smiling human head with a long nose and a little goatee, is a tiny lion-like body with four prancing legs and the poem:

I AM TIMOTHY THE LION

I live in an old sour maple tree
With Happy Jake, who is
A small goldfish;

> *There is also a shortnecked swan,*
> *Two very base players, a bull still wrap-*
> > *ped*
> *In pink tissue paper, and a policeman*
> *Shaped like a watering can;*
> *But they're all afraid of sunstroke,*
> *So me and Jake just sit on our limb here*
> *And shout* Bon Dieu! Bon Dieu!
> *Every time the phone rings up in one of*
> > *those clouds.*

Patchen's poetry and art reveal an incredible dialogue between the world of his reality, his making, and the world that surrounded him with its distortions of war, illness, poverty, politics, death. Out of this dialogue, this search through fantastic realms of color, line, and verbal textures, comes a final triumph, the sense of a man of faith who conquers pain and disaster and finds his own world of love. In the end, as the range of Patchen's acheivements continue to be revealed, there will be cause for rejoicing, a time to re-discover the meaning of the spirit of celebration, to continue the search for wonder and joy at the center of Patchen's life and work.

III

General
Critical Analyses

Amos N. Wilder

Revolutionary and Proletarian Poetry: Kenneth Patchen

We have had occasion a number of times to call attention
to the fact that one school of the new writers should not be included in the cult of negation. This is the group whose concern is
with social revolution. They share the social realism indeed; they
are negative as regards any future for present society; they have
also fallen heir to many of the disillusionments and bitter
knowledge of the modern mood; they recognize the rootlessness of
our culture; they have, finally, been influenced by the changes in
poetic speech and method. But they have not been concerned with
the personal problem or the psychological issues, nor with finding
some individual Nirvana or return to nature. These are ex-
troverts: their alternative or orthodoxy is devotion to a new social
order.

This is a younger generation than the one to which Eliot,
Pound, Aiken, Yeats belong. It came up after the war. In
England its members were at the universities in the middle twen-
ties. Their particular organ *New Verse* appeared around the
beginning of the thirties, and the names that have drawn particular attention have been those of W. H. Auden, Stephen Spender, C. Day Lewis, MacNeice, Madge. They have wished to fight
free from the defeatism and demoralization of the post-war years.
The predicament of Europe after the Peace Treaty, of Britain
with its great strikes and unemployment, the paralysis of remedial
efforts in the face of competitive capitalism and vested interests,
as they saw it, and the challenge of the Russian experiment led
them to their gospel of a new order. The development of fascism
and of Hitler clarified and intensified their zeal. They became
more than ever convinced of the view supported whether by Marx

or Spengler or such Catholic writers as Dawson and Maritain or an Orthodox writer like Berdyaev, that Western society was breaking up, its organic bonds of common faith and morale lost, its inner conflicts constituting an incurable anarchy, and its men and women infected with sickness.

Much of this diagnosis they took over from the new poets before them but they made of it a social program and poetic creed. They also took over the new "public speech" and colloquial style of address. But their lyrical optimism as to the new society inevitably reminds one of the social enthusiasm of Tennyson or Whitman, and their ardor for, and even participation in, the cause of the Spanish loyalists recalls Byron and Shelley. Today with the tragic ambiguity of the U.S.S.R. they have dissociated their revolutionary conceptions somewhat from the Russian formula, though they have not been really identified at any time with the actual proletarian communists in the latter's task of precipitating social strife. As intellectual revolutionaries, like Strachey or the Christian communists, their task has been one of education. Their poetry is made up in part of satirical criticism of the "old world" now as they conceive it, going to pieces; and of calls to sacrifice to the new world, and poetic forecasts of its values. Much of this takes the form of brilliant pamphleteering and topical verse rather than lyrical or personal poems. Here it falls in the tradition of the broadsheet. More recently Auden and Isherwood have written satirical plays or extravaganzas like *The Dog Beneath the Skin*. But they also produce more deeply matured and personal work. William Rose Benet, in reviewing Auden's recent book, *On This Island,* says, "Mr. Auden writes out of the terror and tumult, disillusionment and anger, of his own day. He is profoundly concerned about the state of the world... His book, I should say, is a good deal concerned with the love between individuals perplexed and harried by love of mankind and the hope for a better social order so that it is snatched, as it were, amid perils and imminent treacheries." Some attention has been given in earlier chapters to Auden's charges against the old regime, and the ethical motives in his work.

In the United States similar conditions and the influence of the group have resulted in similar work. The numerous new poetry magazines and annuals show a considerable place given to such themes, and readers of *Poetry, A Magazine of Verse,* as well

as of many of the liberal reviews, not to mention *The New Masses,*
are acquainted with it. We have spoken of MacLeish's radio plays
dealing with the Wall Street panic and the coming of the dic-
tators, as well as of his view of modern poetry as capable of a
social role. Attention has also been called to a few poems in *Public
Speech* in which he points to love as the "Pole star for this year"
and defines the meaning of the word Comrade as something not
determined by the blood.

> Men are brothers by life lived and are hurt for it. [1]

The work of Miss Rukeyser has also been cited. It is especially to
be noted that this group in America includes a definite group of
writers who are or have been themselves workers out of workers'
families. These are properly distinguished as proletarian poets
since they write consciously of their class.

It is ambiguous or misleading to speak of these types of
poetry as communist poetry. The larger part of it represents
merely such a plea for justice and community as any believer in
the future and in mankind feels. It is inevitable that such a social
passion should see the matter in terms of an old and a new order.
The point at which to raise queries is not over the matter of a
change of orders or even over the theme of revolution, which in
some aspects is an intrinsically Christian idea, but over the concepts of man involved. The larger part of this work appears to be
inspired by motives of humanity whose derivation from Christian
values is unmistakable if unrecognized. What else can one say of
such a theme as that of Kenneth Patchen, the American
proletarian poet:

> O be willing to wait no longer.
> Build men, not creeds; seed not soil —
> O raise the standards out of reach.
> New men, new world, new life. [2]

In so far as these poets represent an actual iconoclasm it
must be remembered that the outlook of men is affected by the
conditions of their life, and that the technological changes of the
last century have deeply altered these. New conditions of living
shake men's habitual loyalties and assumptions. We speak of the
changes that came in the nineteenth century with the industrial
revolution. But these changes continue. For techniques continue

to advance. "Advancing, they not only transform the economic system and the social relationships entangled in it, they subtly and profoundly change the scheme of values. Authority may resist the frontal attack of heresy or repair the schisms that it causes, but neither the secular nor the spiritual sword is potent against the habituations and attitudes that respond to new ways of earning a livelihood, to the manipulation of new mechanical powers, to the new resources, new luxury, new leisure, new freedom, and new servitude that their exploitation brings with it, and to the new relations between men and groups of men that they engen- der...new technology, by changing the basis of life, prepares for a change in the very basis of thought. It is thus of particular potency in undermining the established notions of authority held by the masses of men."[3]

The making of a communist is well seen in the case of a young intellectual, whom Charles Plisnier, the Belgian writer, describes in his book *Faux-Passeports,* a book which recently took one of the highest French prizes. The book is transparently autobiographical in many features. In an introduction written for that book but only published in its entirety in a review,[4] the author reviews the forces that played on him during his studies in law at Brussels in 1919. To appreciate the revulsions he felt toward various aspects of the status quo is to understand much of the new poetry.

> When I try to picture what was going on in me I find various sharply contradictory sentiments: a violent an- tipathy towards that contented mediocrity which exhibited itself on every face; a hatred for the hate to which I had ac- customed myself during the war...an abhorrence for the disordered scheme of life that met my eyes in the sordid prosperity of the rich, the sordid resignation of the poor, and that acceptance by both of values that could not possibly lead to the satisfaction of all; a thirst to see this abominable disorder changed; a need to discover something to which one could give oneself without reserve; an attitude of religious awe toward the Russian revolution... the in- toxicating illusion that one found in Marx a complete and coherent explanation of the whole terrestrial globe, past, present and future. As a matter of fact, I always said that I came to communism by way of the doctrine, but I know now

that what decided me were the mournful aspects of life as it was: a working-girl dazzled by false jewelry, the complacent look on the face of some half-washed delivery boy, the line in front of the moving-picture theatre, everything that showed the bourgeoisie luring the poor with its crass materialism and appetite for perdition...I wanted to break with that hateful hierarchy that made me one of the privileged, with that culture whose overthrow I desired.

Such sentiments need not lead to a communist profession. In the case of the character who speaks in this book it did so, but only for a period. He was unable to maintain complete obedience to the party. He still had scruples about his "duty of sincerity." He was not afraid for his skin but they wanted him to throw away with equal alacrity "what he called his honor." He felt perhaps that by comparison with the devoted extremists and martyrs, the "hard," he was only a sentimentalist, a poet who had made an imperfect renunciation. A stern friend had said to him, "You; comrade, take the Party for a house; go in one day, leave another day when you please. The Party is no more a house than the Church is. There are houses in the Party as there are houses in the Church. But like the Church the Party is a fellowship of flesh and spirit... The civil wars, the blood-conflicts have given it this religious character..."

The writer disavowed his communism half-heartedly but what especially interests us here is his account of how he was led to rebellion against the status quo. Through the war and through observation of the life about him and through study of economic laws he felt he had received a kind of clairvoyance with regard to society, insights into the shallowness not to say viciousness of social orthodoxy. Note what a considerable part of his decision against his class is made up of ethical motives. The scorn for materialism, the hot resentment against irresponsible privilege, the sick-heartedness over the corruption of the workers by commercialism and the loss of their simplicity by the peasants; these are ethical protests. The true Marxist goes on to cap it all with an economic doctrine and a program of action. Some of the new poets go on to this. But all or most share the clairvoyant revulsion from traditional life as they see it.

The work of Mr. Kenneth Patchen in his volume *Before the Brave*[5] is of great interest for the light it throws on the outlook of the "proletarian poet" or social radical today, and also for the parallels that appear in it with intense religious motivation. Large parts of it are of extreme difficulty. This is only partly due to the special character of his concerns and his imagery. One would hazard the guess that he has put himself to school to Hart Crane as any poet well may, and he shows some of the powers as well as some of the defects of that method. At his best, and his best is often struck out of a context of obscurity, we find a forcibleness of statement and an eloquence in its kind that indicate a gifted poet. And we may add to this the fact that Mr. Patchen in the frame of reference of his social themes touches deep levels of general human concern. We are not surprised to hear that in his subsequent work still in progress he has sought wider themes, without however abandoning his former sympathies.

The difficulties of the proletarian artist are illustrated well by this case. Mr. Patchen's volume which we shall analyze deals with the mission, the brotherhood, the sacrifices and elation of those who are the spearhead of the new order in the world today. Its intensity and its horizons grow out of the realities of the class struggle. Yet the poet cannot safely read his cause and his allies in terms of the actual class struggle or the actual working classes or the actual political and social front. He will find himself disappointed and betrayed by the workers or by the U.S.S.R. or by the Internationals and his cause will not be theirs. The revolutionary poet must therefore be on his guard not only against the old order, but also against his comrades. Mr. Patchen gives evidence of this in some private notes he has furnished on his present position in which he shows that the writer should keep himself clear of passing phases whether in the social conflict or the literary scene.

It is not easy for me to formulate a credo in regard to 'the poet and the class struggle.' No contemporary poet (or critic) has evidenced a consistent attitude towards any major human problem; he has occupied himself with literary-and-political jockeying for position—not content with changing horses in the middle of the stream, he must change the stream as well; he has spent his energies baying at the moon and mooning at the bay. There is little to go on.

"No poet can write 'for the people' without realizing that current literary tastes (in the hands of the moneychangers) have little to do with literature; i.e., Burns, Heine, Homer, etc.

"Jesus Christ is still a better subject for the poet than the emasculated Lenin of the Stalinists...

"Let the poet be one with his own life.

"Let him read more Dante and Burns and less political mouth-frothing...

"Influences of my life in a steel-worker's home on my work and outlook:

"In the beginning, at least, it gave me a contempt for intellectual writers who intellectualized but did not write — still have it.

"Made me suspicious of people who 'loved the working class.' The working class, by reason of its position in this society, is base, treacherous, ignorant and *cheap;* to say otherwise is to enter upon a major contradiction. The middle class is worse, of course, and still more so, the upper..."

Patchen states that he is at work on a new poem of exceptional length and adds: "I am afraid that it doesn't have a great deal to do with 'proletarian' writing. I am rather bitter about the present set-up in that direction."

We can well understand the objection that a writer like Patchen must feel to have his name bandied about as a "proletarian" poet. He is not interested in being classified, and his convictions are too serious for him to enjoy being made the object of literary gossip. He must go his own way disabused as to both right and left but not discouraged. One of the unexpected notes that recurs in the midst of his bitterest denunciations is a wistful appeal for love or a call to forgiveness. With such an ideal haunting him we can well believe that he finds himself at times disappointed.

There can be no mistaking, however, the ardor and austerity of his challenge to whoever will hear, be they proletarians or not. Nor can one mistake the true doctrine of communism, which appears in his work not as doctrine but as singing and passion. For those who know the language and those that will penetrate the difficulties, here are the themes that have moved mountains in Russia and that work as a well-nigh irresistible ferment in many parts of the world today. This is the faith and the uncompromising boldness of a *church,* but of a church that is a church indeed. Let the guardians of religious institutions and of democracy with their relaxed powers and slackened bows give good heed. Do they believe in the future? Here in any case is certainty of inevitable and predestined victory. Do they recognize the mortal conflict of good and evil? Here is deliberate preparation for the imminent revolution. Do they have the elate abandonment of apostle and martyr? Do they touch hands in a sense of common mission with committed hands in many nations? Here is this kind of vocation and this kind of solidarity together with a sense of glory growing out of ignominy and triumph won out of despair.

Far carrying movements in the world rise ultimately out of conditions where the hearts of men are plowed and harrowed for long periods of time by humiliation and distress. The iron enters into the soul finally and they become capable of single-mindedness. They become capable of disregarding inconsequentials like comfort and safety. This condition among the poor is evidenced in these poems of Patchen:

> their retching sour rage
> Is splendid harvest.(p.110)

The ignominies, deprivation and injury reach a point where profound hungers and urges are felt, not necessarily destructive, but in any case insistent. Not necessarily destructive: it is first of all a crying out for something better, and only if that is denied comes the necessity to destroy the barriers to something better:

> Let us have madness openly, O men
> Of my generation. Let us follow
> The footsteps of this slaughtered age...

But note what follows:

> We wanted more; we looked to find
> An open door, an utter deed of love,
> Transforming day's evil darkness...(p.41)

And again,

> We should love but cannot love being as we are. (p.97)

As the proletarian thinks of a comrade murdered and another lynched and others in other lands shot down by the Fascists he is driven to prefer open revolution to the hopeless inaction of the present interim:

> better to die better to feel that all wisdom
> science and mastery have been turned against
> you that they notice you and kill you...
> better to die while heavy guns shake the
> earth and it's all big and clear   save us
>   from the peace between
> wars Fool fool every man's at war who's
>   hungry and hunted whether
> in Omaha or Tokyo here they come. Here
>   they come. Look out
> they mean business they mean an end to standing
>   in rain waiting for freights out of
>   Toledo and Detroit. Did we ever make
> a town? a porterhouse?   we were always just
>   this side of getting anything
> or anywhere...
>   a hundred million of us coming
> up those stairs in Spain in Mexico in India ...
>   **millions ready**
> to break the back of this muddle-born world.(pp.103 ff.)

For the revolutionary the outcome is certain. Here we have the Marxian version of Early Christian apocalyptic with its imminent and predestined triumph. This is what "all Time has willed."

> Do watch! do wait! the season nears its grain. (p.77)

Yet sometimes the interim appears long. It is like a sultry day when the awaited thunder storm holds off:

> Now this remains: the thunder stopped;
> the stubborn sky grown thick,
> all clumsy, holding back...
>   **this nasty**
> waiting being everything in one, a civil
> war in perfect check
> and then
>   **the rain!** (p. 85)

At times the days of "the major operation" appear at hand:

> Chiefly I prize this loss of patience, deep
> In riot days around us; these swollen

> Times propel the future forward: tear
> Alike my friends and turn about my foes.
> I think not every lesson learned
>   is
> Full of welcome: weeds in suburban streets;
> Stalking gangs who fire at sight...
> These withered times prepared no turkish-bath
> Of comradeship or endless singing in the square... (p.14)

If we ask what the ultimate goal is we find the question waived in a poem called "Graduation." The end of work in other people's industry and world, dancing in the palaces of king and "patriot," the release of prisoners, victories and economic gain: can there be more than this? Perhaps, but it is enough that "the program's under way." Away with speculation.

> We've learned that consummation waits
> And will not rot. O let your Love consume your thought.
>   (p.83)

But what is under way

> starts wheels going worlds growing
> and any man can live on earth when we're through
> with it. (p.35)

To be of the pioneers in this revolutionary procedure is to meet the truncheons of the police, Midwestern jails, tear gas and riot guns. The usual foreshortening of the interim between us and the millennium means that the crisis is imminent and that one lives in the anticipation of martyrdom. Yet without sentimentality.

> We will no martyrs or legends.
> We can't get there by taxi-cab or sentiment. (p.17)

Nevertheless, there is a sense of vocation which gives significance to the role of those who go forward to barrage and barricade: they are "conquerors of time and men,"

> Models for a better maker, propellers of a surer motion,
> Masters in a stricter sense — alive or dead...
>
> We are that thing for which we fight.
> We are the deepest task of centuries; lucky

> To stand where we stand, hardy
> To weather all they can give who have taken
> The every weight of a more hopeless war
>   since the day we were born. O we are not
> Afraid of wounds we've always had. O death
> Is a minor thing to those who've never lived. (p.107)

This hardihood is related to the conditions of life of the workers. As a result of the long underworld existence they have not only the bodies but the tempering and the abandonment to be invincible.

> we're not pretty we're as ugly as hell coming out of the holes
> they dug for us to live in we're proud of our hardness
> we've been picked to live because we could not die
> they could not kill us even when our own were turned
> against us they cannot make a dent in the iron faces
> we've grown in the cellar of the world we've got
> no pretty job to do we are the ugly logic whose beautiful
> bones shall be the frame of all the body of wonder
> which we can never know. (p.125)

The single-mindedness is reinforced by a mystical sense of community with comrades throughout the world who suffer or die, whether famous martyrs like Lauro de Bosis or the unknown. The resolute mood is maintained not by "words or dying themes Of flag or wooden guns": they are

>   a legion whose skill
> Is best put forth by order of a public bond
> In blood we've lost on every field of earth and sea.

And this vocation and solidarity in deprivation and crisis is one of elation, as the same poem says,

> our country is the careless star in man. (p.78)

This theme is best brought out in the account of an execution, "Joe Hill Listens to the Praying." While the chaplain prays, and while the rifles are prepared, the mind of the condemned goes back to the dramatic hours of the social struggle in which he has taken part, various indomitable if forlorn apostles of the cause, the casual laborer's life, the "bumming" over the great West in mid-summer, the bounty and freshness of earth to these free spirits that had taken their lives in their hands, the epic incidents of strike and courtroom, whose epic character had all the more moving quality for the unequal odds and the Main Street setting.

> The homeless, the drifters, but, our songs
>   had hair and blood on them.
> There are no soap boxes in the sky.
> We won't eat pie, now, or ever.
>   when we die,
>   but Joe
> We had something they didn't have:
>   our love for these States
>   was real and deep...
> Let them burn us, hang us, shoot us,
>   Joe Hill,
> For at the last we had what it takes
>   to make songs with. (p.120)

It is most important and a very delicate task to analyze the social judgments that underlie such rebellion. One cannot but respond to the passionate aspirations that voice themselves in it. The devotion to what until now at least has been a forlorn hope in this country is a rebuke to the orthodox in church and state, so inclined to rest on their oars even in times of evident social distress. Even among those that are not communists there is a widespread revulsion against the values of pre-war middle-class life, patriotism as then viewed, and the church. We have seen in most of our modernist poetry that many have been shaken in their confidence in these attitudes and institutions. The aspects of our American order that a worker like Patchen meets are often such as to make understandable the absoluteness of his verdict. We cannot but recognize moreover that where citadels of entrenched and arbitrary power establish themselves — and they establish themselves in all orders — the play of social forces cannot but lead to such crises and overturns as he envisages.

Precise estimates, however, of the good and bad of social institutions and forces is not easy. Whether they are such as to forbid hope of prompt peaceful correction needs more insight and competence than most men have. In particular our supposed disinterested indignation is often complicated by hidden motives of a personal kind. As Robert Frost has suggested there is a vast difference between grief and grievances. Capitalistic culture is, indeed, cursed with a curious stuntedness and complacency which will drive the critic to every form and degree of disgust and lead him to spew out every feature of its arts. But an objective judgment upon anything as complex as a human society is possible to few. The wisdom of such social judgments and such class aversion is only proportional to the amount of love for mankind that the critic brings to them. Otherwise he is making an obscure series of transferences of personal grievances to an imagined social order, and is moving in allusions and fictions. And such is the basis of most Marxism and class conflict. And such is the basis of a certain amount of the art and poetry of proletarian or collectivist inspiration, and of the modernist revolt generally. In so far, it is given its life by illusions and is soon exposed. But if a critic loves and understands men he will not confuse the abiding ills of life nor his personal grievances with the ills of a particular social order. He will then be able to pass an illuminating judgment on his day. Of course elements of such sound reaction are found in our poets, and the modernist literature partakes of good and bad. We do not mean that an ideal critic or artist should take a remote and inactive view of the social order, but that there are few Isaiahs or Lincolns who may permit themselves a dogmatic view or the right to hate or the licence of withering denunciation. The pure fire of zeal is too mixed with the fumes of bitterness in all of us. It is notable that in the personal communication from Patchen quoted above, he shows himself disabused of any other simple assignment of right and wrong in the issue between the classes, and that a plea for solutions in terms of love rather than violence recurs.

Notes

[1] "Speech to those who say Comrade."
[2] *Before the Brave* (New York, 1936), p.18.
[3] R.M. MacIver, "The Historical Pattern of Social Change," in *Authority and the Individual,* Cambridge, Mass., p.150,151.
[4] Souvenirs d'un agitateur, *ESPRIT,* 6e annee, 65 (ler fevrier 1938), pp.723 ff.
[5] New York, 1936. Mr. Patchen has more recently had published *First Will and Testament,* Norfolk, Conn., 1939.

Harvey Breit

Kenneth Patchen and the Critical Blind Alley

> *Foxes have holes, and birds of the air have nests; but the son of man has not where to lay his head. He goes on living according to the pure dreams of his adolescence, and the Christian countries hunt him like a wild beast.*
>
> —Ignazio Silone

Spinoza once reminded men that they were possessed of hearts. Perhaps it is time now to remind the critics of their tasks, those as simple as the fact that men have hearts. To understand and to make a work understood—but that is not possible without a quality of intelligence that is an aspect of imagination; and a quality of mind that is related, directly or indirectly, to the creative process. Otherwise, what was lifelike in the work of art must of necessity become transmuted and an irony, as it were.

In *The Meditations of the Life of Baudelaire* of Charles DuBos there is an ease that the writer seems almost to derive from another source, perhaps from Baudelaire himself. One cannot but be cognizant of the sensibility and the scrupulous taste in the essay and yet what results is closer to a mystery: it is as if Baudelaire had returned at some later date to make these disinterested and knowing observations about himself.

In this sense, Kenneth Patchen's poetry is a last testing of the critic's seriousness. In Patchen the poem's tension is not in the quantities and measurements where the critic is safest, but in what is human: in hate and love, in what men remember and in what men dream, in what they must do, in what they must get. All of it

IN PERKKO'S GROTTO

Everybody
gets along
Just fine
Why
Even
The best
Champagne

Tastes like elderberry wine!

Patshan

MY NAME
IS DOBBLE
AND I
LIVE
IN A
USED
MILK
BOTTLE
What's
with you,
friend?
Patchen

is projected with a kind of unrelenting agony which in itself becomes a terrible statement. Here the critic is farthest from the paper esthetics, the paper rules and the paper pleasures. The critic is pretty much by himself, thrust out into an intensified and heightened, but very real, world. He must say something—as a critic and, more, as a responsible man.

DO THE DEAD KNOW WHAT
TIME IT IS?

The old guy put down his beer.
Son, he said,
> *(and a girl came over to the table*
> *where we were:*
> *asked us by Jack Christ to buy her*
> *a drink.)*

Son, I am going to tell you something
The like of which nobody ever was told.
> *(and the girl said, I've got nothing*
> *on tonight;*
> *how about you and me going to*
> *your place?)*

I am going to tell you the story of my
> *mother's*
Meeting with God.
> *(and I whispered to the girl: I*
> *don't have a room,*
> *but maybe...)*

She walked up to where the top of the
> *world is*
And He came right up to her and said
So at last you've come home.
> *(but maybe what?*
> *I thought I'd like to stay here and*
> *talk to you.)*

My mother started to cry and God
Put His arms around her.
> *(about what?*
> *Oh, just talk...we'll find some-*
> *thing.)*

She said it was like a fog coming over
> *her face*

> *And light was everywhere and a soft*
> *voice saying*
> *You can stop crying now.*
> *(what can we talk about that will*
> *take all night?*
> *and I said that I didn't know.)*
> *You can stop crying now.*

The poems are neither delusions nor pictures of "other worlds"; on the contrary, they are hard and squarely sighted and of this world and express successfully a vision of life. The critical mind is forced to investigate the experiences and the vision. But this is not easy; there are fewer maps.

Crane suffers in this way through the critic's reluctance to experience the poet's life. "One feels the frigidity of Crane's finest work," Yvor Winters says. That is to say, Crane failed in his most serious efforts because he failed to master experience. But is that more significant than the fact that Crane *dealt* with the most complex structures of the mind, that he came to grips with this whirling thick world, and that far more insight, knowledge, revelation, results than in most poems where the experience is mastered? Also, there is finer poetry, in the sense of power, of scope, in much of Crane than in most successful poetry. Winters, perceiving on the edges of things, soars over Crane's conflict and, as it were, over the very materials without which "moral control" is a conceit.

Patchen is getting at something which is neither more nor less than a critique of the things and ideas in our life which determine to a great extent the prospects for such a control. For control, after all, means the ability to unify and relate experience without omitting or perverting all experience. The social order is in question here, first of all. After a lengthy and wearisome struggle, a kind of liberalism emerged; perhaps because of the protracted character of this conflict where the liberalism possessed none of the vigor of the young and freshly-won, it was superseded almost immediately by a new dogma. This dogmatism may have been based on scientific data, but what is certain now is that the consequent attitudes were unscientific. Although the one followed on the other with a speed that was "politically suspect," the adequacy of this most recent ideology has come under question with even more rapidity. Now intelligence alone seems unable to handle the densities of chaos and confusion which exist everywhere; the laws of the movements of progress are revealed as merciless laws. So far they have failed to show a guide to action; they have failed to reflect or create a morality obviously and simply differentiated from the lie, the hypocrisy and the betrayal.

But it is not enough to know it and to name it. A knowledge of right and wrong does not expugn an emotion. Patchen, who is one of the "cut-down" and the "smitten"—just as Rilke was—continues to need the whole sight and the whole view; he makes a morality:

> But I shall endorse no bloody erect
> Murder and go on looking with my own
>   eyes.

True, it is a simplified morality, and though it gives a bias to the "statistical" necessity, it removes action from the sphere of rhetoric and the sophistic conveniences. At a time when people are being conscripted for the bloody murder, when what is in store for most of us is an untold tale of horror, the poet drives for statements which are pitched above the reaches of debate.

But how else is the poet to function? After all, there is little time or room for polemic today, and, in essence, the question is: is the poet to be a factionalist? It is a truism that when the poet argues ideas it is suicide for both ideas and poetry. The poet shows a way of seeing, a way of living, finally, through his own necessary attitudes; and these attitudes, these postures before events, become a medium, immutable, through which the poet makes his criticism of life. In Patchen there are hard and fast assumptions, conclusions which carry no correctives—but then one has not yet learned how to read poetry.

Logical fallibility is an harrassing fact. But what of the imagination, the power, the hard justice, those which are the essences in the immortality of a poem? And what is the scientific fact? Most conclusions in the physical sciences have become working conclusions, tentatives, conveniences; in political economy the entire minute structure of Marxian struggle rests on the concept of *an inspired popular war*. Where in such a final concept are the scientific checks and controls? If Patchen's "facts" are not good therapy, they are good preventative—that which is the basis and ultimate goal even of medicine. The critic who has

dipped into politics and social criticism will ignore that basic
"non-paraphrasable" in Patchen because to have insight into an
agonized vision demands more than a taste of epiphenomenal
science. The horns on which the equivocation of the critic rests are
"truth," that is, the fact, and the truth of the poem, that is, the
consistent vision of the poem. But the resolution settles on neither.
It moves on to a series of imperatives which lie in the reader's own
head. Through the austerity, through the quality of asceticism,
through the hard surfaces and refractions and an explosion of
metaphor as if gotten through the distorting medium of a hundred differently angled mirrors, the poem departs from the things
"spoken about," becomes an insistent first part of a two-part
dialogue with one's self. It is not a comfortable dialogue:

> *Why does this blood scream Liar Liar*
> *Somewhere a door bangs, somewhere a*
> *window flies up.*
> *The hunted are awake. Fear is heavy*
> *as butter over*
> *Their houses*
> *Why does this blood scream Liar Liar*

and

> *Look! There is blood on its arms.*
> *And flesh still warm caught in its nails.*

and

> *Stars that shift and ebb like fog on the*
> *tranquil seaface;*
> *Lights returning, blurred, swinging*
> *away; snatches of old songs;*
> *The rough hand of my father; cities of*
> *my people sinking through vast space.*
> *Troubled stars are staked out in pasture*
> *of sleep...*
> *Turn to me, my darling...face blur-*
> *ring...the human fog...diving*
> *lights...*
> *The solstitial hand over storm and bitter-*
> *ness, over death's awful oblivion,*
> *High, high, holding the dark folly of*
> *clay to the mute drench of eternity.*

> *Look! children are laughing at their*
> *   games...there is no sadness, no*
> *   death.*
> *There is no question, no answer, no*
> *   decay, no pain...there is the quiet*
> *   of earth.*
> *When the lights go out and we walk*
> *   together or lie alone as our fathers do.*
> *There are eyes looking at us and we*
> *   should be beautiful in battle, devout*
> *   in sleep.*

and

> *Before I come again, in my own honor,*
> *Men will have gone down like pricked*
> *   guts;*
> *Murder will walk, and you will be dead.*
> *All the nice young kids will be puked*
> *   clean.*
> *Who will listen? who will care?*

When Ignazio Silone proceeds to an investigation into questions of old standing, orthodoxy is impatient: these have been settled years ago. Precisely! And we have lived according to these formulae as in a charade, in a kind of life without what is life-like. On one level there must be the continual examination, the defining of terms and the refining of definition. On another level there is the actuality still to be dealt with, in another, more direct, more immediate, way. Patchen's way is vast, direct, courageous, and if paradoxically, natural to the poet.

The overwhelming bulk of brutality is unperturbed, at least in an immediate sense, by the statistical image which confronts it. In such a recognition, the poet has, somehow, to match, to race on, in terms qualitatively equal to the giant squid "curling and twisting like a nest of anacondas, as if blindly to catch at any hapless object within reach." We have adjusted ourselves to statistics, they are so many numbers: 39,000 Chinese dead, 64,000 Chinese wounded, 14,000 Spaniards shot, so many and so many soldiers slain in such and such a battle. These mean hardly anything at all! Statistics, so far as I know, rarely suffer censure from the authorities: in the long view, statistics soften the horrors and brutality of war. Patchen, by means of satire and distortion, forces an awareness and even a tenseness as of actual fear; and this has nothing in common with the propaganda of the periodical. So far, I think, criticism as such has stopped short when it is confronted by the phenomenon that "imitates" the full quota of terror and hatred. It seems timid and effeminate alongside of the poem. What is needed, perhaps, is a lonely and tortured enmity to injustice and a recognition that the poems are a superior kind of war.

It is an epoch of wars and revolutions, an epoch of mixed categories, and contrary to Whitman's time. (This is not to say, however, that there is no residue of Whitman's time.) One can no longer enumerate the good things, and, as an old humor has it, one no longer sees signs of what is forbidden but rather he sees signs of what is permitted. Under such conditions a poem does become an instrument of power, just as Lawrence went over and beyond the novel and as Silone is impelled to sacrifice "form" because of what "has" to happen. This is not to say that the poems are not well executed or that there is a minimum of "non-paraphrasable" content, any more than it is to say that Lawrence and Silone have not written exacting works. But that is not central here, and what is important never is perfection of verse: the age of Herrick is far gone and Housman's excellence seems almost to place him in as distant an age.

Eliot's observation that Blake's shortcomings could be viewed through the shortcomings of the British Isles, that the lack of a continuous history, its insularity, blocked the poet, forced him, finally, into non-poetic labors is pertinent. It can be said simply: Blake's Britain is everywhere. The poet is forced into the role of historian, of mythologist, of, what is worse, philosopher and ideologist. He enters into a war of ideas and there, invariably, is submerged. The paradox writes itself: in order to write poetry, the poet must engage in what is primarily non-poetic labor first of all, and what he carries into his verse has been truly earned. For there is no framework of ideas and experience rich enough, true enough, flexible enough, firm enough.

Because of these problems—and one must grasp them in each particular—what is required for an understanding of Patchen's poetry is an understanding into the creative process itself.

And by this process is meant, too, what it feeds upon, that is, the multitude of sources, the values and beliefs, the time, the pastness in it, the credible things and the outmoded things, above all, the sums of these which (though for Dante they were pretty much ready to hand and usable) the poet must create for himself. If for no other reason, Kenneth Patchen's poetry is of significance for us because it reveals more sensitively, more truthfully, the poet's function.

There are few poets today who grasp the nature of the problem. There are fewer still who continue to create moving and whole poems; most are caught somewhere in the pre-history of the poem. Patchen stands pretty much in the middle of the problem and continues, partially because of it, partially in spite of it, to write some of our most important poetry.

David Gascoyne

Introducing Kenneth Patchen

On the dust-jacket of *Cloth of the Tempest* is printed the following brief biographical summary:

> "Born in Ohio in 1911, Patchen speaks for the generation whose destiny has been to grow up during one war and to go through another. He attended the Experimental College of the University of Wisconsin; was awarded a Guggenheim Fellowship in 1936; was one of three new poets to be added to Louis Untermeyer's revised Modern American Poetry; is married to Miriam Oikemus; and lives for the most part in New York."

The first collection of Kenneth Patchen's poems to be published was called *Before the Brave.* I have never had an opportunity of seeing this book, but I understand that the author does not regard it as representing anything but a preliminary and not mature stage of his development. It was followed in 1939 by *First Will & Testament,* 'like no book that has been published in these states,' as the anthologist Untermeyer called it. The unusually strong, indeed violent, if not exactly distinct, personality emanating from each of its 180 pages, made its appearance a memorable event in modern American letters.

In 1942 Patchen consolidated the achievement of his second book with the publication of *The Dark Kingdom,* of which the complete title, occupying the entire front page of the book, runs as follows:

> *'THE DARK KINGDOM stands above the waters as a sentinel warning man of dangers from his own kind. On its altars the deeds of blood are not offered; here are watchers whose eyes are fixed on the eternal undertakings of the spirit. What has been common and tarnished in these poor wombs, here partakes of immortality. In its windows are*

*reflected the unreturning events of childhood. All who ask
life, find a peace everlasting in its radiant halls. All who
have opposed in secret, are here provided with green crowns.
All who have been dragged through the cowled flame of this
world, are here clothed in the bright garment of the tempest. Here all who sorrow and are weary under strange burdens—fearing death, are seen to enter the white throne
room of God'*

This book caused a *New York Times* critic to refer to Patchen as 'one of the poets whom historians will turn to for intelligence about the year 1942. He is the most impulsively romantic and imaginative of the younger writers.'

Since then, Patchen has published two further collections,
the important *Cloth of the Tempest* in 1943, and a little earlier
than this a small volume in the 'New Directions' *Poet of the Month*
series, containing twenty-one poems and entitled *The Teeth of the
Lion*, with the following corollary to the title:

*'In white savage caps make a bloody pasturage where
I am laid down break tear kill in a world of cheats defilers
ratsinpinkwalls through the black camps where murder lifts
the teaching but the girls by the lake and the green quick
laughing kids in the school-yard and the sad wise beautiful
gentle clean strong good loving joys as I am made and you
will know me.'*

On the dust-jacket of *Cloth of the Tempest* from which I
have already quoted, after giving extracts from the entire
American press referring to Patchen in the most laudatory terms,
his publishers assert on the back flap: 'This record of critical
praise and acknowledgement speaks for itself as strongly as Patchen speaks for America,' and conclude by referring to him finally
as 'a modern of...tremendous importance'. Opening the book at
random, a conservative reader, duly impressed by this evidence of
the apparent acceptance by common critical consent of Patchen
as an American poet of serious significance, may perhaps find
himself bewildered, baffled, even outraged, to come upon the sort
of thing of which *Loves of the Tragic Owl*, for instance, will serve
as a fair example:

> Zeeeeen—Stillgrind twing flic. Bleeoook—
> Rattlesoft mouth—
> Lussssssssssss lornhen—

Tubitititit (bloody grass) ferngrim
As an old man's brain —
Sedghart ice-clothed in gray fur —

Turning the pages in search of further enlightenment,
such a reader might well begin to suspect that someone's leg was
being pulled somewhere on coming across pages on which crude
grotesque drawings, scraps of cuttings from newspapers and en-
cyclopaedias are combined with provocative phrases printed
mixed up with the rest in a dramatic lay-out (Patchen calls these
divertissements 'makings'), or a childish outline drawing with the
caption: 'Ragamuffin Playing With a Really Pretty Creature
While His Poor Mother Roams Through the City Looking for
Work.'

If this 'conservative' peruser happened to be one whose
conservatism was simply the rationalization of his lack of intelligence or adventuresomeness or curiosity, as is occasionally the
case with hypothetical readers flaunting this description, it would
probably be simply a waste of his time and my own for me to attempt to mollify him with any sort of argument or explanation.
But if, however, he should be a conservative whose mind were not
quite closed to all reasonable persuasion, and always supposing
that, as I believe, it is in fact possible, notwithstanding the apparently wilful irresponsibility of antics such as I have just indicated, to make out a case for recognising Patchen as a writer
deserving the serious attention of anyone interested in the authentic poetic utterance of our time, — and if it really were necessary to
attempt some 'explanation' or 'justification' of the sometimes
freakish results of Patchen's iconoclasm (to call it that), then the
clearest way of doing so, it seems to me, would be by referring first
to the odd phenomenon known as DADA, and then showing how
Patchen's significance can perhaps best be seen in the light of that
particular context.

To put it plainly: Kenneth Patchen is the lone one-man
DADA of contemporary America.

The true significance, the unique historical importance of
the non-movement (or anti-movement) known as DADA, born
during and out of the First World War, has never as far as I know
been adequately stated (that is, by any writer in English, at least;
Georges Hugnet's comprehensive account published serially in

Cahiers d'Art may be presumed to do it justice in French; it was, of course, in any case, pre-eminently a French phenomenon). Though this is hardly the place for me to start trying to make good this deficiency, the meaning of DADA might very briefly be outlined as follows:

At a moment of universal intellectual and moral degradation when the values on which Western civilization is supposed to be based were every day being spectacularly compromised by most of the official spokesmen of society, DADA was perhaps the sole visible sign indicating the existence of at least a tiny remnant among the living who were still determined not to participate in this general passive surrender of spiritual integrity, not to accept the terms of its betrayal. If this refusal expressed itself only indirectly, as from behind a mask, this was not on account of any prudent deference to civil authority, but because of the determining part that *irony* played in its expression. The mask assumed by DADA in face of the hypocritical official bluff of the *soi-disant* Christian world was that of a ferocious humour (UMOR as Jacques Vaché nicknamed it), the convulsive grimace of frantic absurdity. In a society organized solely for purposes of competitive commerce, the exploitation of subject races and the destruction (whenever necessary, and then with as thorough an efficiency as possible) of landscapes, armies, cities and even civil populations, yet in which that society's official representatives scarcely ever referred directly to the existence of these universally evident evils, though having the words *duty, self-sacrifice, heroism, the good of mankind, Christian civilization* and so on constantly on their lips, — in such a society, DADA's grimace implied, it is impossible to take anything seriously any more; all that is put forward as claiming reverence, respect or honour turns out to be hollow appearance concealing some ugly lie, so that none of the great abstractions by which we are supposed to order and justify our lives any longer makes sense: What other honest and sincere expression can we give to our reaction to such a situation than a burst of furious, incoherent laughter? You have to laugh, since to weep is too embarrassing, and even sorrow is a 'noble' emotion that one has therefore had to learn to distrust at last...

Most of those who actively participated in DADA were either writers or painters; which amounted to saying that nothing could be calculated to arouse their disgusted derision more effectively than literature and art. The *Mona Lisa,* for instance, was eminently suitable, they considered, for painting moustaches on; Rodin's *Le Penseur* made an excellent trade mark for a patent laxative; if a poem was to be expected of one, a page or two from the telephone directory would always serve. The Art of Letters, to a dadaist, meant no more than a random item in a catalogue including poultry-farming, semantics, ludo, phrenology and colonic irrigation.

If, as Vaché wrote to André Breton in 1917, 'it's necessary to disgorge a little acid of old lyricism, let it be done abruptly, rapidly...' And: 'ART of course doesn't exist—so it's futile to go into a song and dance about it...So we neither like Art nor Artists (down with Apollinaire and HOW RIGHT TOGRATH IS TO ASSASSINATE THE POET).'

The review which eventually became the 'organ' of most of the dadaists after the defeat of DADA, — that is to say, after they had realized that 'DADA could only continue by ceasing to exist,' — had a title which seems plain and straightforward enough at first sight, but which actually was fraught with complex implication. It was called simply *Littérature.* For the contributors to this review, 'literature' was no more than a term of contemptuous ridicule; it was adopted as a label out of a sort of wry self-depreciation, rather as a collegiate 'mag.' might style itself *The Tripe-Hound,* and in much the same spirit as that which led Eric Satie to label a really unexceptionally serious group of piano studies: *Dried-up Embryos.* This self-depreciation and defensive sarcasm was due to it being only as it were shamefacedly, as a result of an absurd, all-too-human feebleness of mind, that these writers wrote at all. The soundest justification of the habit that they could find was that of Knut Hamsun, quoted by André Breton: 'I write to pass the time.'

The close similarity between the dadaist attitude to literature and the attitude of Kenneth Patchen is so obvious, I think from the following passages, that I need but quote them to dispense with further commentary:

> 'And in particular ask me to tell you
> What I think of the present state of our American Letters
> As I think
> It stink—

Together with the drippy jerks who commit it.'
                (The Impuissant Surrender to the Name & the
                Act & the Tensions of Ratheda.)

'It is an absolute mistake to ladle out stress like a cook measuring off the ingredients for a cake. We've got a country full of cake-baking poets now, one just as good and just as bad as the next. — Poetry is writing. Maybe what I am talking about is not poetry (the stuff the critics are yammering about)…I am a writer and I shall write. The term "poet" is a convenience of the middle-class. I declare myself a writer. I want room to move around. Spare me from the pawings-over of the cake-bakers.' — (Preface to *The Hunted City.*)

'It is more than unusual to write about anything now. Hours of each day I pass in the work of perfecting a little racket which is designed to interest spinsters and schoolmarms of either sex. Tomorrow I have an appointment to visit a certain well-known poet whose work is done altogether under the influence of large checks from his mama who never quite went to bed with him. All his poems begin with x.' — (*I Never Had Any Desire So Strong…*)

Just as DADA expressed itself through a mask of absurdity the adoption of which was determined by the irony inherent in the dadaist attitude, Kenneth Patchen, we find, has evolved in his more recent work a sort of *dramatic convention* for the expression of his attitude, which more or less amounts to a *persona*. The convention might tentatively be formulated somewhat like this: The poet, hypersensitive representative of humanity's loftiest ideals, is so appalled by the brutal realities of the contemporary scene that finally he has been driven literally out of his mind by the sheer horror of it all. And in his derangement, wandering bemusedly about the Bedlam of New York, from time to time he gives vent to poignantly incoherent fragmentary utterance. . . delirious. . .outpourings in which, among much that is strictly meaningless, there nevertheless shine forth now and then the cold hard gleams of a kind of truth which a merely sane writer would never have the face to articulate except in a very much more roundabout, watered-down way. For instance, in a poem rather significantly entitled *None Stay the White Speech of His Wandering*, after a couple of stanzas of unadulterated dementia, he suddenly hits out with:

'Death. Because when you are very naked
You cannot clothe yourself with the partydress
Of state or church or opinion or of being
An article of merchandise on a country's
Bloodlist. You will confine yourself to The Kingdom.'

As another example, here is the end of a poem called *The Temple of Diana:*

'I am too angry to bother with this poem
About the beauty of the world
Who cares a damn about that now.'

Or again, here is a small piece of truth about the life of Man as it is lived in America every day at this time:

'Rain dripping down from a rusty evespout
Into the gray-fat cinders of the millyard...
The dayshift goes on in four minutes.'

The Kingdom to which the demented poet of Patchen's dramatic convention is said to confine himself is nothing more nor less than the domain of the solitary individual's irreducible integrity: the expression *son fort intérieur* describes it exactly. It is that unique corner of subjective chaos which has been colonized by his creative imagination, as Blake colonized Jerusalem, not as a sensitive dreamer's cosy hide-out against the hostility of the kingdom, forever inescapable after all, of mundane reality, but in very earnest as a guilt-determined *symptomatic reflection* counterbalancing our unpleasant 'real world' and standing as in a certain sense an indictment of it. Just as the enraged burlesque of DADA really constituted an indictment of the 'universal intellectual and moral degradation' that called it forth as a protest, at the time of the First World War. Time since then has lurched uncontrollably on, carrying all dadaists well into their middle-age; Andre Breton, in 1942, was reproaching himself that he still had 'an eye for the sad recantations' of Louis Aragon, author in his youth of one of the most notorious of dadaist poems (called *Suicide* and consisting simply of the letters of the alphabet), who had then recently been describing himself as 'looking very respectable indeed with all my decorations and my hair whitened by age,' and Breton a year or two later was himself to be found at least sufficiently respectable to be invited to deliver an official address to the Year's Leaving Class at Yale. The coming of the Second World War can hardly be said to have brought with it a very marked improvement on the intellectual and moral condition that I have described as being universal at the time of its predecessor. But if its coming found the first dadaists settling down to middle-age, it could discover no alteration in the pure intransigence of the original DADA spirit, for that is something that cannot be tied down by dates. In the poetry, or whatever you like to call it, of Kenneth Patchen, it is to be found flaring as wantonly and gratuitously as ever.

[Editor's Note: the following statement appeared immediately after the conclusion of Gascoyne's essay, on the same page, when the essay was first published in *Poetry Quarterly.*]

A STATEMENT

Putting aside whatever disagreement I may have with Mr. Gascoyne's interpretation of DADA, I am at a complete loss to see what his essay on this movement has to do with my work.

Mr. Gascoyne quotes from certain of my poems to substantiate his thesis; were there space, I can think of no better refutation than to reproduce these same fragments here—especially since it should be obvious even to that 'conservative peruser' that satire is often best served by a satiric approach.

'What other honest and sincere expression', asks Mr. Gascoyne—stating the DADA position—'can we give to our reaction to such a situation (the hypocrisy and vulgar falsehoods of society) than a burst of furious, incoherent laughter?' Oh, but there are a lot of others! As poets we can reassert our belief in the essential nobility of human beings, our love of and humility before the art of poetry itself—for without these we are not poets at all...we can weep, and our tears will not be those of spoiled children but of men who have serious lives in this world of horror and wonder...we can kneel, because the Beautiful is kneeling beside us, and the Mystery is watching us with its eyes that are the cold flowers of the sky.

KENNETH PATCHEN

January, 1946 (New York)

Richard G. Morgan

The Journal of Albion Moonlight: Its Form and Meaning

What is astonishing about *The Journal of Albion Moonlight* is not that it was ignored for so long by critics and colleges alike, even as was Patchen himself, but that it was written at all, particularly on the chest-thumping, flag-waving eve of America's entrance into World War II. Its initial reception notwithstanding, it was eventually appreciated by and had an effect upon such diverse figures as William Carlos Williams, Henry Miller, Samuel Beckett, Jean Wahl, René Daumal, T. S. Eliot, and Jack Kerouac. The *Journal's* worth as an early form of anti-novel and as an artistic work of genius, are beginning to be recognized, and an in-depth critical analysis is long overdue.

The book was written during the "plague-summer" of 1940, when the heady odor of war was in the nostrils of the entire civilized world. Patchen describes it as follows:

> (*JAM*) is a journal of the summer of 1940 — that plague-summer when all the codes and ethics which men had lived by for centuries were subjected to the acid test of general war and universal disillusionment. I have tried to make an imperishable record of that time.[1]

In its simplest concrete form, it is the tale of a group of people who journey, half in headlong flight, half in missionary pilgrimage, from New York to an indeterminate place of heavenly being called Galen, where they hope to find Roivas (Savior). This is, however, only the external framework of the journal, and is largely irrelevant to much of its actual purpose and meaning. In fact, the entire book's action occurs as if between parentheses, a moment between dreams in the mind of Kenneth Patchen and his narrator-persona Albion Moonlight.

The critical inaccessibility of the book until now is due to a number of factors. Patchen left no extensive personal literary reflections behind, and according to Miriam Patchen, the wife to whom all his books are dedicated, "K. P. didn't write many letters [and] he didn't discuss his work to any extent to speak of."[2] In addition, Patchen's views and mode of life mitigated against formal inquiry into his work. When the *Journal* was composed at the onset of World War II, he had not undergone the "appropriate" changes from an artist living in a Depression economy to a soldier-poet writing in service of a wartime boom. Rather than disown his radical pacifism in the name of national unity, as so many did, he continued to regard fascism and capitalism as indistinguishable evils, both awash in a lust for war. Kenneth Rexroth wrote,

> With almost no exceptions, the silentiaries of American literature have ceased to be able to tell good from evil. One of the few exceptions is Kenneth Patchen.[3]

Patchen's own inner morality and his sense of artistic integrity caused him to purposely attempt to put his work outside the framework of modern critism, and to consciously reject any effort to place him within the aegis of any group or movement. He has been classed as a Proletarian writer, a Surrealist, a Dadaist, an Anarchist, a Socialist, a Mystic, and a Beat; and these groups have all been denounced by him in turn.

His objection to easy identification with a group resulted in obscurity, an obscurity deepened by his refusal to define the aims of his work in terms of popular notions of art and classifiable forms. James Dickey says of Patchen, "He is a poet not so much in form as in essence."[4] And here is the point. Despite oddities of construction, one cannot view the *Journal of Albion Moonlight* as a rebellion against form, but rather as both a parody and a rejection of the very idea of form. In fact the early concentration on and disapproval of the irregularities of Patchen's form were so great precisely because of the disturbing strength of his content, particularly in this book.

I

With subjects unacceptable to the social system, the retreat to a commentary on form was but hastened. The *Journal*, of course, containing no clear linear path of action, was frustating in that respect as well. Since the particular genre was not openly apparent, familiar critical patterns and measurements became useless. The only conclusion possible under these circumstances was that the *Journal* is incoherent. That surface "incoherence" is, however, one of the points of its existence, a conscious abandonment of literary form in favor of direct personal discourse paralleling a rejection of society as then constituted, in order to thrust forth more effectively the actual themes. At one point in the *Journal* we read,

> I have thought it over, Jetter — what you told me tonight of your ideas about poetry. Why the large, messy rebellion against form? What do you care? What difference does it make? What does it matter that you don't like this sort of whistling in the dark? The whole thing is somehow silly anyway. But to get excited about it. . . . Don't be a poet; be a prime minister, a garbage collector. The point is, I think, how many lays do you get? Do your shoes fit well? These things are important. (pp.6-7)[5]

In large part then, the actual content of the *Journal* is its form. It is necessary, however, to examine the manner and process of the book to gain the requisite perspective for appreciating and understanding the content. Criticism of the book must be undertaken according to the terms of the *Journal* itself, and a stylistic or structural analysis is thus primarily a definition of them in direct relation to its content. Henry Miller's statements on the book are significant in their analysis of those terms and are worthy of consideration. In his review he asserts:

> It is a journal of a state of mind, a seismological record of an inner explosion. It does not record or describe the outer chaos produced by the dissolution of a world but reproduces that chaos as it is experienced hour by hour in the heart of a sensitive being.[6]

This "sensitive being" is Albion Moonlight, who is both author and character in his own and his author's books. Late in the book, he himself defines the terms of the journal:

> The journal, whether real or imaginary, must conform to only one law: it must be at any given moment what the journal-keeper wants it to be at any given moment. It is easily seen from this that time is of the greatest importance in the journal; indeed, there can be as many journals as there are days covered. The true journal can have no plan for the simple reason that no man can plan his days. (p.304)

As such the "form" is that of the internal psychology of its creator, to paraphrase Randall Jarrell, "a dream among objects," leaving a work that is a novel by length, poetry by language, philosophical treatise by intent, but none of these to the exclusion of the others. Reality as an objective quality is thus meaningless; the book forces the reader to move from spectator to participant.

Without the externally-imposed order of a standard literary form (except the journal, which here is far from standard in a traditional sense) we must, to "understand" the book, disregard intellect for instinct and proceed through Albion's line-by-line growth and development. Our response to the *Journal* must therefore be based upon the actual events therein and not upon preconceptions of literary form. The only way to become truly cognizant of the development of the *Journal* is to enter into it as a co-equal respondent to the stimuli projected by the characters.

The development of the book is achieved primarily by a process of dissolution, and the journal is a narrative (in its underlying aspect) of the roles and social and literary framework of the various Albions dissolving to reveal a bare psyche which is part of external nature. Albion Moonlight is the central character and the unifying factor of the narrative though, in truth, all of the book's characters may be viewed as Albion or reflections of him, and they in turn are individually quite different Albion Moonlights.

Throughout the book we are reminded of Patchen's presence through intrusions and "interruptions," and also of the fact that Albion is his own creator, that his existence comes from writing the events of his own life. The multiplicity of his identities includes all those he creates, and those who create him. Likewise, the movement toward Galen is primarily a movement within his own heart.[7] At one point Albion says,

> I have spent ten years becoming a saint. It was not easy because always the man I was got in the way. This man's name is Albion Moonlight. He has been puzzled by my behavior. I feel that he is nearly dead now. (p.37)

On the next page, however, a voice declares,

> *I am Albion Moonlight. I do not know the being that says these things. I fear it. It is but another trick of our enemies. My head is heavy with fighting it.* (p.38)

The divisions and inclusions in the character of Albion Moonlight are numerous. Among the most important of these is the distinction (and unity) in him between creator and created. At one point we are told of "the story that was coming to life under his fingers." (p.107) This authorship is set in the following light later in the *Journal:*

> it was necessary for me to go out of my way to write *that which I did not want to write* to put it simply: I had to become a person it would kill me to be. . . . I wanted to make a book that I could read for the first time *after I had written it.* . . .
>
> . . .this novel is being written as it happens, not what happened yesterday, or what will happen tomorrow but what is happening now, *at this writing.* . . . I am desperately anxious to discover what will take place next in this book. (pp.144–145)

This primary role, that of writer of the journal, is analyzed by Hugh McGovern in this way:

> Albion Moonlight, the author-character, is hopelessly insane, because he is the consciousness of the perception of an organic world in which no reference point for sanity exists; but Albion Moonlight, the author-observer, possesses in his distance from the action an absolute sanity that can diagnose his own condition and in its living body, fling it in-

to the consciousness of the reader so that the reader too, may
touch the madness of his brethren.[8]

McGovern's perception of this organizational schizophrenia is
correct on one level of the book, but stops short of the rein-
tegration inherent in the *Journal's* plan and purpose on a more
profound level. To understand that deeper significance, it is well
to look into the main character's name and its origins both in
history and in the works of William Blake.

Historically Albion was the ancient giant of Britain, later a
symbol of Britain itself. He is mentioned in Holinshed (*Chronicles
1577*) and in Spenser's *Faerie Queen* (II.x.ii) among others.[9] As
early as the Morality plays, Albion Knight was a familiar character representing mankind, a generalized quester following various
rituals of education and illumination.

This symbolic interpretation was accepted by Blake and
used in several of his major works, most notably *Jerusalem.* When,
in 1946, Patchen wrote an introduction to Blake's *Job,* he mentioned *Jerusalem,* and *Milton* as Blake's greatest books. Concerning Blake's symbology, Patchen writes:

> Many have attempted to penetrate the identities of the
> "things" in Blake's poems — Geoffrey Keynes, S. Foster
> Damon, Ellis Yeats, Sloss, Wallis, etc., etc., this iden-
> tification (which I think is the most interesting) is by Mr.
> Damon, and appears in his book, *William Blake, His
> Philosophy and Symbols,* 1924, O. P. Los (sol) equals what
> the Poet can know; *Vrizen* equals Reason: *Enitharmon*
> equals Inspiration, Orce. a union of Imagination & Reason;
> *Tharmas* e. The Senses (of this world); Luvah e. The
> Emotions (from the moon); *Eden* e. The Site of Inspir-
> ation. . .[10]

This allegorical transposition, in addition to its similarity
to sections of the *Journal* is significant in its exclusion of Albion.
In the book Patchen cites, S. Foster Damon states

> Albion, the ancient British giant, is the symbol of Man, and
> around him revolve such familiar characters as Jesus,
> Jerusalem, Vala, Los, Enitharmon, and Rehab.[11]

and in his *Blake Dictionary,* Damon further clarifies the matter,
saying,

> Albion is the father of all mankind (EZ ii: 43). . . .He
> corresponds . . . to Swedenborg's Grand Man and the
> Adam Kadmon of the Kabbalists.[12]

That Patchen subscribes to this view of Albion is apparent,
and equally certain is his early and total familiarity with Blake.
Miriam Patchen writes,

> Kenneth read Blake at all times, from his earliest days to his
> last. He read everything.[13]

As a result, we may safely assume the centrality of the character
Albion Moonlight and move toward an estimation of his symbolic
role. The entire "plot" of the book (if such a word is relevant at
all), is the record of the progress, or even the mere functioning, of
the mind of Albion (and of Kenneth Patchen) in the "plague-
summer" of 1940. Near the end of the book the implication is
made that Albion/Patchen has never left the room.[14] And yet the
narrator's control over our knowledge is faulty. Whereas there is
conscious commentary on the literary style of the journal, and a
continuing sense that the book is a living body being examined by
its physician-author, at other times Albion explodes into such
discussions as,

> You will realize that my characters are dangerous to me.
> God knows! they may decide to walk out of the book at any
> time, leaving me to carry on as best I can. I had no
> suspicions of Thomas Honey. Yet he managed to turn
> Jackeen against me. Jetter was my dearest friend. . . . I in-
> sist upon knowing why Turnbull and Fenn forced themselves
> into my journal, taking up a space I meant to fill with an ac-
> count of how my mother wanted me to study for the
> priesthood. . . . I have been compelled to struggle every
> inch of the way against the sheer bullheadedness of these
> people. I had not the least wish to tell you about Leah, but,
> dead as she was, in she came. (pp.146-147)

Under the circumstances, the form of this "chronicle of the
human spirit" (p.145) becomes whatever happens to fall between
page 1 and page 313.

To see how this form functions, it will be useful to explore,
first in an objective, 'literary' sense the nature of the other characters. H. (Harry) Roivas, who lives in Galen, is the savior to whom

Albion and his party are journeying. He appears variously as a beautiful and wise man, a Christ-like, gentle creature, as a drooling, hideous dwarf, and as Albion himself. Among the other significant characters are Jetter, a "Negro" and man of violent aspect; Billy Delian, a hypocrite and degenerate who becomes president of the United States; Joseph Gambetta, a phantom who is also Jackeen's father; Jackeen, Chrystle, and Leah, all incarnations of womanly purity, who in various ways signify both the saving and the damning aspects of love; Carol, similar but flawed and thus realized as a sexual partner; Thomas Honey, a man of artistic nature; Adolf Hitler and Jesus Christ, as themselves; a number of interchangeable bed partners for Albion, among whom the most identifiable is Ann Deaken; Keddel, the "most important man in the book," who is revealed as one aspect of the true savior; and many other minor figures. All are in some way related, and all die, a number of them more than once, usually at one another's hands (like Blake's four warring Zoas).

In the *Journal,* we are given several interpretations of the characters. The first reads as follows:

> I have brought into being people of my own size: Jetter, the careless murderer; Billy Delian, in whose useless heart treachery and betrayal lie; Thomas Honey, the physical man who has no endeavor worthy of his strength; Carol, the woman like any other; Jackeen, the visible body of man's desire on earth; Chrystle, the pure child who is in all of us — and I did this thing because I was afraid; I had to perform for you; I had to distract you from failure — my failure to tell you what all of us are waiting so faithfully to hear. (p.23)

Shortly thereafter, in a conversation with Roivas, Albion (the author) decodes the characters as follows: Galen, paradise; Jetter, the crippled gunman, crippled because "before the State can get him to do its murder, the State must first kill his soul" (p.30); Billy Delian, Hitler; Carol, Dante's wife — his "good bedfellow;" Joseph Gambetta, a phantom; Jackeen, "every woman that every man has ever wanted — and couldn't have;" and Thomas Honey, Beethoven.

And yet on the next page we read

All this rot about who is what! . . . Billy Delian is no more
Hitler than you are . . . Beethoven was Beethoven and
Thomas Honey is Thomas Honey . . . my people have
meaning in themselves. (p.31)

This derangement of literary sensibilities, coming early in the
book, can be eased only by accepting the characters on several
levels at once (a point which will be dealt with further as it applies
to the thematic content of the work).

The actual framework of the book is divided into several
different journals, novels, interruptions, and asides, to match the
non-linear nature of thought, human development, and indeed,
life itself. (A supplement delineating these parts is appended to
the end of this essay). The book must thus be examined as a circular entity rather than a sequential arrangement of events.

Despite the complex nature of the narrative, the main
journal does remain, proceeding from May 2 to "terminate" on
the promised August 27th. There is a consistent (though
physically impossible) movement around the American continent,
through small Middle American towns and large cities. The entire
story occurs against the background of a huge, endless war, whose
guns the pilgrims can usually hear in the near distance. Cleveland
is bombed. The big guns are heard outside Detroit. We are
greeted by the stupidity of cowboys, and visit various whorehouses
across the land. Interspersed are philosophical dicta, comments
on literary figures, topographical and social surveys and
typographical oddities in the form of oversized print, odd spacing,
and pictures. This combines with a sexual atmosphere now tender
and beautiful, now raging and cruel. And the literary tone as well
varies between lyric tenderness and vicious, angry depravity.

II

The story line of the *Journal of Albion Moonlight* is,
however, secondary to the actual matter or themes of the work. As
the plot becomes more indefinite, the naked visage of Albion
Moonlight becomes clearer, and by the end of the book we find a
stark figure of moral and artistic statement, and a novel which has
disintegrated into fragments and isolated thoughts. It is not the

story here, but the themes it embodies, which are of central importance. Those themes are: (1) Art and the role of the artist. (2) War (and murder) and the sociopolitical madness which breeds it. (3) Love, natural (or animal) religion, and the primacy of the soul. (4) The unity of being, and communality among all creatures.

In general, the movement of the *Journal* may be viewed, as may Patchen's intention, as being away from organized Society (and literature), and towards nature and the wonder of the natural soul. Thus it is in one respect a stripping away and rejection, and in another a move toward unity, a divergent motion apparent both in Albion himself and in the actions of the other characters in the narratives.

A valuable initial reference point for approaching these themes is through Patchen's view of art and the artist. Ray Nelson believes, on a critical level, that

> Patchen's novels mark him distinctly as a figure in that tradition of American literature that emphasized the artist's moral responsibility. In the moral tradition and artfullness of the writer are applied to an expression of the truth he perceives in his own person rather than to fulfilling the demands of structural and emotional symmetry.[15]

But even beyond this, the cogent point in the *Journal* is that "literature" (and its "tradition") is not merely a neutral but a destructive force, itself an inhibiting factor in communication. Thus when we are told, "Man has been corrupted by his symbols, Language has killed his animal," (p.15) we must realize that the basis for artistic consideration has shifted. The intent here is to strip away the literary baggage and situational expectations which have accumulated around the instincts and thereby to permit direct communication between artist and audience. Patchen writes,

> My purpose? it is nothing remarkable; I wish to speak to you. (p.22)

In order to accomplish this we are led through numerous attacks on literary figures and various concepts of form. The object is to avoid creation of a proscenium.

The problem for Patchen with holding a mirror up to life is that it can readily be recognized as a mirror. The goal is to reject all forms of distancing between points of origin and reception. In the entry for June 19, we read:

> I was troubled, thinking: they will not trust me because I grew weary and told lies; they will not really listen because at times I became afraid and tried to clothe my spirit in art; but I was a fool to think this — they can *feel* me coming out at them. (p.23)

The reader is given no means for escaping from the meaning of the words into a false-front artistic creation. Albion offers his heart " — take it! I hold it out to you. . . . Close the covers of this book and it will go on talking." (p.200). The audience is importuned directly:

> There are buildings falling. I am cold. Put your arms around me. (p.13)

Albion as author writes the book "as it happens," and the communication is thus between souls engaged in the common pursuit of wonder and flight from social madness. Of this McGovern says,

> We are led in *The Journal of Albion Moonlight* to where art should always take us: behind the scenes of the so-called "real" thing to the perceptions and evaluations of the spirit.[16]

Patchen's assertion is: "I am alive in every part of this book. . . . I write this book as an action." (p.261). And this reaches to the heart of his view of the artist:

> The reader will remember that A. Moonlight is not a reformer, nor is he an informer, an out-former, an underformer nor an overformer; he is a *former* — savvy? (p.143)

The purpose of art, for Patchen, is just this — to form, to form a new world. As he writes in his introduction to Blakes's *Job:*

> TO FORGIVE IS TO UNDERSTAND
> ART IS GIVING
>   THE SAVED MUST SAVE THE REST.[17]

and in the *Journal,* Albion tells us

If you will listen to me, you will learn to create laws. You
have none, you know. What did you get from Shakespeare's
hooting and howling? A bit of stuff about an idiot and a
king. And you threw up in sheer ecstasy. That won't do. The
noble speeches aren't enough. The thread-bare and
ridiculous plots aren't enough. Men were made to talk to
one another. You can't understand that. But I tell you that
the writing of the future will be just this kind of writing —
one man trying to tell another man of the events in *his own
heart.* (p.200)

It is the socio-literary stereotypes which both prevent effective
communication and encourage vicious behavior. At its worst
literature becomes merely the systematic completion of expected
patterns.

A means of understanding this problem may be as an extension of Wendell Johnston's concept of "verbal nesting,"[18] which
employs the idea that standard terms and models grant asylum
from thought, and also diffuse attention. For example, the simile
"red as a rose," fails to capture any attention on our part, being
inexact through extensive use and cultural saturation.

Patchen's reaction is to reject common methods of literary
development in favor of directness and a strength of statement.
He assures us,

I won't pull any tricks with mirrors on you.

Later I may see a mistake in this. Later I may say: what was
the use in not resorting to all the old, boring stage sets; the
imitation teeth and spreading, false mustaches — why did
you trouble to show yourself as you are? (p.142)

Later in the book he states,

I want it clearly understood that I am not an entertainer.
Get a load of this:

Carol was dying.

Blood dripped down her face.

Her legs had been hacked off at the thighs. (p.258)

The method is made even more explicit by his informing us of
what he intends to do, is doing, and has done. We are told to expect a novel, then that we should not have expected one; he daz-
zles us with a lyrical passage or beautiful description, then says, in

effect, "How'd you like that one?" Near the opening of the book, while we are groping for a frame of reference, he gives us an allegorical translation for each of the characters, changes it, then steals it away entirely.

The outcome is that we are left alone in a room with Albion Moonlight, a man busy with being born, with discovering and inventing his own life. He says, "I have stepped onto a new planet" (p.201), and we are to accompany him. For here the role of the artist is not to create literature but to uncover life:

> You will be told what I write is confused, without order — and I tell you that my book is not concerned with the problems of art, but with the problems of the world, with the problems of life itself. . . . (p.200)

Life and art in *The Journal of Albion Moonlight* are inseparable. The artist, far from taking entertainment or the perfection of a genre as his province, has as his purpose the redefinition of art and the assertion of a basic morality. The means for accomplishing this is not a system of thought, for as Albion states,

> If the mind does not function in a logical way, by what right do we demand ordered thinking? . . . If there can be no logic outside the mind, and if the mind rejects logic, is not the desire for logic a form of madness? (p.148)

Rather it is the spontaneous and purposeful creation of that specific quality — madness, madness, that is, as it appears in the eyes of a larger social insanity. Even Patchen's own mode of composition is parallel to this scheme. Miriam Patchen writes,

> When Kenneth started writing his own work (not letters which were very difficult for him!) it was almost as if he were working from instant re-play tape. In a way of course he was — for he was always working — even when asleep. I'd hear him talking and singing in his sleep poetry which was not yet down on paper. When he started to write — longhand — it came out perfectly.[19]

So in Patchen's mind the act of creation, itself madness in the eyes of a martial society, was the means to salvation.

> The word is the way a child thinks
> The word is a green face in a marble thicket

> The word is an acrobat in the land of cripples
> (p. 238)

It is the duty of the artist to create such a word, which is in turn the means by which to confront the "problems of life" as Patchen sees them.

Of these problems, the problem of war (and murder) is paramount. If there is a concrete superstructure to the *Journal,* it is that of organized, worldwide murder, and we are told,

> In a world of murder the artist must be the first to die. He must lead. *Otherwise no one's death will have meaning.* (p. 204)

Henry Miller responded to the book by saying,

> The purpose of *The Journal of Albion Moonlight,* it seems to me, is to kill off the war. In this book, all the characters are killed off excepting the Voice which is, I presume, the voice of conscience.[20]

And Patchen himself makes an overt declaration on the subject in the *Journal:*

> I write along a single line: I never get off it. I said that you were never to kill anyone, *and I meant it.* (p.48)

Several years later, in the only foreword he ever wrote to one of his own books, he verbalized his feelings in a more extended manner:

A WORD

> These poems cover the ten years of my writing life. There shouldn't be any point here in trying to add to what the poems say; but perhaps a few flat statements might not be wasted (people sometimes protest that "modern poetry" is too obscure) so, in plain English:
>
> I am opposed to all war.
>
> I don't believe human beings should kill each other.
>
> I am opposed to all violence — *for whatever reason.*
>
> I believe that wars will only end when men refuse to murder one another — *for whatever reason.*
>
> I believe wars will only end when the present murderous forms of society are allowed to die — and all men are at last permitted to live together as brothers.[21]

The multiple murders in the *Journal* are functions of the need to "kill" murder. By presenting murder in all its various forms, it becomes not glory under furled banners, nor defense of national boundaries, but the gory, agonized rippings of flesh of dazed beasts. *The Journal of Albion Moonlight* is an effort to stop the war:

> Anything you may think to be the truth, will be a lie —
> otherwise there could be no war. In a world where truth was
> worth a damn, this book would stop the war. Everything is
> on my side. I speak the truth — *but all of this is a lie because
> nobody will listen.* I will stop the war for anyone who
> reads this — you will listen to my war, until I am
> done. (p. 40)

The attempts to destroy murder extend to the level of the individual characters' actions. The narrator says that in order to write the book,

> I had to become a person I was not; indeed to become a per-
> son it would kill me to be. (p.145)

We hear Jetter say,

> How will my killing someone change all that killing — that's
> what you don't see. Well, it does change it — it blots it out
> for me . . .
> . . . the only escape from war is to become a soldier, to lose
> all touch with your own identity, to become part of one
> huge, quivering mass of fear and horror. . . . (p.9)

The trip is described at one point as a "journey to death" (p.191), and never is the atmosphere of murder allowed to escape our consciousness. Albion writes,

> There is a new plague. There is a plague from which there is
> no escape for anyone. *The great grey plague* — the plague
> of universal madness.
> My journal is its record. I have traced its origins, defined its
> boundaries, shown its course. (p.305)

This madness is the "cancerous fear of our own species" (p.3) which results in war, and defines Albion's task:

> You see, and this is not meant to startle you, I am at my
> work of murder now. A soldier kills after the fashion of

> soldiers; a writer must kill with what he says. . . . How sim-
> ple to kill a man's body! I choose to kill his soul . . . the fact
> that I wish to put a purer soul in its place does not alter the
> fact of murder. (p.40)

Albion on one level is certainly a murderer; we are not permitted to forget, however, that,

> When men wage war they are not moved to destroy one
> another; their struggle is against *what they themselves
> are.* . . .(p.192)

This state is seen to be embodied in, and perpetuated by, governmental systems. The entry for July 30 includes the statement

> Because of property every good impulse has been defiled
> and lost. (p.203)

War in the *Journal* is a result of the action of socialization on the
human spirit. In an essentially beneficent world, humanity has
been induced to create terror and destruction by the demands of
herd security. In speaking of history, Albion says,

> I refuse to hear how some besotted madman set whole
> nations at each others throats . . . I won't listen to a word of
> it!
> A leaf falls to the ground.
> The eye of a rabbit has seen it.
> Make me such a design. (p.33)

The political nature of this is made clear:

> It has been said that property is theft: I say that property is
> murder. The hands of dying children reach up through your
> bread. You beat me with your stick. You made the war.
> Even now you take the side of murder; no one must have
> your money. Your dollars become rifles. You will protect
> with the last drop of someone else's blood what was never
> yours. You walk over my face. I am the poor. I am the
> one in whose house you live. It is my food you
> eat. (pp.25-26)

The war is an extension of both capitalist and fascist governmental systems; both are fed by, and flourish in it. Two places
the travellers visit are indicative of this belief, reflective

allegorically of capitalism and fascism respectively. On June 27, they arrive in a strange village:

> Something unreal about the information furnished us concerning this place. It seems — though this is hard to believe — that the inhabitants here *do not have enough food.* The barns and sheds groan with it; money spills out of the banks in a flood the color of snake skin. Everyone is working like mad — his fingers peeled to the bone. But they don't have enough to eat. Yet this is truly the odd part: The few who are sitting about at ease are as well fed as shoats. Amazing! *Only the loafers are taken care of: The bread-makers have no bread.* (p.53)

On inquiry, the inhabitants are found to know the situation but to be in such great fear that they will hardly acknowledge it, much less act upon it.

Another important and entertaining incident in the novel concerns the party's visit to Topenville, a village "impossible of approach from the world." (p.82) The entire population lives in baskets "suspended from captive balloons." Topenville's economy is based on the fact that the citizenry continually shoots down one another's balloons. No one is unemployed because "there are always balloons and planes to be built, and damaged ones in need of repairs and new parts." In this consummate war economy, the greatest dread is life.

> The real truth is that these people are dead; what they fear is life. When they 'die,' they are transported to Hannibal, Missouri, where they must remain for all time. Their chief sage has said: "Life must come to all men; much as we may struggle against it. (p.136)

And the Topenvillians ask:

> Death is so sweet in Topenville — God! why must we live in Missouri? (p.136)

In the *Journal,* wonder and the beauty of life are brought into direct opposition to the idea of property, and all political systems are condemned for honoring the latter. Albion states,

> Your backs are bent under the junk of property, which you came by because of your fear. You were afraid to possess

LITTLE CHIEF
SON-OF-A-GUN-
DON'T-GIVE-A-SHOOT

the last
surviving
member of
the
Blackfeet
Tribe

bl ue

—Boston-branch

your soul, so you went by the wayside and acquired property. (p.25)

The means for sustaining these systems of acquired property is
war, a war which further enriches those systems and causes more
war, and which impoverishes the heart, and destroys life. Beyond
that, war becomes a necessity in any non-egalitarian society,
because it focuses the idea of "enemy" outside the perameters of
that particular society, thus draining energy and motivation from
internal criticism and rebellion. Albion intones,

> Wars are conducted that the people may lose sight of their
> own need to wage war. (p.205)

Patchen's purpose is just that, to "wage war," and to bring
war into sharp relief as an immediate personal experience. By
making it clear against whom our war should be waged, the murders in the book become murderings of death itself, and of the
current social reality which propagates war, thus freeing us from
the war. He writes,

> The only thing that should be surpressed is supression;
> should be killed is killing; should be restrained denied re-
> tarded is restraint denial etc., etc.[22]

Thus Albion's revolution, and his belief in future
revolutions, dictate that they be "concerned with altering the
minds of man, with vomiting out all that is insane for his animal."
(p.299) The intent is just that, the destruction of war, and the
assertion of faith and animistic beauty.

In a book of murder, the true subject then is love, a love
both social and pantheistic. Albion discusses the motivation for
his journey:

> It was essential that we bring our message to the people who
> had lost hope in the world. It was our duty to go into the
> villages and cities — Our message was this: we live, we love
> you. Our religion was life. Flowers, brooks, trees . . . Now
> we are held here and the world will perish because no one is
> saying we love you, we believe in you. (p.17)

We approach the core of the tale, and indeed of Patchen's
sense of his poetic mission: against a background of death and

economic slavery, the unshakeable assertion of life. The mission is reiterated in Albion's entry for June 25:

> It must be clear to you now, what I am trying to do. With what sense of shock you must have realized that it is not we who are fleeing from the world: with what joy you exclaimed, "No, Albion and his friends are not running away — they are speeding to us; we were in headlong flight, and they have overtaken us — they have stopped the runaway world, and it is awaiting their further orders. Now we are to hear of love and hope — we are to be instructed in salvation."
>
> Yes that I must do for you, that I must do for you. . . . (p.52)

The belief, the "matter," once again transcends form.

Of the surrealists, with whom Patchen is invariably compared, he writes:

> There is no such thing as superrealism. (The surrealists have managed to put on a pretty good vaudeville act for the middle-class: *but there isn't a religious man among them.*) (p.307)

The subject matter of the *Journal* can, in fact, be viewed as being religion, the attainment of cosmic unity through mystic illumination, illumination arising from nature. "Life itself is the only church" (p.265), Albion states. Religion in the *Journal* is centered in a Romantic or even Transcendental view of the earth, and like Blake, Patchen believes, "each thing that truly lives is sanctified."[23] As for heaven Albion says,

> My great idea is that man does not need God. God needs man for his existence. . . . I believe that man is God. (p.38)

To believe in oneself, to believe in one another, is to believe in, and to honor God. Albion believes, "all that is dangerous lives in us," and conversely, all that is holy lives in us as well. It is a matter of recognizing the grace and beauty inherent in the world, and rejecting social order. In a conversation between Albion and Joseph Gambetta, Albion responds to a question:

> "I am telling the truth. Man has been corrupted by his symbols. Language has killed his animal."

"And you are resurrecting it?"

"No. It has never had an opportunity to live."

"What will you do about it?"

"I shall continue to ask How."

"How to what?"

"To the strange, unborn thing which is in all men."

"You'll be easy picking for the scoffers."

"I have no interest in that. I see men engaged in activities that would shame a grub under a rock. Their codes and ambitions leave me sick with disgust."

"You'd like to try your hand at being God."

"I'd like to try my hand at *being*." (p.15)

What is demanded is the courage to remain alive, and to love in a world of horror and death. The means by which we reach life is through faith in creation and retention of a sense of wonder. Albion promises,

> I will not forget you: we will follow the fleet, green deer into the thunderhead together. I can't sleep tonight. I walk into the field and throwing the windows up watch God undressing for bed. A woman is singing somewhere in His house. (p.36)

As in Patchen's later *Memoirs of a Shy Pornographer,* where Priscilla sees the angels and the green deer through faith and a trust in the transforming power of love, so we are guided here.

The movement of the entire book is clearly away from intellectual derivation and its manifestation in literature, and toward the natural "chaos" of the soul. Patchen's systematic disruption of literary formulas, and the number of simultaneous narratives, makes it impossible to engage in a linear analysis and forces us to consider the story "by field'" as it was constructed, and to suspend our disbelief in the events contained in those fields of action. Jackeen, surprised that Albion believes an unlikely explanation she has given him for her pregnancy, asks,

> "How can such a thing happen?"

and he responds,

> "It can't. That's why I know you're telling the truth." (p.166)

Logical impossibility is far less significant than a failure in the soul. Albion elaborates on his faith:

> "For my religion I assume the bold style of a naked man.
> Who can think of nature without ecstasy? Solomon was wise
> because he liked wisdom. I like faith more." (p.197)

The only means by which we can arrive at truth is to discard intellectual traditionalism, to transfer our faith from the purely human accoutrements of industrial society, the breeder of war, to the "animal" organic systems of the universe. As we presently live, "we serve no purpose in nature" (p.148), and though our actions are guided by, and our reality defined by, our place in the social system, in truth, "only our organs are sane" (p.96). In the *Journal*, Patchen has created a new world, with its own particular order and causation, and it is a world which works by the laws of nature rather than of man. Patchen wrote, in *They Keep Riding Down All the Time*,

> Sometimes I think that every man's life has a meaning in a
> greater life which is being lived by a single creature whose
> nerves and cells and tissues we are. Just as there is no star,
> but stars; no tree, but trees; no brook or hill or sea which
> exists alone from all others of its kind; no road, but roads
> whose direction is everywhere; just as there is no pain or joy
> or fear which has not been felt by all of us; so must there
> forever be no man, but men whose lives cross and recross in a
> majestic pattern, unknowing, unstained, and beautiful,
> therefore, beyond comprehension. We are, to put it another
> way, cells in the brain of God.[24]

This Romantic concept of a unifying bond connecting all things is perhaps the single most important factor for interpretive study of the book, and will be the final matter considered.

A sense of unity with all creation permeates *The Journal of Albion Moonlight*. It is stated at times as a common humanity ("I'm as full of people as a city," p.102) and elsewhere as a sequence of being. In his journal, Albion writes,

> The child picks a flower: our bodies lie in her hand. A deer
> bends to drink at a mountain stream; our blood enters his
> throat. (p.78)

Such a vision is significant in two important respects, both central to the book. First, it is the feeling of common essence which Patchen presents that is the main factor opposing the war and murder in general. The desire to propagate war, in Patchen's view, arises out of artificial differences between people, created by governments for the purpose of maintaining themselves in power. In a society where murder is "our most sacred institution" (p.160), the most radical sentiment possible is that of community (or commuality). All existing governmental systems, universally discarded in the course of the book, fail equally to respond to the basic problem, that of social differentiation leading to class, nationalism, and thereby, to war. In the panhuman character of Albion Moonlight, Patchen addresses just this problem. When Albion murders, he is murdering another Albion. When he fears murder, it is something within himself which he fears. The characters Albion creates are likewise himself. He writes,

> Each day I begin a new life. An endless procession of men runs through me. (p.219)

And in the same entry,

> There can be only one thing in the world. Each is *its own part* of all. (p.226)

In these two quotes also lies the other aspect which is vitally important to the story, and which is reflected in its form—continuity. If one is to disregard both the technological and the formal Christian views of growth and eternity, then for the sake at least of spiritual solace, another concept must be substituted. For Patchen, the concept is that of universal mind, a state of sheer pantheistic existence, which must be recognized as a state rather than a path.

The concept prevades the action of the book, and is finally the key to understanding its structure and its content. In terms of plan we are told near the end of the book:

> I ventured forth early this summer with a definite project in my mind: It was my intention to set down the story of what happened to myself and to a little group of friends — and I soon discovered that what was happening to us was happening to everyone. . . .

> . . . It was too late to write a book, it was my duty to write
> all books. I could not write about a few people; it was my
> duty to write about everyone. (p.305)

Within this all-inclusive framework, the characters are themselves combined. Albion says, "I am the world. I know of no other
world but the one which is in me." (p.298) The identification is
made even more manifest in the proceeding action.

It is said that Roivas can be known by a missing finger;
later Albion is found "fondling the stump where his finger had
been." Jackeen is at once the daughter of Albion, Roivas, and
Joseph Gambetta. Near the beginning of the book Albion hands
Billy Delian a square of cheese which the latter stuffs into his
pocket. A hundred pages later, in a different subdivision Christ
hands Moonlight a square of cheese which Albion disposes of in an
identical manner. Similar actions interconnect all the book's
characters.

In terms of space, a similar union takes place. The
pilgrims at one point leave a forest inn, travel for days, and arrive
at an inn tended by the same inkeeper. The movement around
the country is physically impossible, and in the different
narratives and novels the various characters are in different places
on identical dates. All places are thus made equivalent. In addition Albion states,

> I believe that what we have in our heads now is only one of
> millions of possible *seeings*. . . . (p.298)

which renders even the senses irrelevant to the establishment of a
single conception of the world.

The unity of time is equally significant. The narrator announces,

> I propose to make the future and the present and the past
> happen all at once. (p.146)

As in Blake, there is no 'Berashith', no beginning, no end. Time is
only "an illusion of our senses,"[25] a concept borne out by the close
of the book.

Albion is walking down a road, and finally sees the house
of Roivas:

> Don't you understand? I have arisen not from the dead but
> from the *living*. It is my own face I see in the blazing win-

dows of all the houses on earth.

There is no darkness anywhere. There are only sick little men who have turned away from the light.

God is seeing.

My eyes are watching you.

But I must tell you that what I have said is not true.

This is all a damn lie. The real truth is . . .

What the hell do I care! Go bury your head in a pile of old bones. Get out of my way!

I am going to . . . I am . . . *What am I going to do?*

There is no way to end this book.

No way to begin   (p.313)

And so the book does or does not end, depending on one's definition. The important thing to consider is that we are not led to a pre-emptive conclusion; our role as participant (as opposed to reader) is carried through to the very place where the book stops. This is both natural and necessary when we realize that the continuity (and unity) of the narrative is organic (psychologically internal) rather than literary.

In the *Journal,* Patchen does not sketch a line along which we are to follow; instead he describes a circle within which the book exists. Because of this, it is not necessary to take the conclusion of the book as the "end." Several encounters between Albion and a 'Savior' occur, and each is another point within the circle. When he reaches an island in one of the book's novels, Albion drops down, then:

For the last time I open my eyes . . . Keddel is there above me . . . filling all the heavens . . .

What do you see?

An EYE . . .

It is trying to tell me something . . .

Yes!

Roivas!

The Book of the Living slips from my fingers.

Savior!

(p.209)

The fulfillment does come, or it does not, depending on the individual and one's relationship to the events of the journal. As in

Jerusalem, where Albion's last words are "Hope is banish'd from me,"[26] the path toward salvation is variable and inconstant. It is through love, however, and faith in both man and nature, that it becomes finally possible. He says,

> I wish you no harm; please God that the way be not too hard
> for you.   (p.124)

The attitude is a benevolent one, despite the cynicism of the closing lines of the book. The next year, he writes a radio play, "The City Wears A Slouch Hat," which in many ways follows the same pattern as *The Journal of Albion Moonlight;* it appeared but briefly in the public domain, for one airing, and then vanished from view. It closed as follows:

> I am coming into your house with my hand outstretched. I
> am your friend. Do not be afraid of me.[27]

So, here, finally, is the message of Kenneth Patchen. It is a simple one: "We believe in you. There is no danger. It is not getting dark." A man's hand reaches out through the cold of a "human winter" and the darkness of his own pain to offer hope to a beleaguered world.

Supplement

1-57:   The main journal (1). Actually all the various divisions are part of one entry or another in the main journal

57:   The first novel (1) begins — chapters in arabic numbers.

59-156:   The novel (1) and journal (1) are interwoven.

Novel (1): 57-9, 60-1, 64-81, 96-124, 140-156.
Journal (1): 59-60, 61-4, 81-96, 124-140.

156:   The second novel (2) begins in chapter 14 of novel (1) — chapters in roman numerals.

160-167:   The second journal (2). Duplicate entries at this point, organically as part of novel (2), chapter VI.

163-164:   The first story (1), in dialect, also part of novel (2), journal (2) entry for June 15.

168:   Novel (2) ends with "to be continued," novel (1) resumes.

169:   Novel (1) ends with "THE END" but resumes immediately.

171:   Journal (1) resumes at July 20, and continues.

177:   The first bold-face marginal comment: DOST THOU/ IMAGINE YOU/ CAN WIN/ THROUGH/ TO GOD, beside journal (1) entry for July 27. Other marginal comments appear on pages 179, 189, 191, 192, 193, 204, 218, 220, 221, 236, 237, 238, 240, 241, 243, 249, 253, 254, 255, and 256.

179-183:   Story (2), written in the margin beside the continuation of Journal (1) entry for July 28.

187:   Novel (1) resumes with chapter 15.

193:   Journal (1) resumes at July 30.

196-200:   Story (3) in margin beside Journal (1).

207-209:   Novel (1), chapters 16 and 17.

216-257:   As part of the journal (1) entry for August 10, Albion includes "The Notes," a varied body of material which "could not be handled adequately in the journal." It includes a great many sections: "the notes" themselves, interspersed throughout, giving suggestions for inclusions in the book or the novel, short descriptions, observations, brief journeys and events along the route, etc.; a long Whitmanesque poem (227-232, 234-244, 246-256); four separate margin stories (227-232, two on 232-234, 253-256); an article on military attack (235-240); six brief fragments on 233; two more on 234, a concrete poem (245); and three separate endings on page 257.

257:   The main body of the journal (1) continues, with the entry for August 11. At the end of the page, Albion writes: "You may just as well consider the book begun and ended right here. It is time I started my little show. Hold on to your hat, you sonofabitch."

268:    In the entry for August 19 (which begins on page 266): "I have reached a place where I feel I can begin this book." Six lines K later: "END OF THE JOURNAL"; "THE NOTES" resume.

281:    Part two of chapter 14 of novel (1) begins.

282-283:   Table of contents of *The Enchanted Assassin* (which is not in the book) appears as part of novel (1), chapter 14, part two.

290-304:   Table of contents of *The Island* (which also is not in the book) appears, as part of novel (1).

302:    Continuation of chapter 13 of novel (1), examination of drawings.

304-306:   "The Little Journal of Albion Moonlight," interspersed with parts of the table of contents of The Island. Duplicate entries for May 2 and 3, the first two days of journal (1). Pages 268-306 are contained within the journal (1) entry for August 19.

306-313:   Main journal (1) resumes with August 23, ending August 27. We were told earlier (p.130): "We shall enter Galen on August 27."[28]

Notes

[1]"The Journal of Albion Moonlight." An advance flier for *The Journal of Albion Moonlight*. No publication data.

[2]Letter to Richard G. Morgan, March 14, 1975.

[3]Kenneth Rexroth, "Kenneth Patchen, Naturalist of the Public Nightmare," in *Bird in the Bush* (New York: New Directions, 1959), p. 97.

[4]James Dickey, "In the Presence of Anthologies, III," *Sewanee Review* (Spring 1958), 303.

[5]All page references in the text are from Kenneth Patchen, *The Journal of Albion Moonlight* (New York: New Directions, 1961).

[6]Henry Miller, Review of *The Journal of Albion Moonlight*," *Experimental Review*, no. 2 (November 1940), 76.

[7]In fact, a chapter called "Albion Moonlight survives a night in Galen" occurs in the middle of the book.

[8]Hugh McGovern, "Kenneth Patchen's Prose Works," *New Mexico Quarterly*, XXI (Summer 1951), 74.

[9]See S. Foster Damon, *A Blake Dictionary* (Providence, R. I.: Brown University, 1965), p. 9.

[10]Kenneth Patchen, "Introduction," in *Job: Invented and Engraved by William Blake* (New York: United Book Guild, 1946), p.[1].

[11]S. Foster Damon, *William Blake, His Philosophy and Symbols* (Boston: Houghton Miffin Co., 1924), p. 185.

[12]Damon, *A Blake Dictionary*, loc. cit.

[13]Letter to Richard G. Morgan, February 28, 1976.

[14]See pp. 305-6. There is also the implication that the author is writing in a room in Galen, while being hunted in the town outside (p. 206).

[15]Ray Nelson, "The Moral Prose of Kenneth Patchen," *Steppenwolf*, III (Summer 1969), 59.

[16]McGovern, 184.

[17]Patchen, *Job*, p.[2].

[18]Wendell Johnston, Professor of Speech Pathology at the University of Iowa, introduced the concept in 1963. To my knowledge, nothing concerning it was ever published.

[19]Letter to Richard G. Morgan, Sept. 4, 1975.

[20]Miller, *Experimental Review* 76.

[21]Kenneth Patchen, *An Astonished Eye Looks Out of the Air* (Waldport, Oregon: The United Press, 1946), unpaged.

[22]*Job*, loc. cit.

[23]Cf. Damon, *William Blake*, p. 151. "Everything that *lives* is holy."

[24]Kenneth Patchen, *They Keep Riding Down All the Time* (New York: Padell, 1947), p. 17.

[25]Damon, *William Blake*, p. 140.

[26]Damon, *A Blake Dictionary*, p. 12.

[27]Kenneth Patchen, "The City Wears a Slouch Hat," written for the Columbia Radio Workshop, and produced May 31, 1942.

[28]A rudimentary form of this outline appeared in Ray Nelson, "An American Mysticism, the example of Kenneth Patchen," an unpublished dissertation (1972).

Bibliography

Damon, S. Foster. *A Blake Dictionary.* Providence, R.I.; Brown University, 1965.

Damon S. Foster. *William Blake, His Philosophy and Symbols.* Boston and New York: Houghton Mifflin Co., 1924.

Dickey, James. "In the Presence of Anthologies." *Sewanee Review* (Spring 1958), 300-304.

Glicksberg, Charles I. "The World of Kenneth Patchen." *Arizona Quarterly*, VII (Autumn 1951), 263-275.

McGovern, Hugh. "Kenneth Patchen's Prose Works." *New Mexico Quarterly*, XXI (Summer 1951), 181-197.

Miller, Henry. *Patchen, Man of Anger and Light.* New York: Max Padell, 1946.

Miller, Henry. "Review of The Journal of Albion Moonlight." *Experimental Review*, no. 2 (November 1940), 74-76.

Nelson, Ray. "The Moral Prose of Kenneth Patchen." *Steppenwolf,* III (Summer 1969), 59–87.

Patchen, Kenneth. *An Astonished Eye Looks Out of the Air.* Waldport, Oregon: The Untide Press, 1945.

Patchen, Kenneth. "The City Wears a Slouch Hat." (1942). Unpublished Radio Play. Special Collections, Northwestern Univ.

Patchen, Kenneth. *In Quest of Candlelighters.* New York: New Directions, 1972.

Patchen, Kenneth. *Job.* New York; United Book Guild, 1946.

Patchen, Kenneth. *The Journal of Albion Moonlight.* New York: New Directions, 1961.

Rexroth, Kenneth. "Kenneth Patchen, Naturalist of the Public Nightmare." in *Bird in the Bush.* New York: New Directions, 1959, pp. 94–105.

See, Carolyn, "The Jazz Musician as Patchen's Hero." *Arizona Quarterly,* XVII: 2 (Summer 1961), 134–146.

Taylor, Frajam. "Puck in the Gardens of the Sun." *Poetry,* LXX (August 1947), 269–274.

Wilder, A.N. "Revolutionary and Proletarian Poetry: Kenneth Patchen," in *Spiritual Aspects of the New Poetry.* New York: Harper and Brothers, 1940, pp. 178–195.

Williams, Jonathan. "Out of Sight, Out of Conscience." *Contact,* II: 7 (February 1961), 149–155.

Charles I. Glicksberg

The World of Kenneth Patchen

Kenneth Patchen is a twentieth-century Shelley who no longer beats his angelic wings ineffectually in the intense inane. Unlike Shelley, however, Patchen, a sensitive child of his age, experienced a profound change in his radical political outlook, and this has greatly affected the kind of poetry and prose he has written since then. For Patchen, to believe is to act. Faith is a passion suffusing his whole being, controlling the furious energy of creation, coloring his *Weltanschauung*. In a sense, *Before the Brave* and *First Will and Testament* constituted the most forthright, the most inspired "proletarian" poetry of our time. But his spirit was too independent, too innately creative and prophetic, to remain long within the Marxist orbit. It is probable that the outbreak of the Second World War hastened his precipitate retreat to the fastness of the self.

Before the Brave sounded a call to revolutionary battle. In the very first poem, the theme is defiantly announced: the lights illuminating the statues of our ancestral heroes should be turned out; let us pray for the coming of men, though without forgetting what our forebears have accomplished.

> Do not destroy. They built a world we could not use;
> They planned a course that ended in disaster.
> Their time is up. The curtain's down. We take power.

That is the leitmotif: The young must take courage into their own hands and act boldly if they wish to set this disjointed world right. Though man cannot live to see the fruition of his labor, he has his duty to the earth and to the unborn generations—a task that he is urged to fulfill by the imperative of conscience.

The conflict is not only inevitable but imminent. To prepare ourselves for this catastrophic but redemptive event, we must rid ourselves of the dangerous nonsense of religion, the rank folly of patriotism. Patchen prays that the revolutionary fighters will not be deceived by words and creeds. Power, he declares ringingly, "is in hate." Of the exploited and the rejected of earth he asks: What are you waiting for? What fate can possibly be worse than the one you endure so tamely now? This early class conscious poetry of Patchen gains tremendous power by its concentration of aim. But with the publication of *First Will and Testament* in 1939, a significant change came over Patchen's work. This volume is largely an effort at self-understanding. Like Whitman's "I" in "I celebrate myself," Patchen's lyric ego is but a symbol of the universal, a projection of the self that is common to all mankind. Patchen now wants to reveal what goes on within the soul of man: the fear, the pain, the conflict, the lacerating anguish. Man must fight hard if he is to conquer himself. There is no other war. This perception of all that man has to suffer, the cosmic cruelty of things, lends a touch of compassion to his savage tirades of condemnation, even when he beholds men preparing for war and cries out:

> I know a word like God and I write
> Poems. I put one thing beside another
> Thing and sometimes
> I want to kick the whole damn
> Gang in the teeth with it…

Even in *First Will and Testament,* Kenneth Patchen had already taken a new turn, startling us by his audacious disdain of traditional methods of poetic composition. His spiritual kinship with the Surrealists is revealed in his ability to circumvent the guard of censorship and allow tabooed reports to trickle past the frontiers of censorship. He is drawn between two poles of creative desire: one leads him toward the creation of poetry that is hard, sensuous, direct, of the earth, earthy; the other prompts him to experiment with "metaphysical," dissociated, spiritualized images and lines distilled from the alembic of the unconscious, nebulous as mist, puzzling and "aberrational" as a Surrealist painting by Salvador Dali. More and more, Patchen is setting himself in opposition to the world of reality by seeking to escape from it. He has become, as in *The Teeth of the Lion,* an intrepid explorer of the underworld of the unconscious. Obsession with the cruelty and

evil of contemporary life is in this volume masked beneath a surface of Surrealist imagery, but now and again the conscious hurt
leaps forth in a piercing cry of horror. It is the madness and
homicidal hatred of men which Patchen cannot bear, and this
serves to explain "the neurosis of escape," "the Surrealist
paranoia," from which he seems to suffer. He has reached the
stage where his love of life, his worship of its overwhelming
beauty, its infinite variety and profusion of forms, leaves him
almost inarticulate, grasping for words that will shadow forth,
however dimly, the mystery of this radiant super-reality, but
unlike the professional Surrealists he is never irresponsible. His
violent dissociations of ideas and "free" imagery are controlled by
a prophetic ideal, a fundamental personal integrity. Where Freud
found the death-wish implanted in human beings, the poet
discovers it in the civilization of his time. *The Dark Kingdom,* for
example, is the poetic, imaginative expression of Freud's essay,
"Thoughts on War and Death," published during the height of
the First World War. Patchen's poetry is an outpouring of horror
and an outburst of compassion. Man must make his peace with
death; the savior must be born anew.

    Panels for the Walls of Heaven, like *Cloth of the Tempest,*
is a concentrated cry of horror at the insanity of the world,
especially the insanity of hatred that leads to the mass slaughter of
war. Oh, if he were only God, Patchen would see to it that there
would be no hunger, no needless suffering, no anxiety neurosis
about the next war, but he realizes that all this is futile. In his
heart he knows it is too late. Love has been slain; death has entered the kingdom of life. Repeatedly in *Panels for the Walls of
Heaven,* Patchen breaks into the prophetic, ejaculatory strain, as
if his heart can no longer contain itself and leaps beyond the con-
fines of art. There must be a beauty, a greatness of life, greater
deeds than lying and murder. The world is in the power of mad-
men bent on its destruction and there is nothing left for the poet
to do but praise the grandeur and goodness of God. Life is the
supreme value; no man stands alone. We must acknowledge
God, that is life in all its fullness, and throw off the power of the
murderous maniacs who rule the world. "Art has no place for
lies." Unfortunately this work, like *Cloth of the Tempest,* is
marred by typographical vices, the use of diagrams and drawings,
surrealist tricks, inscrutable symbols, and glaring capitals, all in-

tended to announce that the poet can smell death all around him.
It tends to suggest the delirium of paranoia. The whole book is a
plea for the absolution and finality of death.

II

As if seeking a larger audience for his message, Patchen
finally turned to prose, but the fiction he has produced, five
volumes in all (with others waiting to be published), is as disor-
dered and frenziedly mystical as his later poetry. It is practically
impossible to suggest the substance and structure of a book like
The Journal of Albion Moonlight, which has no logical structure,
no determinate principle of continuity, no plot that can be traced
consecutively from beginning to denouement to conclusion. In its
deliberate incoherence and sensational discontinuity, it is more
original and disconcerting than either *Sleepers Awake* or *Memoirs
of a Shy Pornographer.* It is Surrealism run amok. It is the cry of a
tortured soul in hell, a choral chant heard in bedlam, the
hallucinations and transcribed ravings of a madman. The boun-
dary line between fantasy and reality remains tenuous and elusive.
That is perhaps the principal intention of the book: to bring home
to us the insanity of our civilization. Mad with the lust to kill, we
invent the institution of war, the fine art of mass murder, and
clothe it in high-sounding, sacred names. It is the dream of the artist that is the reality: the dream of peace, the ideal of living to the
top of one's bent, fulfilling all his higher potentialities, his
capacity for love and productive work. *The Journal of Albion
Moonlight* is full of shooting, killing, murder, the horrible sights
and sounds of war, all meant to symbolize the sadistic fury of our
age, its terrible, self-destructive mania, against which the poet
protests with all his might.

All sorts of crazy things happen in *The Journal of Albion
Moonlight.* Characteristic of Patchen's method is his use of planned incongruity, the conjunction of the sacred and the profane,
the sublime and the trivial, the infinite and the microscopic. As
Patchen phrases it, he is trying to achieve "that sense of propor-
tion which comes from a planned deformity." Plop, in the middle
of things, he will introduce some violent imagery: a palpitating
biscuit rubbing some elderberry jelly into its womb. And all this is
intended to heighten the effect of the horror — the wholesale death

and destruction, the madness of our war-minded world, the impossibility of leading a sane, decent life on earth. Everything is included in this strange novel: puns, quotations from Shakespeare, Keats, Bacon, epigrams, jokes, reflections on the art of the novel and the writing of poetry, the problem of form. Patchen himself tells us:

> You will be told that what I write is confused, without order — and I tell you that my book is not concerned with the problems of art, but with the problems of this world, with the problems of life itself — yes, *of life itself.*

If anyone should accuse him of grotesque exaggeration, his reply is that he is describing the world of today as he found it. He does not have to invent or do research.

> What have I to do with the cult of hallucination? Derangement is for the too-sane — everything under heaven cries to be *arranged.* I demand order and precision in what I do. The supreme cultivation of chaos has already been done. *That is what I am talking against.*

The one function of the modern State — what is it but murder? "I ask for an unconditional overthrow of the world you will risk your life for tomorrow." His one sustaining measure of sanity is that he is still convulsed with rage and horror.

In *The Journal of Albion Moonlight,* Patchen is not interested in writing a novel about private people, their loves and hates, triumphs and tribulations, success and failure, but about the fate of man, the possibility of redeeming the world. He would induce in us a profound feeling of love for all created beings, without the wish to exploit or kill our neighbor. The world will perish, he fears, because "no one is saying, we love you, we believe in you." To achieve his end, he will strip himself naked, speaking to us not with words of studied wisdom but with the wisdom that is deep and instinctive. There can be no doubt that *The Journal of Albion Moonlight,* first published in 1941, represents the recorded agony of one wandering in a hell whose scenes and towns clearly suggest the United States of the twentieth century.

If Patchen has learned from any of his literary predecessors, it is chiefly from Joyce (in his playing with words and puns, his parodies of conventional plots and the grandiloquent style), from Kafka (in the use of enigmatic symbols and a tortured, mystically ambiguous "plot"), and most of all from Freud, though he uses these influences with remarkable freedom and independence. But the truth is that all these freakish, Alice-in-Wonderland marvels are put in for only one purpose: to reveal "the message" of the author in this hour of deadly crisis. The doom of the world is about to befall us, and he wants to warn us, to get the accursed horror out of his system, and to affirm the spirit of love. The questions Patchen asks, the problems he wrestles with in the night, are the eternal ones: Who are we? Why do we live? What do we make of death? How can we bear it that war is going on in the world? We are all implicated in the collective guilt. According to Patchen's naturalistic humanism, man makes his own decisions, confronts his destiny, bears his own burdens. Men will have to learn a new language, new symbols, new objects of worship, new principles of freedom and faith. Believing that the people can achieve their own salvation, he bids them strike for their own emancipation. In the manner of Whitman he declares: "I demand that the body of no one be degraded." Patchen has stepped outside the laws and institutions devised by man. He has reached the unknown, the absolute, the last shore, the end of night. Murder is murder, however it is spelled. There are no excuses, no justifications. Patchen cries: "We must learn to live *for the first time.*" That is his categorical imperative: Man as God must learn to worship himself and the murder in his heart must be torn out by the roots.

Thus Patchen builds up his non-conformist, mystical philosophy of anarchism: his repudiation of material success, his denunciation of practical wisdom, his tempestuous resistance to established values. "It is *natural to go mad.*" The artist as leader must give meaning to this universal carnival of death. The stink of death is in our nostrils. Even our art is decadent. The individual needs no defence; it is the State that is on trial. In the realm of the spirit, there are no nationalities, no races, no classes, only human beings. At present we are incapable of the liberation that love brings. Death is our fate. Since this is so, he cannot remain silent. With the fiery earnestness of the Hebraic prophets, he calls out to us to throw off the body of this death, to be fully alive, if we wish to survive at all on this planet.

In *Sleepers Awake,* another Surrealist nightmare, what Patchen, a poet with a bleeding conscience and a messianic yearning to save mankind, is trying to do is to warn us of the terrible danger that is before us, the destructiveness that is all about us and in the heart of man. He would wake us out of the lethargy of sleep. What horrifies Patchen most violently is the fact of war, the fact that men will kill, that they will imprison those who take seriously the Christian injunction not to kill. With an obsessed imagination he describes the phantasmagoria of war; then he breaks into a prophetic chant, using capitals and large print to make his message emphatically plain. Patchen is stressing modern man's need for belief. Man, deprived of his vital powers, has lost the road to salvation. Positively Patchen's creed is summed up in the statement that he believes in life and in human beings. He is the inveterate enemy of any force which deprives any one of life.

Not that Patchen has any ordered system to offer. He has no magic panaceas, no sure-fire formulas. What he hopes to do is to widen the boundaries of consciousness, sharpen our senses, rouse us out of sleep. This accounts for the interpolation of squares with letters either meaningful or meaningless, the broken skein of fantastic and melodramatic incidents, the counterpointing of the sacred and the profane, the holy and the vulgar, the mystical and the erotic. The circus of freaks Patchen trots out, the various impersonations of the hero of the tale, the series of abductions, seductions, rapes, druggings, killings, all are forgotten as the author suddenly whispers that death is still with us, always present. One hears the thunder of the guns against a sky filled with beautiful stars. The earth can be made a place of wonder and joy. Love must transcend hate. To do so, however,

> It would be necessary to return to the human being his individual faith in himself, and in his life on earth. There only lay the road of brotherhood which the prophets had schooled the stars in. It would be necessary to find importance in the least act of the least of men.

Books, Patchen declares, must provide a channel of communion with the unknown, provide real food for the spirit, unfold the mystery of being fully alive. Man must be made to understand "that all the gates are still open, that all the Wild and Beautiful are beckoning to him *now.* "

We have forgotten how wonderful a thing it is to be a human being. What binds man together today is the bond of hatred. The world is dying, but before it perishes Patchen delivers his Sermon on the Mount:

> I tell you that what has to be changed is the whole conception of human life—that men of every race on this earth may have the same opportunity to live beautifully—to live in purity without fear or hunger or hatred—as brothers, not as brutes tearing through these hideous swamps of ignorance and war. Men speak of a belief in God. I am beginning to understand what every Christ—and their skins have been every color—what every Christ has taught:

> That love of God is love of mankind. That no one can profess to love God while he hates the least of his fellows. Jesus, if He were on earth now, would fight to free men from oppression and evil and war, and you who have made a pious mockery of His every commandment—you would kill Him.

Patchen, essentially a "religious" prophet, looks forward to the day when all men will be brothers. This hunger for a better life cannot be stopped. It is stronger than the forces that instigate war.

Sleepers Awake mirrors the welter of modernity, all the evil and destructive passions of our age. The ultimate madness is the phenomenon of war. How could anyone believe in anything and still kill a man? If this is a lie, he declares, then everything is a lie, and the universe we live in is stripped of all meaning. "Where is not faith; there is death." And the darkness will remain over us until the lights of love finally go on. The artist, Patchen feels, is "always the spokesman of God," the pioneer who strives toward the light, the liberator of mankind. Give humanity a chance, Patchen cries. The supreme question is what we are going to do with our life. The main thing is to know what we are living for. All that leads to life is good; all that makes for death is evil. If the murderers hate the artist, it is for a good reason, for no art can come out of evil.

> I say it—art is giving life—art is talking to God
> if the artist loses now this world is doomed
> and I think the human imagination is being murdered

The Memoirs of a Shy Pornographer, Patchen's most popular work for reasons that are not difficult to fathom, follows the same general pattern: it is Surrealism with a difference, mad as any dream, disheveled, lecherous, absurd, fantastic, though always under conscious control. The tissue of amazing incidents is given some degree of credibility by the use of sober, realistic details and a deliberately colloquial style. This work holds up a candid mirror to our age and its culture: the traffic in pornography, the ravening schemes of success and personal omnipotence, the drunken orgies, the cruel murderous competition, the killing, the wars, the psychopathic people in the world, each with his private dreams and obsessions, his delusions of grandeur, his hidden fears and anxieties. It is not easy to suggest the madcap kind of irresponsible talk and delirious action to be found in this work. The action gets wilder, madder, more nonsensical and nightmarish. And in the midst of this riotous foolery we hear thunderous words of denunciation directed against those who betray the truth, the prostitution of art to the rage of chauvinism, the greed and hate which lead to perpetual wars. What Patchen is reiterating with all the force of conviction at his command is the truth that the enemy is war. Only through the pathways of love can we find our way out of this diabolical darkness. We must learn to love, not to hate; to believe in life, not death, and then no power on earth can defeat us.

Patchen is affirming his own faith. These works of fiction are his testament in prose. Man must throw off the lie, walk in the path of integrity for his soul's sake, honor the bright image of the God within, reach the heights of salvation by knowing his kinship with all created beings and by breaking down the obstacles that stand in the way of love. Then we are given a fearful picture of the legions of the lost and the damned speaking to the lost and the damned. No one knows what it means to live. And the scene reaches a scream of horrified protest in the words:

> Why should anyone kill?
> WHY SHOULD ANYONE KILL!

It is not enough to reply that the world was made that way. Who made the world that way? Why this terrible madness? Is it sane for man to murder himself? For Budd, the central character in the novel, God exists, God is everything — everything he can dream of or imagine or wish for. God stands challenging, accusing, inexorable, before every man, for God is everyman. In short, man is capable of reaching the highest, for he contains within himself undreamed-of potentialities, greater than any attributed to God. Perhaps what people consider life is really death. What kind of purpose can life have if death is the end for man? It may be that the dream gives us the truest knowledge of life, and that one must "die" in order to come to life. What counts supremely is not the doing but the being, the knowledge of whence we come and whither we are going. But people are afraid to believe in the miraculous, the marvelous, the reality of a green deer, whereas it is beliefs such as these that are the only hope of the world.

> No man who honors Caesar but dishonors God. No man who willingly snuffles and roots in the slimy rubble of this hatred and greed but shall be stained beyond the idiot dog which slobbers up his own filth. Let me tell you that it is not getting along in the world to eat when your neighbor is hungry; to add to your income when he has nothing; to build a new house when he is homeless. There is no bread but the bread which shall feed your least neighbor; there is no possession but the possession which you shall share with him; there is no dwelling but the dwelling whose doors shall be opened joyfully to him.
>
> Wars and the plague-sores left by wars shall not be ended until mankind turns from the murder *which is practiced by everyone.*

Thus *The Memoirs of a Shy Pornographer* is on one level a search for identity, for unification, for faith. Man must know the meaning of life and death. Each one must love his fellowman and prepare the way to God.

III

These are the prophetic revelations that burst out from the pages of these wilfully distorted "novels." This is the madness that has overcome us. Every kind of ingredient—fantastic incidents and incredible dreams—is thrown in to sustain our interest. But there is a fundamental pattern within this fictional chaos: the recurrence of the cry of protest against the mass murders going on in the world, the agonizing death of the young on battlefields, while no one seems to care in the least and even the victims acquiesce in their own doom. And as if to remind us that he is well aware of what our daily routine consists, Patchen dwells on the banal, the commonplace, the hideously familiar: the robbing, killing, drinking, plotting against others, waging war, till, seared by the image of our horrible irrationality, our eyes fail to distinguish between the normal and the abnormal.

From an aesthetic point of view, however, the final question concerning *The Journal of Albion Moonlight, Sleepers Awake,* and *The Memoirs of a Shy Pornographer* is this: what is the purpose and value of such a violently incoherent confession? Why did Patchen use the form of the novel, though deliberately disrupting its structure, if his aim was really to denounce the evils of our world and, through the healing mediation of art, put an end to the collective insanity of our time? His defence that he is simply telling the truth about life, is no defense at all, for the truth of art is not a matter of literal representation or photographic verisimilitude. It is not a transcription, nor even in Surrealist imagery, of all that is perceived, felt, thought, and experienced. Selection and order are inescapable. Obviously even in composing these works Patchen must have had some architectonic principle in mind. Why, then, does he labor so frantically to keep it concealed and disguised?

The chief critical objection to Patchen's experiments in this genre, astonishingly original and revealing as they are, is that they fail to achieve the desired effect. Patchen, it is true, is no cultist, no conforming Surrealist. If he dwells on the fantastic, it is because these imaginatively heightened elements of the irrational are the very warp and woof of contemporary civilization. He is in command of his material and his techniques; he presumably controls the flow of images and the series of fictional events he unfolds. Apparently he knows, even if the reader does not, what these extraordinary characters and their sensational, illogical actions are supposed to symbolize, though one often gets the impression that he is tired of the whole story-spinning device and perfectly delighted when he can at least discard the pretence of constructing a narrative and get down to the really important business of communicating directly his anxiety neurosis, his paranoiac horror, his religious vision of redemption for humanity. And these are, one must confess, the most rewarding sections to be found in these bewildering, cabalistic books.

But precisely because our civilization suffers from this psychotic confusion it is incumbent on the artist, whether he write a novel or poem, to impose some order on the contemporary chaos, precipitate a meaning, wrest harmony out of savage discord. Patchen frequently verges on the unintelligible. It is not the disease but the aroused creative consciousness that must be at the controls. Yet when Patchen speaks in his own voice, unleashing his hatred and confessing his creed, he is immensely worth reading. For at bottom, whether he writes verse or fiction, Patchen is a prophetic poet, the Shelley of our age. He is forever trying to reach us directly, to drop the make-believe that he is writing a story. If he writes about epidemic wars and is virtually obsessed with the theme of murder, it is because he is convinced there is nothing else worth writing about. In *The Journal of Albion Moonlight* he declares: "When you have understood this, you will be through with novels...I write this book *as an action.*" To the devil with literature!

If he bleeds for all the senseless murders committed on earth, he also believes that the minds of men will change, that our vision of things can and will be radically transformed. The revolution of the future will be concerned with curing men of their murderous insanity. A time will come when men will grow aware of the whole world and thus catch a glimpse of the murder and the madness that is in the consciousness of all of us. This explains the nature of his creative purpose, his religious motive. He is trying to make the light shine in the universal darkness. He would do without the protective and distorting garments of Art. If he does not reveal the whole truth, it is because he fears going mad. He is afraid to face all the implications of the tragedy that has over-taken the world. There is no real communion in America, the land of the spiritually homeless. Unlike Dostoyevski, whom he resembles closely in his underlying spirit of compassion, he wastes no pity on the poor and has no faith in the heaven that Christianity promises them for their patient endurance of misery on earth. The poor must be eradicated if a new society is to emerge. Let their minds as well as their bodies be filled with the best food. That is the urgent, emergency message Patchen at-tempts to communicate in a strange hybrid of art which disdains the uses of art.

Tom Ložar

Before the Brave: Portrait of Man as a Young Artist

> Tomorrow I expect to take a trip to the planet Mars and, if so,
> will immediately commence to organize the Mars canal workers
> into the I.W.W. and we will sing the good old songs so loud
> that the learned stargazers on earth will once and for all get
> positive proof that the planet Mars really is inhabited.
>
> —Joe Hill to Ben Williams.
> *Solidarity,* October 9, 1915.[1]

    Patchen's *Before the Brave* celebrates socialist themes: the
Soviets, Marx, THE TEMPLE IN RED SQUARE, THE RED
WOMAN.[2] But also in form and ambition it is a work of socialist
realism, or revolutionary romanticism. Of socialist realism
Malraux had written: ". . . if the will to realism is an effective
one for the U.S.S.R., it is for the reason that it is brought to bear
upon a romantic reality: civil war, wartime communism, the five
year plan, socialist construction, frontier guards, autonomous
republics, all this serves to create a tragic and picturesque reality
which confers upon realism all that is necessary to enable it to out-
strip itself."[3] America in the Thirties was not that photogenic. But
like the first poets of the October Revolution the young Patchen
was more interested in thousand year plans than in five year ones.
    The poets of a revolution are anarchists. In 1968, predic-
tably, Patchen ends up as the patron saint of an anarchist
magazine, wherein he calls Blake "a social realist."[4] In 1917
Mayakovsky said that "the revolution of substance—socialism-
anarchism—is not to be thought of apart from the revolution of
form, futurism."[5] Yesenin thought that the revolution would stop

time in an ideal Russia of the villages. Any poet who joins the revolution feels the pull of the simpler past and the perfect future. Sometimes in anarchist vision he can join the two. Trotsky had such poets figured out: "They do not grasp the revolution as a whole, and the communist ideal is foreign to them. They are more or less inclined to look hopefully at the peasant over the head of the worker. They are not the artists of the proletarian revolution but her artists' fellow travellers. As regards a fellow traveller, the question always comes up, how far will he go?"[6] The answer with Mayakovsky and with Patchen is: too far, too fast.

But this is predictable. Socialism outstrips itself to become anarchism. Socialist realism outstripping itself resembles science fiction or cosmic fantasy. The science-fiction artist, Lenin, in the midst of the Volga famine planning a fully-electrified self-governing U.S.S.R., says to the visiting Wells: "If mankind ever comes to other planets all our philosophical, moral and social assumptions will have to be re-examined."[7] In *Before the Brave* we can see the revolution become cosmic revolution, Revolution, and revolutionary romanticism become science fiction. The revolution in *Before the Brave* is Zamyatin's revolution. Its law "is not a social law, but an immeasurably greater one . . . a cosmic universal law — like the laws of the conservation of energy and of the dissipation of energy."[8] Its art Mayakovsky described:

> No one can know what immense suns will light our future. It may be that the artist will turn the grey dust of cities into multicoloured rainbows, that the never-ending thunderous music of volcanos turned into flutes will resound from the mountain ranges, that the ocean waves will be freed to play on the nets of chords stretching from Europe to America. One thing is clear to us, that we have opened the last page of the latest chapter in the history of art.[9]

Before the Brave is part of that chapter. Perhaps in 1935, with their revolution still just around the corner, only American poets could write the pure old socialist realism. Mayakovsky and Yesenin were dead of the revolution; socialist realism was dogma in the U.S.S.R.; and the huge Soviet projects were more often monument than factory. If the Patchen of *Before the Brave* is heir to the early socialist poets, his heir in America (if in imitation of these poets we may pass too quickly beyond the work at hand) is a poet like Richard Brautigan. In *The Pill versus the Springhill Mine Disaster,* in a poem which surely would have pleased Mayakovsky and Yesenin, "a cybernetic ecology" makes us "free of our labors" and we can

> return to our mammal
> brothers and sisters
> and all watched over
> by machines of loving grace.[10]

* * *

The last words of *Before the Brave* are the words of the title (BTB 131). This rounding out of the book imitates the infinite energies inside. It also signals that we are meant to read the book again and again. In a second reading we will know for certain what we might only have suspected at first, that the site of *Before the Brave* is not our earth. The careful reader will know that there is an earlier launch into a new world or at least into a new way of reading, for the first section of the book, INTRODUCTION, ends with a poem which, after praying "O give us words that shrug/Giant shoulders at the false display of poetry," also ends with the words "before the brave" (BTB 25). The first poem of the section immediately following these words is called THE MAGIC CAR (BTB 29). In it we are still at the Jules Verne stage of space and time travel, with old hardware for new tasks, but the magic car takes us to THE TEMPLE IN RED SQUARE (BTB 30). Only at first reading is this a poem of a recognizable earth, of Russia. Although as sentimental in the Red Thirties as one of Benet's American names, Red Square is conveniently also a shape. A futurist might have called the poem "Composition in Red." The power of the temple is indicated by the way the sonnet seems to come out of the title:[11]

THE TEMPLE IN RED SQUARE

Shall hold the world, comrade, shall help the wild
Joy contain itself: not break the soft touch;   (BTB 30)

With its power to "hold the world" it is no mere Moscow shrine; rather, as our first landmark in "the landscape/Of tomorrow" (BTB 30), the temple resembles nothing more than Borges' Aleph, the place moment which contains all time and space.

But what we notice first in *Before the Brave,* through our old eyes, is the enthusiasm of a young poet in a first performance. The volume is a portrait of the artist as a young revolutionary. Much of the poetry is versified speeches.[12] The first words of the volume are:

> Turn out the lights around the statues.
> Unlock the vaults of unhewn stone; put down
> An order for new men . . . (BTB 13)

The language, especially in the INTRODUCTION, is overly ceremonious and saved from sentimentality only by the impatience of the poet. The poetry is always interrupting itself to get more messages in. It sounds a little like that committed Thirties talk which sounds translated from Russian. Or it is the curious punctuation which turns the sentimental into a code. Poems are mere jottings. Colons abound: perfect chutes to bring the future in. The poems would have made great leaflets for Lauro de Bosis, the ideal poet of the volume, who was shot down over the Adriatic after dropping leaflets on Rome from his plane Icarus. In POEM IN THE FORM OF A LETTER: TO LAURO DE BOSIS (BTB 94-98) he is addressed together with Shelley.

The ambitious Patchen is finding his energy as the revolution begins to gather strength. But if he expects to arrive at Revolution he cannot remain the romantic individualist. In DEMONSTRATION we first meet a very old kind of poet who sounds like Poe and Millay combined:

> I thought your face as lovely
> As mind knows silence in mansions
> Read about, so slowly real and long ago:
>
> Here words are pigeon-toed schoolboys
>   lisping
> Through the halls of sunny love on earth, (BTB 45)

After an awkward transition the revolution comes to the rescue of the lover and the writing, and begins to lead:

> For at the moment, and sudden,
> While kissing you,
> The sound of a crowd in the street
> Gave the kisses double homes, (BTB 45)

The proper music for the ceremony of love is now "the sound of a crowd in the street." The next lines are the young poet's attempt to describe the beloved, but the chaotic metaphor also attempts to describe a new energy:

> And the press of your lips was a toast
> To the torch which they carried,
> Was a flame tossing above the shoulders
> Of an unloosed wonder where are no words
>   like hairy dreams to squat
> Above the wild sweet grave of our honor. (BTB 45)

In this poem love goes out of doors as the young poet joins the revolution. The kisses still have "double homes." Soon love will go out of this world, as the revolution itself changes. In the very next poem, THE OTHER SIDE, THE GREEN HOME the lovers are lost among the stars. The poem seems full of the nostalgia of a cosmic traveller for his earth home.

> The earth is near tonight: O slow
> within that wonder, turning
> mouth to mine, the million laws of world
> forgotten, love: . . . (BTB 46)

In such times the poetry of the lover turns into the poetry of the young revolutionary and turns then into the poetry of a crowd in the street. *Before the Brave* gives the poems of "the engine WE" (BTB 72). It is not only that in the volume we meet "we" as often as in most first collections we meet "I," but that the book seems designed as the hugh voice of first an earthly revolution and then a greater one. It makes use of echoes, memories, and premonitions to create itrs sound. The lines OUR EYES ARE THE EYES AT YOUR WINDOW, GEN-TLEMEN/OUR HANDS ARE THE HANDS AT THE LAT-CHES OF YOUR DOORS first appear in the book as a section title in the more than functional Table of Contents in neat businesslike upper case letters. But they are also the italicized epigraph of one of the nine sections of the book, and sit isolated on an otherwise empty unnumbered page (before p. 89). But they appear as two quietier still lines within a poem thirty-one pages before their appearance as an epigraph. This poem of "I" appears chaotic but has an underlying relentless rhythm:

> I shall be with you when hollow faces
> on time's screen stare at you leaning forward
> leaving no distance from here to Berlin or Rome
> leaving no roses under the wheels of the traitors
> or hate's tractors tearing up earth . . . (BTB 56)

Out of this chaos comes the lines of a guerrilla warning of ambiguous intent:

> Good-by to golden
> technique of grain till attacks the landscape
>   background
> of fists police bombs till staged a comeback being
> our eyes are the eyes at your windows gentlemen
> our hands are the hands at the latches of your doors.
> (BTB 56)

The revolutionary wants and does not want these lines heard. But we need not only explain these lines' appearances from the point of view of the revolutionary. His is only one of the voices which contributes to the huge voice of the revolution.

Another is the poet's. A glorious revolution need not deliver its messages secretly, but flaunts them. Patchen, in effect, quotes his poetry in the Table of Contents, uses his own lines as epigraphs, and thus works on his own legend. But the lines all belong to the revolution. In capitals they are banners; in italics, a mythic presence. *Before the Brave* is a workers' pageant. This is evident from the appearance of the book. It is full of empty pages and paraphernalia. The first poem comes only on page thirteen, or if we discount the INTRODUCTION, only on page twenty-nine. Perhaps this represents rather the sensibility of Random House, but the contents repeat the pageantry of the form. Socialist realism is certainly closer to aestheticism than to expressionism. The ceremonies begin with the titles of the INTRODUCTION, excerpted from the Declaration of Independence and the Gettysburg Address (BTB 12-25). Out of their context, reduced to fragile italics, the phrases are requisitioned to provide a small starting pipe sound which will bring history, as the rest of the book will bring the masses, from the American Revolution to the revolution which is in all things. The first section's banner title reads WE BRING NO BOXED SOLUTIONS: OUR FLAGS/STREAM OUT FOR USE, NOT

TRUMPET MASSES and we are marching perhaps into Madison Square Garden with the Paterson textile workers, but at the head of the last section, excerpted from THE RED WOMAN, comes the slogan *The timeless bride of all our loving,* and we seem ready for more than a wage hike.[13]

THE RED WOMAN is the woman of man's new public love. "Man has loved an image whose core/is hard/And bright as rifle's fire: . . ." (BTB 49) "Tall as/Thank You's from a beggar's lips" and with "the Kremlin lamp of her eyes" (BTB 49) she is at least the size of socialist realist statues. "There is the fire of love for man to love" (BTB 49). Making love to her will not be a little death. Although she begins as an orthodox socialist woman, born of history, she stands to woman as the cosmic revolution does to the socialist. Soon we see her "Grinding out of day's agony/A vast and teeming star" (BTB 50). Our final vision of her includes love, birth and death:

> Comrades, the Red Woman!
> She is dream's image made real.
> She is the timeless bride of all our loving.
> I give you dawn on the face of death.
>
> On the huge prone wonder of the earth. (BTB 50)

Soon children of this new love will begin to appear. Their real life and poetry will be outside this book, as socialist realism will make art obsolete. It is the breakthrough into new man which is photogenic. In AN INVITATION TO THE DANCE they resemble normal children but their dance is not at the Palomar Ballroom, nor is their revolution a mere barricades revolution. The poem begins as the poem of a socialist revolution:

> Come to the corner of Cross and Sickle
> at eight sharp Put on your masks Look to
> your bayonets Don't mind the barricades
> take your lives into your Hands off the morning's
> tall sun straight through the question. (BTB 33)

But from a revolutionary enthusiasm in which it is exciting to die picturesquely ("They too are craftsmen whose fingers close/Over careful triggers whose targets we are" (BTB 17)), we pass to a time when the children seem invulnerable, beyond the revolution:

> men will ask How did you fare Tell them
> our love was like a town with gods there
>   Our love
> was like the top of time and we above to look down. (BTB 33)

"Men is to be read as "mere men." It is what these children once were, or rather, would have been. The answer to the old irrelevant questions is a new language:

> And were we sad or dead or simply tired
>   Tell them
> dynamos were toys and towers and joy joy was hired. (BTB 33)

In the "tell them" there is a reluctance, as if the answer will not be believed; a stubborness, because after all the old men have to be initiated; and a great joy. We are watching the gathering of energy in mythic times. There is no need for punctuation as the lines come from new lungs. This is the birth of the revolution and the poet. The last line of the poem, difficult to read, is one of his first products, and passes without a period into the world. Words stumbled describing private feelings, but these are the private feelings of Man. The two "joys" coming together bounce without even the help of "toys." The line is a child's line, but speaks of great power. In the disrespect to the dynamo is a spirit beyond socialism. But the new race is only beginning to use its muscles. Finally, as was hoped, they have become "an engine rearing at eternity" (BTB 24). Since "time and love/Are our ancestors, these and these alone" (BTB 55), Man's ambition is huge:

> Whose bodies are already bargained for and bleeding ...
>   vow
> To alter nothing of living but life in our time,
> To plant the dynamite of hate in all our seeding
> O to build and break and march and climb and climb
>   (BTB 47)

After the socialist tasks of dynamiting, seeding, building, breaking, marching, at the last "climb" we are ready to escape the bonds of earth.

But it is not only the occasional science fiction cliche which makes *Before the Brave* a work of cosmic fantasy. The very insubstantialness of the language first encourages such a reading.

The attempt by the poet to say everything before it is too late makes the language less substantial. To show the new man acting in the universe the poet must, in effect, make the earth disappear. We have been watching quantitative change. Patchen's language signals qualitative change. There is nothing like the inexact adjective and the dangling participle to make the language of poetry other-worldly.[14] This is not a mere excuse on behalf of the young poet. The failings of the poet are often the best aid to the science fiction writer. In *Before the Brave* Patchen insists on his failings. He decides it is his task to present: "The graphs of love's scant honor:lungs,/Star-hunger, bird's cry, flowers" (BTB 84). To these elements of a fantastic setting are added, to make a kind of recipe for *Before the Brave*

> The "moving," "drawing near," "coming
> On"; enormous wings in steaming hash
> Of sun, night, rivers,
> And the loveful "having been." (BTB 84)

Full of such language, *Before the Brave* might well have been called, after a juvenile poem of Patchen's, "The Color of Air."[15] Soon the dreams of the new men begin to replace reality:[16]

> Do watch! do wait! the season nears its grain
>   in heart the lusty rain
> Of newness spends its yield in wonderment.
> Day's joy! Day's jewel! we wait content
> Where dreams already crowd the corn in field. (BTB 77)

The new men may still merely be the toughest of the old but there is already the hint of organic change:

> we've been picked to live because we could not die
> they could not kill us even when our own were turned
> against us they can not make a dent in the iron faces
> we've grown in the cellars of the world . . . (BTB 125)

The new men and the new world are not merely a culmination of social causes:

> O my countrymen
> the seasons moving on in a cycle
> of night and of death

> are surely moving in the pulse of the earth
> a better race of men are surely moving. (BTB 97)

Here is a cosmic change beyond socialism: "a mystery . . ./is
thrilling through the heart and power/of the stars of the vision's
blood is yours/to use" (BTB 98). Compared to this change not
only socialist power but all earthly power is found wanting:

> The fences of the ocean's shore
> the chill hands of the dynamo
> every power known to function in this time
> what are they as power O comrades
> compared to the driving wheels of our purpose. (BTB 98)

These comrades are preparing for an existence beyond earth.

> Power is in living clean before our love
> has written what we are
> on every distant corner of tomorrow's sky. (BTB 98)

One day we will wake up to find

> The cities peoples living
> Flesh of stars the firmament of joy
> In first vast stir of jangling eternity
> Of fellowship and spring where good and law
> Is thicker love and every day shall spawn a god. (BTB 108)

The new men are no longer given to playing but watch the
changes taking place inside themselves. In a poem such as NIGHT
HAS BEEN AS BEAUTIFUL AS VIRGINIA, America is only a
memory in the title. The whole earth is on the threshold of the
future:

> This ends: entering the show of silence
> voices gone: the outposts of glory given
> bare to stillness. Traps are sprung on day: (BTB 57)

The poet then paints a night on the planet: "blunted by dark the
trees/draw back, . . . then, as we watch,/ . . . they lunge/ at
space, in full gulp getting the first star" (BTB 57). Against this
background we watch the strange thoughts of the new men:

> Through hours intent on fields within ourselves
> exploring maps that lead from womb
> to will of being where every flower closed

> where every use of light goes late to memory
> and good awaits tomorrow's massive towns. (BTB 57)[17]

More aware of the shape of the planet than of Virginia we last hear "the dark curve of eternity go coughing down the hills" (BTB 57).

The isolation of the new men from the old world reminds us that in a time when the poet was the size of "I" rather than "WE" this epic of the birth of a new race would have been just another portrait of the artist as a young man. We are, after all, watching the birth of Kenneth Patchen, a poet with the voice of millions. The product of the introspection of those "through hours intent on fields within ourselves/exploring maps that lead from womb to will" is visionary poetry. But within socialist vision, with Man, not only Patchen becoming the poet, and the elements of poetry thus changing, the process which normally separates the poet from humanity here separates the New Man from humanity. There is no time for poetry because it works with words. The new artist Man works with worlds.

The puzzlement at the new world soon passes. The lines in the penultimate poem of the volume trip over themselves as the old world is given up to the old men:

> he wanted to take the earth with all the rivers
> lakes and hills with all the towns and all
> the mountains seas and plains thrown in
> and he can have them and he can take them. (BTB 129)

Then finally, apparently still in the name of socialism, man is transfigured with the earth:

> the earth opening into flower into the long deep flame
> of our bodies
> the splendid words upon our coins Comrade. (BTB 129)

But we have come from the dynamo to "Dark sweetness weaving/dynamos of lily and the rose. . . ." (BTB 114).

As all of the poetry of the volume has been headed to the words immediately following "the splendid word upon our coins Comrade," towards the title of the last poem, A WORLD WHOSE SUN RETREATS BEFORE THE BRAVE (BTB 130), so the revolution has been headed towards a world whose very sun retreats before the brave. The last poem is the book done again,

perhaps the first true product of the new man. With "Magnificent
the harvest" in the first stanza we remember our socialist begin-
nings.[18] But this is not a harvest of wheat culminating a five year
plan, but of worlds and man, culminating a thousand year plan.
And from old poetry we come to a new language: "the heart that
mocked at camp/And followers has learned another language,
name." In the third stanza, "Far out, beyond this common scene
and country of words," as the poet confuses life and art, we are no
longer on a solid earth. The dam which breaks then is not a
socialist realist Dnieprostroi. Out of it comes the future, not
water. "The dam breaks: we try to stem the flood, the silver wonder./Standing close together, new, our heads are split by
birds/Returning home to the silent lands of our wilderness." By
the poem's end man will be in the stars. The momentum of the
mysterious energies of *Before the Brave* is only momentarily held
back in the middle of the last stanza:

> Who were the property of every dunce and prophet,
> Of every gust of wind, of every goutish giant on earth,
> Are come now to claim ourselves and the profit
> Of an ownership which has been our own since birth,
> We are not cool: our hate has made us wise, not clever.

Then the new world is born:

> Beloved, listen, the stirring of life from the grave —
> The heart breaks with the groan and the grind of a lever
> Which lifts a world whose very sun retreats before
>   the brave. (BTB 130-131)

The motion which lifts the new world breaks the heart of the old.
It is an appropriate ceremony. "The groan and grind of a lever"
has also the sound of a down-at-heels-carnival trick but there 130
pages to support the last sentimental scene in which Man does not
so much ride into the sunset as he is the sunset. *Before the Brave* is
only a tour de force. Perhaps the beauty of size and strength is the
only justification of socialist realism.

The culmination of the book and the final hymn may also
appear anti-climactic. We need music and have only words. But
art is irrelevant now. The end must appear dramatic *and* matter-
of-fact. "Tell them." The new Man cannot march out but must

fade into the distance. Our eyes are not up to his speed. The last line is over before we know it. We are left at the end with the title in our minds. But travelling as it is at such speed and at such a distance from us, the line makes of the book a miniature. Our huge red book becomes a little red book, as poetry becomes obsolete. We are invited to read it again as a souvenir. Or at least, one is encouraged into such a reading by the elegance of this socialist work.

* * *

Patchen starts out as a poet of the revolution and becomes a poet of Revolution. A shrewd party eye, remembering Trotsky's warning, would have noticed the presence of Joe Hill as a hero in *Before the Brave*.[19] To make the volume a more orthodox socialist work it is necessary to ignore the poems to Joe Hill and Dostoevsky. These point to Patchen's next volume, *First Will & Testament*, a second volume necessarily called "first."[20] *Before the Brave* is the sky of Patchen's poetry. If it is the book of the apotheosis of man, then *First Will & Testament* is the book of an incarnation. It is a long way from the last words of *Before the Brave* to the first words of *First Will & Testament*. There in the first poem we seem to be fleeing with a Christ returned to suffer again (FWT 9). And with him Patchen comes down from his pure poetry to the poetry of earth. He must start again at least for political reasons. He speaks of this in THE EXECUTIONS IN MOSCOW (FWT 130-32). The second section of this poem, a formal poem written for the occasion by the bard of a fugitive nation that once was a vanguard, signals a new kind of poetry in Patchen, a small poetry more of the peasant than of the worker, again the poetry of "I."

> Like a woman in a warm room
> Will make a church of her hands
>
> When she touches her lover:
> I put my heart to the revolution. (FWT 130)

The love that went outdoors in DEMONSTRATION goes into hiding. And in A REVOLUTIONARY PRAYER a rhythm which might very well have lifted us to the heights of the ending of

Before the Brave again, bring us not only down to earth, but even takes us underground where we wait for "the miner Love" (FWT 36).[21]

Notes

[1]Quoted in *Rebel Voices: An I. W. W. Anthology*, ed. Joyce L. Kornbluth (Ann Arbor: University of Michigan Press, 1964).

[2]Kenneth Patchen, *Before the Brave* (New York: Random House, 1936). Page references are included in the text as BTB followed by page number. I have left the titles of individual poems in the upper case letters of the original. Sooner or later the student of Patchen decides that to do anything but photocopy a Patchen poem is to misquote the poet who became a painter.

[3]André Malraux, "Literature in Two Worlds," *Partisan Review*, II (January-February, 1935), 18-19.

[4]The first issue of *Whisper & Shout* (Mickleover: Derby, 1968) is in effect a "Selected Works of Kenneth Patchen."

[5]Vladimir Mayakovsky, quoted in *The Life of Mayakovsky*, ed. Wiktor Worosyzlski, tr. Boleslaw Taborski (New York: Orion Press, 1967), p.193.

[6]Leon Trotsky, *Literature and Revolution*, tr. Rose Strunsky (New York: International Publishers, 1925), p.57.

[7]Lenin quoted in *Other Worlds, Other Seas: Science Fiction Stories from Socialist Countries*, ed. Darko Suvin (New York: Random House, 1970), p.xxii. The development of my theme of the connection between socialist art and science fiction owes much to Darko Suvin's preface to *Other Worlds, Other Seas*.

[8]Yevgeny Zamyatin, "On Literature, Revolution, Entropy, and Other Matters," in *A Soviet Heretic: Essays by Yevgeny Zamyatin*, ed. and tr. Mirra Ginsburg (Chicago and London: The University of Chicago Press, 1972), pp.107-108.

[9]In Woroszylski, *op. cit.*, p.193.

[10]Richard Brautigan, *The Pill vs. The Springhill Mine Disaster* (New York: Delta Books, 1968), p.1.

[11]This is the only poem in the volume in which the title serves as the first line.

[12]See Edwin Rolfe, "Poetry," *Partisan Review*, II (April-May, 1935), 37.

[13]Daniel Aaron reminds us in *Writers on the Left* (New York: Avon, 1965) that the intellectuals staging workers' pageants were often more enthusiastic about them than the worker participants.

[14]Randall Jarrell complains about Patchen's and Muriel Rukeyser's inexact adjectives and dangling participles in a no longer sympathetic *Partisan Review*, 10 (1943), 471.

[15]I have seen this poem in manuscript at the Patchen house in Palo Alto. During my visit with her in the spring of 1975 Miriam Patchen could not have been kinder or more helpful.

[16]Limitations of space do not permit me to develop fully a relationship between *Before the Brave* and a science fiction novel. *Before the Brave* is one of the many works of science fiction about the birth of a new, no longer quite human, race.

Perhaps the most famous example of this kind of science fiction novel is Arthur C. Clarke's *Childhood's End* (New York: Ballantine Books, 1975, thirtieth printing). I suggest the parallel with science fiction in an attempt to encourage a reading of what may first appear to be unreadable propaganda. *Before the Brave* is interesting for the atmosphere and the landscapes.

[17] In *Childhood's End* this is the parallel scene:

> He would stay quite still for hours on end, his eyes lightly closed, as if listening to sounds which no one else could hear. Into his mind was flooding knowledge from somewhere or somewhen, which soon would overwhelm and destroy the half formed creature who had been Jeffrey Angus Greggson. (p.179)

[18] In *Childhood's End* an "Overlord" speaks: ". . . we till the field until the crop is ripe. The Overmind collects the harvest" (p.200).

[19] Leon Trotsky, *op. cit.*

[20] Kenneth Patchen, *First Will & Testament* (Norfolk, Conn.: New Directions, 1939). Subsequent citations are included in the text as FWT followed by the page number.

[21] My article on *Before the Brave* may be seen as a response to Allen Guttman's call that more attention be paid to the proletarian poetry of the Thirties. See his "The Brief Embattled Course of Proletarian Poetry" in *Proletarian Writers of the Thirties*, ed. David Madden (Carbondale: Southern Illinois University Press, 1968), pp.252-70.

Peter Yates

Patchen's Poetry and Jazz

"The blues," Leadbelly told us, "the blues is a lonely man goin' down a lonesome road at night, alone, singing." The scene changes a little here but it signifies the same, in these *Lonesome Boy Blues* by Kenneth Patchen. Read very slowly. Let the sounds of the words fall slowly with space and silence in between.

> Oh nobody's a long time
> Nowhere's a big pocket
> To put our little
> Pieces of nice things that
> Have never really happened
> To anyone except
> Those people who were lucky enough
> Not to get born
> Oh lonesome's a bad place
> To get crowded into
> With only
> Yourself riding back and forth
> On
> A blind white horse
> Along an empty road meeting
> All your
> Pals face to face
> Nobody's a long time

That's poetry, but you can sing it if you think of a tune. The melody is made of words, placed so that every one of them may be heard, poetry that distinguishes itself not by any rhyme-scheme or faithfulness to the iambic pattern that is supposed to be the "natural rhythmic fall of English verse," as somebody said some time, having rectified the verses of Shakespeare so that each would come out as closely as possible to two-times-five and forgetting to

observe how more effectively they are distributed in the first Folio;
the melody is the sound of words falling each surprisingly and
rightly, right in unexpected place. The rhythm is made by the fall
of this syncopation against fixed time. Your purist will ask: Which
fixed time fixed to what? Which is the proper question for him to
ask, because he is accustomed to a ticking of syllables, each,
whether or not it can be heard, accounted for by a procedure of
counting out with little marks, called scansion. Now just as
nobody who really writes ever stops to parse a sentence to be sure
that it will pass the canons of intelligibility and good taste, so no
poet worth throwing to the critics as a poet ever can remember
how to scan a line. When Patchen is reading he beats time with his
foot: I do, too, whether reading aloud poetry or prose. The
rhythm is not this fixed beat but what you are hearing in relation
to a similar fixed beat, which the words by their rhythm are
requiring you, too, to beat, if you have any rhythm in you, unconsciously, in your own muscular system and inside. This is
rhythm, and the more any poet can substitute in this rhythm silence for unneeded syllables that would not be heard, the more
will he be using wherever they are needed syllables that can be
heard in their own right. This is mostly the way by which
American poetry nowadays is distinguishing itself from English.

Because some poems so written are their best tunes, Kenneth Patchen has chosen to have some of his lyrical poems set to
jazz music that plays around them while he reads. His resonant
voice doesn't need singing, as deep and rich in natural overtones
as that of his friend Dylan Thomas. Stravinsky reckoned with this,
the effect of such a voice, alone, reading, when he set Thomas' *Do
not go gentle* to music as a memorial for him. The musical setting
grieves in the clash of canonic melodies passed between string
quartet and four trombones, while the singer simply and clearly
sings. Thus the emphasis is transferred from the voice alone to the
relationship between words and music. Patchen, remembering
the lost voice, objected to this setting; he couldn't accept that grief
could be like this, impersonal, objective, and be grief. But that is
Stravinsky's way, and I feel it as he means it to be felt. Thomas
reading needed no music, nor does Patchen.

Patchen and his composer Allyn Ferguson have found a
way different from that of Stravinsky. They began like Stravinsky

with the poet reading. They taped many of the poems as Patchen
read them, then Ferguson began building his jazz designs around
the reading.

> It's dark out, Jack
> The stations out there don't identify themselves
> We're in it raw-blind, like burned rats
> It's running out
> All around us
> The footprints of the beast, one nobody has any notion of
> The white and vacant eyes
> Of something above there
> Something that doesn't know we exist
> I smell heartbreak up there, Jack
> A heartbreak at the center of things —
> And in which we don't figure at all.

Take a poem like that — is it a poem? oh yes, it's a poem
— and set music around the slow, timed, tired-seeming, almost
monotone, so rigorously placed in slight deviations from the
monotone, entry and wait and reentry of the words. You wait for
the next words — Patchen can make you wait — as you would wait
for someone slowly telling out what is in his heart, one of those
times when a man's heart-beat does toll out while you listen to
him; and the music is all the world going on all around. You don't
quite listen to it; you listen for the words. The music heightens
your attention. One of the poems they have set to music is nothing
but the word "Wait" repeated in different rhythmic relations with
the silence, the music, what is not said. Such a poem cannot speak
for itself fully on the page. Indeed many of Patchen's poems do
not altogether come alive, until the sound of them has been timed
and placed in the memory by reading. Then you can understand
how some of the hollows in some of Patchen's longer poems are no
more than a dropping off, relaxing before the resurge of power,
the vocal climax, that can be so very moving when he reads his
poems. Some of that, the voice, cuts below the level of reason.

There's art in all this. If it's jazz you want, I'm not sure that
what Ferguson is writing is just jazz. He's a longhair who cut it
short, a sharp circle that was square. In the circumstances, the
music has to be composed. Haphazard music to haphazard reading
would defeat the timing. Does the music use too many in-

struments? In his Chamber Jazz Sextet — the name tells very clearly what it is he believes he is doing — Ferguson's six players get around on enough instruments, three or four apiece, so that if there were players at one time for all the instruments, the group would be an orchestra: besides the usual piano a reed piano, which sounds like a sort of disembodied harpsichord; non-jazz items, French horn, oboe, bassoon, flute. That comes back to what one believes is the exact line between jazz as jazz and classical as classical and sound as music. American jazz, American music, partly out of jazz, is an art of polyphony in sound. Ferguson is the first I know who has successfully interpenetrated the wider intervals of music with the finer intervals of the speaking voice. He imitates phrases but contrasts the sound. (I make these distinctions to keep Harry Partch out of it, who has invented a scale, nearly as fine as the overtone series, to approximate the narrower intervals of speech.) I could offer many qualifications as to what this music isn't. Any critic with a minimum of effort can do that sort of thing to any art-work. New listeners are constantly finding out that Debussy isn't Beethoven, and that late Beethoven is not for the half-baked. If you care to ask what Patchen and Ferguson are doing: there's a record. [Kenneth Patchen reads his poetry with Chamber Jazz Sextet, Cadence CLP-3004] What they have done together should surprise you the first time and hold your attention for a good many hearings. The vogue may be as great as it has been for the Dylan Thomas records.

I have to pick shorter poems by Patchen to work with. The longer are easier to grasp when he reads them aloud. This doesn't invalidate the publication of such poems on their merits apart from sound; it does explain why Patchen has never been a figure of the little magazines. You can't lump him in with everything else that gets lumped into the little magazines. He doesn't refuse them but he doesn't seek them. Little magazines are too often little in everything, prejudice, point, particularity, and passion. Some poets, whose work fits in the picture, have done very well in the little magazines, for example W. C. Williams. There are little magazine poets, and good ones, just as there are anthology poets. Wallace Stevens ennobled two generations of the little magazines by his inventions, but he didn't come to his full stature as a poet until his poems were collected and we learned that his inventions were meditations, and at what range.

Patchen, who has made poetry a full-time profession, has brought out the larger part of his poetry in books. There we can have it, all his, all together, prejudice, point, particularity, and passion, unblunted by the elegance of inelegance of the poetry or prose next page. That's a hard way to get a living. I first met Patchen in the course of business, interviewing him across a desk, in 1939, and didn't meet him again until this last winter, but I didn't forget him. Big, handsome, full of personality, and determined, he convinced me during a few minutes conversation that he would be a poet, nothing else, and would somehow make a living at it. Football got him into college; he was injured, and that same year I met him the injury recurred; during much of the time between '39 and '57 he lived and wrote in bed. He didn't make a living entirely through his books. In our society even the ruggedest, most individual disbeliever in the right of money and the good of organizations may have to turn sometime or other to the organizational givers of monetary gifts. Usually one of them will help him, regardless of beliefs. Our society is not quite so bad as some of us would paint it. In a large, disinterested way, a few of the big men with big money have learned that a civilization can't exist without its artists, and that some artists had better be helped and let alone. No money can buy the integrity of an artist who stands for our civilization against our civilization where a man like Patchen stands.

There was also the time when Patchen became so physically helpless, the best of our American poets went together with the best poets of England to raise money for him. When a thing like that happens to a dedicated man it sets him apart from literary commerce. He becomes a lighthouse against the uncommunicative darkness.

In or out of bed Patchen wrote constantly and published, sometimes at a loss to the publishers—wrote perhaps too much. His books, like those of Wallace Stevens, contain a residue of poems that are sketches, manneristic blurbs, sentimental extravagances, a fault to which Patchen is especially subject, oversniffed prejudices, the same point made too often, particularity turned mannered, the soft smear of a foiled passion. He can scold uselessly; he can condemn or damn unfairly; he can let the generality of a virtuous notion sound as if it had a purpose. And he can also ring them like the Creed, these generalizations:

> Pause.
> And begin again.
> It would take little to be free.
> That no man live at the expense of another.
> Because no man can own what belongs to all.
> Because no man can kill what all can use.
> Because no man can lie when all are betrayed.
> Because no man can hate when all are hated. . . .
> Pause.
> I believe in the truth.
> I believe that every good thought I have,
> All men shall have.
> I believe that what is best in me,
> Shall be found in every man.
> I believe that only the beautiful
> Shall survive on the earth.

(It deltas out: with a shrug of the shoulders you could leave it there. But see what happens, not only the passion but the particularity—without which passion can be painless as a good intention.)

> I believe that the perfect shape of everything
> Has been prepared;
> And, that we do not fit our own
> Is of little consequence.
> Man beckons to man on this terrible road.
> I believe that we are going into the darkness now;
> Hundreds of years will pass before the light
> Shines over the world of all men. . . .
> And I am blinded by its splendor.
> Pause.
> And begin again.

This leaves me to say that Patchen, like Emily Dickinson, can afford to throw himself away, working outwards through the dark towards the half-dark, until epiphany. In that light the seven stations of failure are made meaningful. It is not what a poet thinks that matters so much as what he does: that he is there, thinking, a poet. He has then only to wait, working, and be worthy.

Kenneth Patchen and Emily Dickinson are the two supreme American lyricists. Others have written lyrics not less ample, but these two can say all they have to say in the lyrical form.

Both are narrow of scope and subject, reflectors of an immense, slow-hurrying cosmic vision, in their deep wells points of light, light-years tall. Both are inclined to a homeliness of expression, to be familiar with death, to exult by hymn-singing, to being very small, lost, and sorrowful, and to sprouting fire and brimstone as naturally as volcanoes. Their technical accomplishments are concealed, their faults evident. In comparing Patchen with Dylan Thomas one would find the obvious advantages all on the side of Thomas, who seems at times to have swallowed the bardic lever of verse and at other times to be playing dominoes with rhymes. Both are inclined to nightmare and nonsense, good nonsense and bad sense nonsense. It's when you come to the simple things you learn where Patchen exceeds Thomas. (I know they were good friends, but who else in their like, though they were so different, are you able to compare them with!)

> *Rifle goes up:*
> *Does what a rifle does.*
> *Star is very beautiful:*
> *Doing what a star does.*
> Tell them, O Sleeper, that some
> Were slain at the start of the slaughter.
> Tell them, O Sleeper, that sleet and rain
> Are falling on those poor riderless heads
> Tell them, O Sleeper, that pitiful hands float on the
> water. . . .
> Hands that shall reach icily into their warm beds.

Now go back and look at that one word: "riderless." Observe how carefully the two unexpected rhymes finish the poem. Or . . . at this praise fragment:

> In thee the quills of the sun
> Find adornment.

Each of Patchen's books manipulates the material of words according to a different style. Sometimes the form is held to a single design. Sometimes he splashes out with his big personality, uncouth, graceless, determined to have his say without bothering to wait and comprehend how, if it is worth saying, this should be said. Dylan Thomas would jewel up a piece of this half-sort until all the diamonds ran together in a glare of invisibility. Scholars

are now busily going to work to prove that in this type of Thomas-
poem the paste diamonds are all jewels or the jewel diamonds all
paste. Really, it doesn't matter. This is the sort of poem Thomas,
in the freshness of youth, could write when he could write no better; and there is a remnant of this same highly competent in-
vertebracy of meaning in his work at the most potent. He was a
life torn between power and inadequacy. He ran like a rapids
every direction through the chasm downwards. With Patchen you
have at first very often the same feeling. After a while you begin to
see that there is a backside to his thinking as well as a front side.

> They are all intent on an object or ideal
> Which seems to be harbored just above me.
> The heart moves its head from side to side,
> And in each of its eyes there is a tiny slit
> Through which a cross looks.

Ambiguous, as ambiguous as Thomas, but no scholarship
required. The language is quite simple. This is not notably a good
poem. But you don't have to scan the *Metaphysicals* or learn Bardic Welsh before you accept it or reject it. The purpose of this
perhaps unjust comparison of Patchen with Thomas is to help
readers understand that the significance of what's there may be
sometimes less than the significance of what isn't.

I shall confess that I make nothing of the poems with
scraps of drawing or the drawings with scraps of poems that Patchen intersperses through his volumes. I am a doodler myself; I
have a bird period and a dragon period. And I am unacquainted
with the Painted Books Patchen turned out as limited press items
during his years of physical confinement, printing them on a silk
screen press laid across his bed. I do enjoy his habit of printing an
occasional poem in his own bold script. Only the sketches in his
recent little book of almost-nonsense poems, *Hurrah for
Anything*, occasionally strike me, for instance the one on the
cover, *The Celery-Flute Player*. As good a choice as any of this
wonderful book's poems.

> There was a celery-flute player
> Who got himself caught burning fire
> On top of some old hoodlum's lake;
> They wanted to hit him with a hammer,

> But couldn't get up the admission
> He would have charged them to see it.

You can take your time with that, waiting for it to register. Nonsense poems are not epics, but poets who can write nonsense
poems, that stand up on their texture as poems and are not intended to be jokes, are rarer than old masters. Patchen's humor,
mordant, morbid, is there, like sunlight at the edge of storm. It
thrives in context.

Finally, I would say that Kenneth Patchen, when you
begin walking through inside the rooms of his volumes, has caught
the modern lack of art in poems about men and women, the
loneliness, inability one might say to subsist unconfirmed by
woman, the sexual immediacy that can be both raw and embarrassing and more, can seem too important in context to be
honest, and he has transferred it into lyrics and love-songs that are
no longer, sentimentally, what they ought not to be, because they
are simple, beautiful, and honest. (His novel *See You In The Morning* begins this way but ends distressingly otherwise.)

> As we are so wonderfully done with each other
> We can walk into our separate sleep
> On floors of music where the milkwhite cloak of childhood lies
> Oh my love, my golden lark, my long soft doll
> Your lips have splashed my dull house with prints of flowers
> My hands are crooked where they spilled over your dear curving
> It is good to be weary from that brilliant work
> It is being God to feel you breathing under me
> A waterglass on the bureau fills with morning . . .
> Don't let anyone in to wake us

Quotation like poetry needs art and can't be too artful. Need I
point to the waterglass.

> Light thickens,
> And the Crow makes Wing to th' Rookie Wood . . .
> And my poore Foole is hang'd: no, no, no life? . . .
> Neuer, neuer, neuer, neuer, neuer . . .

These, iambic or trochaic? these, rather than "the multitudinous
seas" or "Ripeness is all," should serve us for a touchstone. If one
have the first, the second will be consequent. I have tried in these

pages by quotation to give you a poet, one not yet taken up by the
anthologies, not popularized by those public avatars of cheerful
rumor whose praise has turned Kenneth Rexroth aside from his
true art; a man of principle and force who has stood up for his
generation as a poet. Not a lost generation, though an angry one;
not a lost poet, though his witness calls down the stars to rain
upon us because we are inept.

> So I cry out against these living gates (at me, Lord
> Look at me! why must Thou assume
> That this wild wrong face despairs of Thee? . . .

Carolyn See

The Jazz Musician as Patchen's Hero

The recent experiments in the new poetry-and-jazz movement seen by some as part of the "San Francisco Renaissance" have been as popular as they are notorious. "It might well start a craze like swallowing goldfish or pee wee golf," wrote Kenneth Rexroth in an explanatory note in the *Evergreen Review,* and he may have been right.

Under the general heading "poetry-and-jazz" widely divergent experiments have been carried out. Lawrence Ferlenghetti and Bruce Lippincott have concentrated on writing a new poetry for reading with jazz that is very closely related to both the musical forms of jazz, and the vocabulary of the musician. Even musicians themselves have taken to writing poetry. (Judy Tristano now has poems as well as ballads written for her.)

But the best known exploiters of the new medium are Kenneth Rexroth and Kenneth Patchen. Rexroth and Patchen are far apart musically and poetically in their experiments. Rexroth is a longtime jazz buff, a name-dropper of jazz heroes, and a student of traditional as well as modern jazz. In San Francisco he has worked with Brew Moore, Charlie Mingus, and other "swinging" musicians of secure reputation, thus placing himself within established jazz traditions, in addition to being a part of the San Francisco "School."

Although Patchen has given previous evidence of an interest in jazz, the musical group that he works with, the Chamber Jazz Sextet, is often ignored by jazz critics. (*Downbeat* did not mention the Los Angeles appearance of Patchen and the Sextet, although the engagement lasted over two months.) The stated goal of the CJS is the synthesis of jazz and "serious" music. Patchen's musicians are outsiders in established jazz circles, and Patchen himself has remained outside the San Francisco poetry group, maintaining a self-imposed isolation, even though his conversion to poetry-and-jazz is not as extreme or as sudden as it may first appear. He had read his poetry with musicians as early as 1951, and his entire career has been characterized by radical experiments with the form and presentation of his poetry. However, his subject matter and basic themes have remained surprisingly consistent, and these, together with certain key poetic images, may be traced through all his work, including the new jazz experiment.

From the beginning of his career, Patchen has adopted an anti-intellectual approach to poetry. His first book, *Before the Brave* (1936), is a collection of poems that are almost all Communistic, but after publication of this book he rejected Communism, and advocated a pacifistic anarchy, though retaining his revolutionary idiom. He spoke for a "proletariat" that included "all the lost and sick and hunted of the earth." Patchen believes that the world is being destroyed by power-hungry and money-hungry people. Running counter to the destroying forces in the world are all the virtues that are innate in man, the capacity for love and brotherhood, the ability to appreciate beauty. Beauty as well as love is redemptive, and Patchen preaches a kind of moral salvation. This salvation does not take the form of a Christian Heaven. In Patchen's eyes, organized churches are as odious as organized governments, and Christian symbols, having been taken over by the moneyed classes, are now agents of corruption. Patchen envisions a Dark Kingdom which "stands above the waters as a sentinel warning man of danger from his own kind." The Dark Kingdom sends Angels of Death and other fateful messengers down to us with stern tenderness. Actually Heaven and the Dark Kingdom overlap; they form two aspects of heavenly life after death.

Patchen has almost never used strict poetic forms; he has experimented instead with personal myth-making. Much of his earlier work was conceived in terms of a "pseudo-anthropological" myth reference, which is concerned with imaginary places and beings described in grandiloquent and travelogue-like language.

These early experiments were evidently not altogether satisfying to Patchen. Beginning in *Cloth of the Tempest* (1943) he experimented in merging poetry and visual art, using drawings to carry long narrative segments of a story, as in *Sleepers Awake,* and constructing elaborate "poems-in-drawings-and-type" in which it is impossible to distinguish between the "art" and the poetry. Art "makings" or pseudo-anthropological myths did not meet all of Patchen's requirements for a poetic frame of reference. Many of his poems purported to be exactly contemporary and political; so during the period approximately from 1941 to 1946, Patchen often used private detective stories as a myth reference, and the "private eye" as a myth hero. Speaking in terms of sociological stereotype, the "private eye" might appeal to the poet in search of a myth for many reasons. The private detective (at least in the minds of listeners and readers all over the country) is an individual hero fighting injustice. He is usually something of an underdog, he must battle the organized police force as well as recognized criminals. The private detective must rely, as the Youngest Son or Trickster Hero does in primitive myth, on his wits. The private detective is militant against injustice, a humorous and ironic explorer of the underworld; most important to Patchen, he was a non-literary hero, and very contemporary. In 1945, probably almost every American not only knew who Sam Spade was, but had some kind of emotional feeling about him. In *The Memoirs of a Shy Pornographer* (1945) Patchen exploited this national sentiment by making his hero, Albert Budd, a private detective.

But since 1945, Sam Spade has undergone a metamorphosis; he has become Friday on *Dragnet,* a mouthpiece of arbitrary police authority. He has, like so many other secular and religious culture symbols, gone over to the side of the ruling classes. Obviously, the "private eye" can have no more appeal for Patchen. To fill the job of contemporary hero in 1955, Patchen needed someone else.

It was logical that he would come up with the figure of the modern jazz musician. The revolution in jazz that took place around 1949, the evolution from the "bebop" school of Dizzy Gillespie to the "cool" sound of Miles Davis and Lennie Tristano, Lee Konitz, and the whole legend of Charlie Parker, had made an impression on many academic and literary men. The differentiation between the East Coast and West Coast schools of jazz, the difference between the "hard bop" school of Rollins, and the "cerebral" experiments of Tristano, Konitz and Marsh, the general differences in the mores of white and negro musicians, all had become fairly well known to certain segments of the public. The immense amount of interest that the new jazz had for the younger generation must have impressed him, and he began working toward the merger of jazz and poetry, as he had previously attempted the union of graphic art and poetry. In addition to his experiments in reading poetry to jazz, Patchen is beginning to use the figure of the modern jazz musician as a myth hero in the same way he used the figure of the private detective a decade ago. In this respect, his approach to poetry-and-jazz is in marked contrast to Kenneth Rexroth's. Rexroth uses many of his early poems when he reads to jazz, including many of his Chinese and Japanese translations; he usually draws some kind of comparison with the jazz tradition and the poem he is reading — for instance, he draws the parallel between a poem he reads about an Oriental courtesan waiting for the man she loves, and who never comes, and the old blues chants of Ma Rainy and other Negro singers — but usually the comparison is specious. Rexroth may sometimes achieve an effective juxtaposition, but he rarely makes any effort to capture any jazz "feeling" in the text of his poems, relying on his very competent musicians to supply this feeling.

Patchen does read some of his earlier works to music, but he has written an entire book of short poems which seem to be especially suited for reading with jazz. These new poems have only a few direct references to jazz and jazz musicians, but they show changes in Patchen's approach to his poetry, for he has tried to enter into and understand the emotional attitude of the jazz musician.

It is difficult to draw the line between stereotype and the reality of the jazz musician. Everyone knows that private detectives in real life are not like Sam Spade and Pat Novak, but the real and the imaginary musician are closely linked. Seen by the public, the musician is the underdog *par excellence*. He is forced to play for little money, and must often take another job to live. His approach to music is highly individualistic; the accent is on improvisation rather than arrangements. While he is worldly, the musician often cultivates public attitudes of childlike astonishment and naivete. The musician is non-intellectual and non-verbal; he is far from being a literary hero, yet is a creative artist. Many of these aspects will be seen as comparable to those of the ideal detective, but where the detective is active and militant, the jazz musician is passive, almost a victim of society. In order to write with authority either about musicians, or as a musician, Patchen would have to soft pedal his characteristically outspoken anger, and change (at least for the purposes of this poetry) from a revolutionary to a victim. He must become one who knows all about the injustice in the world, but who declines doing anything about it.

This involves a shift in Patchen's attitude and it is a first step toward writing a new jazz poetry. He has shown considerable ingenuity in adapting his earliest symbols and devices to the new work, and the fact that he has kept a body of constant symbols through all of his experiments gives an unexpected continuity to his poetry. Perhaps tracing some of these more important symbols through the body of his work will show that Patchen's new poetry is well thought out, and remains within the mainstream of his work, while being suited to a new form.

Henry Miller characterized Patchen as a "man of anger and light." His revolutionary anger is apparent in most of his early poems. The following passage from "The Hangman's Great Hands" illustrates the directness of this anger.

> Anger won't help, I was born angry.
> Angry that my father was being burnt alive in the mills;
> Angry that none of us knew anything but filth and poverty.
> Angry because I was that very one somebody was supposed
> To be fighting for.

This angry and exasperated stance which Patchen has maintained in his poetry for almost fifteen years has been successfully modulated into a kind of woe that is as effective as anger and still expresses his disapproval of the modern world. In his recent book, *Hurray for Anything* (1957), one of the most important short poems — and it is the title poem for one of the long jazz arrangements — is written for recital with jazz. Although it does not follow the metrical rules for a blues to be sung, the phrases themselves carry a blues feeling.

> I WENT TO THE CITY
> And there I did Weep,
> Men a-crowing like asses,
> And living like sheep.
> *Oh, can't hold the han' of my love!*
> *Can't hold her little white han!*
> Yes, I went to the city,
> And there I did bitterly cry,
> Men out of touch with the earth,
> And with never a glance at the sky.
> *Oh, can't hold the han' of my love!*
> *Can't hold her pure little han'!*

Patchen is still the rebel, but he writes in a doleful, mournful tone. Neither of these poems is an aberration; each is so typical that it represents a prominent trend to the poet's development.

Patchen is repeatedly preoccupied with death. In many of his poems, death comes by train: a strongly evocative visual image. Perhaps Patchen was once involved in a train accident, and this passage from *First Will and Testament* may have been how the accident appeared to the poet when he first saw it—if he did:

> Lord love us, look at all the disconnected limbs
> floating hereabouts, like bloody feathers at that — and all
> the eyes are talking and all the hair are moving and all the
> tongue are in all the cheek. . . .

This chaotic image has been refined by the poet, made ironic and even slightly humorous, by reducing the number of victims to one and having that one person cut into two. In "The Body Beside the Ties" the train image appears again:

> Can't seem to wake you kid, guess it
> put you to sleep getting cut in two
> * * *
> Hello Kid
> Still dead?

Patchen's later short prose work, written in oracular style, and dealing with the inevitability of death, *They Keep Riding Down All The Time,* had as part of its grisly comic relief, the recounting by the hero of an anecdote from his hometown. This was told in tough talk not unlike Kenneth Fearing's. It then

abruptly switches to the oracular tone that is held through most of
the book.

> Ned Bolton was always afraid of his father. Why his old man
> used to scare the living daylights out of him by just saying
> pass me the butter huh. One day last week a trolley went off
> the track in good old Scranton Pa., making an upper and a
> lower Bolton St. Nobody saw the thing that gave the trolley
> a nudge nohow. They just keep riding down all the time. No
> one can ever stop them.
>   O Which one do you want to ride down for you?

This same image is used in a humorous limerick (Patchen's own term for some of these short poems, although they actually do not follow the limerick form). This poem is read to a jazz
riff that was written especially for it and for other humorous
poems of the same length and mood.

> There was a tame streetcar conductor
> Who one day was considerably surprised
> To have it suddenly bite his behind;
> So next morning he reported for work
> Disguised as a broad-minded chambermaid . . .
> And now lives with the company president's daughter.

In much of his lighter poetry and prose, the poet uses the
acting out of puns. This is a surrealist device, possibly derived
from Henry Miller. In much of his work, it appears out of place,
but at times it is fortunately conceived, as in this passage from
The Memoirs of a Shy Pornographer. Albert Budd is on his first
case as a private detective, and is following a man who repeatedly
drops secret notes that Mr. Budd picks up. On every note is written, "Your hat's on Backwards," and every time that Budd takes
his hat off, it is. Later on, a sinister gentlemen says:

> "It may amuse you to know the name of the man who has
> been wearing your hat. May I present Herman Y. Back-
> wards — Mr. Budd, Mr. Backwards."

In *Hurray for Anything*, the book of peripheral jazz experiments, Patchen does not exactly act out a pun, but he has the
unidentified narrator of one poem act from good intentions, and
do what appears to be a good deed, but which ends in disastrous
results. The poem has a loony humor and naiveté that suggest an
addict at work.

PROMINENT COUPLE BELIEVED PERMANENTLY
STUCK TO PORCH

On impulse, to impress you, and remembering
How much in grade school you liked them,
It was I who had those thousand taffy apples
Delivered to your house —
After so many years!
Me, a humble but honest filing clerk,
And you O little pig-tailed one, the Mayor's wife!
How was I to know you'd be off vacationing?
Anyhow, think how lucky you are . . .
For I might have sent roses —
And then you'd of had big sharp-nosed bees
Lappin' at you instead of them contented bears.

Another of Patchen's surreal images shows the general precariousness of man's existence. In *The Journal of Albion Moonlight* (1945), the hero says:

"You see — we are all on the water but there is no need to build a boat because it would be burnt in an instant. I know history."

This same image is incorporated into a humorous jazz poem, with a shifted emphasis:

There was a celery-flute player
Who got himself caught burning fire
On top of some old hoodlum's lake;
They wanted to hit him with a hammer
But couldn't get up the admission
He would have charged them to see it.

Patchen's angels of death recur in almost all of his works. Typically, in *They Keep Riding Down All The Time,* he speaks of the angels:

O They keep riding down all the time. Nobody can ever stop them. Some from the light and some from the darkness — O see with what stern tenderness they keep riding down on this world!

And in his jazz poetry, Patchen mentions angels:

I stand
Under the blazing moon and wonder
At the disappearance of all holy things

From this once so promising world;
And it does not much displease me
To be told that at seven tomorrow morning
An Angel of Justice will appear
And that he will clean up people's messes for them. . . .

It would appear from these instances that Patchen has not changed too radically in his imagery since he has become aware of the possibilities of jazz as a springboard for his poetry. He has become at the same time less militant and less pompous; he is less angry, but many of his newer poems appear to grow directly out of his older work. He has been, on the whole, cautious in his approach.

There are only three direct uses of the jazz idiom in *Hurray for Anything*. One short poem is called "Far Out," which is a slang term for musicians, but the poem, outside of being very strange, has nothing to do with the title. Another poem is entitled "Players in Low See" has certainly musical implications, but these are not followed through in the poem. Only once in the actual text of a poem is there an allusion to jazz:

I am Timothy the Lion
I live in an old sour apple tree
With Happy Jake, who
A small goldfish;
There is also a short necked swan,
Two very base players, a bull still wrapped
In pink tissue paper. . . .

There is one other mention of jazz in the volume, this time, typographical. One of the poems is called "Flap*j*acks on the Piazza," which has nothing to do with jazz or flapjacks either for that matter.

The next logical step in this fringe experimentation, is a long work exploiting the vocabulary of jazz as well as the attitudes that are commonly thought of as connected with jazz. Patchen is now writing such a work. It is untitled, but almost complete, and the poet now reads excerpts from this work, which is a play, with the Chamber Jazz Sextet. The entire play will probably not be constructed to be read to music, but it utilizes many jazz idioms, and it is a deliberate effort to "marry" poetry and jazz. The play is centered around an addict, a musician addict, and the play's speeches are larded with all kinds of "hip" talk.

In the beginning of the play's excerpt for jazz recitation, entitled "Glory, Glory," Patchen reviews again the state of the world and notes again that culture is in the hands of the villains, that an honest artist (in this case a musician rather than a poet) doesn't have a chance. He speaks of the futility and pathos of trying to "make the scene." Patchen identifies the musician with Christ; when an honest horn player tries to blow, "The good people nail him, they fix him," and this phrase is very good, for besides recalling the crucifixion, "nail" and "fix" are part of the addict's slang. The artist is driven by the "others" to a world of addiction, which is a strange and terrible "Dark Kingdom," but no worse in its terror than the rest of the so-called civilized world. Then Patchen catalogues the names of the sparkling capitals of the world, ending with Paris, France, and says, "Yes. Glory, Glory." Patchen says that we are all in the dark, "with some pretty awful hands over the light switches." He ends the speech with the advice to try to "Make your own scene, while there is still any scene left to make at all."

There is a problem of communication with this kind of poetry. Most of the words in the jazz vocabulary are part of a "special" language, and like all such languages, may not convey much to people outside the tradition of that language. Most of the phrases in the jazz vocabularly are purposely vague and non-literate. These phrases may add something to poetry when they are used in moderation, but when the language is used to carry the burden of the whole "message" of the poem, there is a danger of almost total lack of communication between the poet and his reader, or listener.

Patchen manages his "hip" talk rather well, but he sometimes gives the listener the impression that he is not altogether sure of what he is talking about. The listener is constantly afraid that the poet is going to make some gaffe with the language, and when the poet doesn't, the listener is relieved. Yet to avoid an error is hardly the goal of a work of art.

Because Patchen is experimenting cautiously, and has taken over the parts of the jazz form were essential to his ultimate success — that is, a fairly strict and simple poetic form and a quality of disaffectedness or "coolness" that has never before been in his work — there is a good chance that Patchen will be able to effect the merger of poetry and jazz, perhaps more than any other contemporary poet.

Many musicians (to say nothing of the poets) do not believe this is possible. In an irate article about Kenneth Patchen, Ralph Gleason, a San Francisco music critic, writes: "Not until a poet comes along who learns what jazz is all about and then writes poetry will there be any merger, what we have now is a freak, like a two-headed calf." But Gleason does acknowledge the popularity of the experiment and expects to see soon a trade paper ad that looks like this:

> WANTED — Avant Guard poet. Must have book published. Needs tuxedo; read, fake, plenty hot. Must travel. No boozers, no chasers.

Patchen has answered this theoretical ad, but will he be a success at his new job? He thinks so. He says he sees hope for a new medium.

Ray Nelson

The Moral Prose of Kenneth Patchen

> who dreamt and made incarnate gaps in Time and Space
> through images juxtaposed, and trapped in the arch-
> angel of the soul between 2 visual images and joined
> the elemental verbs and set the noun and dash of con-
> sciousness together jumping with sensations of Pater
> Omnipotens Aeterna Deus
> to recreate the syntax and measure of poor human prose and
> stand before you speechless and intelligent and
> shaking with shame, rejected yet confessing out of the
> soul to conform to the rhythm of thought in his naked
> and endless head. . . .

Allen Ginsberg, Howl

Allen Ginsberg was describing an ideal American of his own, but this passage from *Howl*[1] makes a remarkably apposite appreciation of the purpose and achievements of the strange, visionary novels Kenneth Patchen wrote in the years during and just after World War II. Even more than the poetry for which he is far better known, Patchen's novels mark him distinctly as a figure in that tradition of American literature that emphasizes the artist's moral responsibility rather than what might be called his "literary" responsibility. In the moral tradition the resources and artfulness of the writer are applied to an expression of the truth he perceives in his own person, rather than to fulfilling the demands of structural and emotional symmetry.

Literature that focuses on the moral nature of the in-dividual, and attempts to communicate the urgency of moral demands at the expense, if need be, of a beautiful or consistent artistic surface is, of course, characteristic of America from the first; and the act of literary creation has often become, in this country, a means of personal salvation. It is this concern that led Hawthorne and Melville to identify with morally threatened characters in their own novels, and Emerson to call for a literature casting off traditional restrictions in order that moral truth might be expressed in a new way, appropriate to the fresh vision of the infinite that American life made possible. Walt Whitman was the first American artist to gather up all the implications of this concern and make his art of them. He defines the literature of moral responsibility, and those few writers — Thomas Wolfe and Henry Miller among them — who have abandoned traditional literature to create an intensely personal art that is finally inseparable from their own lives, look to him as their source and standard. Those who follow Whitman's way have been influenced by his rejection of traditional forms, which he considered structures of the moral failure of history and an imposition of false perception upon new glimpses of eternal truth. More important, they have been influenced by his characterization of the poet as priest of a new morality, and by his "bardic" role, the prophetic stance he took toward human experience and human destiny.

In this century these writers have been especially concerned with doing battle against the highly influential attitude that finds the value of art in technique and surface, and is willing to allow verbal beauty to justify the moral implications the surface might contain — particularly of the rage for artistic order. Ezra Pound's fascism is the classic case in point. Reacting harshly to the demand for form, and the disappearance of the artist from his work, Patchen and others have declared that attention to artistic effect for its own sake is treasonable and fraudulent; they have insisted on the function of the artist as a moral leader. For Patchen, the religious and prophetic implications of the writer's role become explicitly and crucially significant. "The artist —" he tells us in *Sleepers Awake,* "and I am speaking very carefully now — is always the spokesman of God." (p. 317)[2] The disturbing novels he has worked out of his concept of art, out of the overly neglected Whitman tradition, earn him a major place in that tradition, and the stature of a representative and important American writer.

Working always with great artfulness, to make tangible the moral truths with which his consciousness is bursting, he offers, when listened to carefully, the tormented questioning of Melville, the tenderness and compassion of Whitman, and, above all, the angry refusal to compromise, the toughness, the lonely moral dignity that we associate with the Henry Thoreau of the anti-slavery papers.

In view of his achievement it is disappointing, even if not entirely surprising, that his work has received so little attention. When his novels have not been ignored altogether, they have been treated with condescension and grossly misunderstood. Review of *The Memoirs of A Shy Pornographer,* the first of his prose to be reviewed at all, were remarkably irrelevant, and thoroughly misleading. *See You in the Morning,* his one vastly inferior production, was the only Patchen novel given anything approaching serious consideration in the literary publications that influence book sales. Reasons for this neglect and dismissal are not hard to find: the very tradition out of which Patchen writes, the literature of Whitman, has been judged by criteria foreign to it, and never fully accepted by either the popular audience for which it was intended, or the intellectual audience that has struggled to understand it in the context of other movements. And critics who had given their lives to their work were puzzled by, and considered irresponsible, a writer openly at war with all they stood for, who accused them, literally, of murder. In addition, the unpopular stance Patchen took during World War II seems to have hurt badly the reputation he was earning as a representative of the then-fashionable "proletarian school."[3] Despite the general radical disillusionment at the end of the 'thirties, Patchen refused to shift from radicalism to patriotism when war broke out. He maintained instead his intense hatred for both capitalism and fascism, using these political terms as metaphors for the moral evil to which he opposed his absolute pacifism. His concern in these years was scarcely political at all. A dialogue from *Sleepers Awake* illustrates his position:

> ". . .I like poets when they're not damn punks."
> "You could use a little tolerance. It's a pretty lonely business trying to write poems in this madhouse of a world."

"But most of them aren't really poets," a stranger
said.

Kell grinned, "You wait. In a couple of years you'll
discover they hated war all along."

"In a pig's eye. You don't get no Sergeant or
Lieutenant in front of your name by refusing to kill people
— and for my money, poet and killer can't be used to
describe the same person," the stranger said.

"Something along that line occured to me in prison."

"How much'd you get?" I asked, watching the
stranger disappear through a small hole in the ceiling.

"Three years."

"Because you refused to break one of God's com-
mandments."

"Yeh. So long, Best. Think about that tolerance
angle." (p. 74)

In the post-war years, as the "classicism" demanded by that
group loosely — and helplessly — characterized as New Critics
became increasingly the public idea of an "official" literature,
Patchen's reputation remained submerged, and his work grew increasingly distasteful to many of the writers and critics who were
regarded as authoritative.

Another important reason that Patchen has remained obscure arises also out of the background from which he writes, and
is related to the characteristic strangeness of his prose. Like many
of the young writers of his generation, he was influenced by the
revolutionary intellectual movements of Europe — notably
surrealism; unlike them, he retained after the first period of ex-
cited experimentation an essential loyalty to these movements,
and adapted them wholesale to his own distinctly individual ends.
His novels are surrealistic in their glorification of the imaginative
world of childhood, their refusal to be resigned to hopelessness,
and their adherence to what Georges LeMaitre outlines as the
surrealist program:

> According to the surrealists, the liberation of our
> subconscious mind can best be effected through an attitude
> of deliberate censorship towards all the accepted forms of
> traditional thinking. . . . Therefore, all means are
> legitimate which might bring about its [intellect's] total and
> final disintegration. Irony, ridicule, sarcasm are our most
> efficient weapons in this struggle for our complete inward

enfranchisement. Every fixed form of opinion or expression must be discarded as arbitrary and absurd. Every established law about aesthetics or morals must be ruthlessly swept away. . . . Surrealist humor is a grotesque parody of all things in which the ordinary "unenlightened" man still implicitly believes. . . . When destructive humor has definitely cleared the field of all conventional obstacles, man can at last have access to the enthralling *surréel*. . . . Of course such contact cannot take place if we look at the world analytically. . . . We must grasp through mystic intuition the totality of energies offered to our experience. . . . Thus would be resolved the age-long antagonism between the subjective and objective.[4]

It would probably be erroneous to classify Patchen as an orthodox surrealist; he is a person who deliberately defies classification, and it is unlikely that he is willing to accept the Freudian reverence for the subconscious at face value. In the person of Albion Moonlight, Patchen makes some disclaimer of surrealistic intent: "There is no such thing as super-realism. (The surrealists have managed to put on a pretty good vaudeville act for the middleclass; *but there isn't a religious man among them.*)" (p.307) Despite his reservations, however, Patchen has retained much of the method and imagery of surrealism, while rejecting many of its philosophical underpinnings; and the influence has caused him some trouble in this country. Not only is an American surrealist suspect, but to critics who have little experience or understanding of its methods, surrealistic literature makes no sense. The impulse is to compare a writer of Patchen's generation with Faulkner, Steinbeck, Hemingway, when his true contemporaries — outside of Henry Miller and some European novelists like Hesse — are painters: Klee, Chagall, Miro. The painter's technique is important to Patchen; he is himself a prolific painter, and relies heavily in his prose on imagery adopted from the visual arts. The "heaven" of *The Memoirs of A Shy Pornographer*, for instance, is described as a painting:

> The first thing I noticed was the sky. It had a lot of drawings of birds and fishes and funny little trees on it. But I should have saved funny to say that these drawings were flying around and swimming and had real apples and pears and oranges on them.
>
> Also there was a big golden ball with lines shooting out from it. That must be the sun, I thought — and just

then one of the lines reached down and touched my sandal
— it was the sun all right. (p. 225)

And the landscape of *The Journal of Albion Moonlight* is often
established by classic surrealistic images: "Put this book on a glass-
topped table and fire a bullet through it; it will drip a woman's
face in its own blood." (p. 157)

The interaction of the two essentially revolutionary influences of Whitman and surrealism reinforces the American tendency to break through historical limitations to a new moral grandeur with the surrealistic impulse to explode rational limitations
and grasp transcendent truth. In Patchen these influences con-
tribute to the development of a writer determined to destroy
traditional forms, and the attitudes toward reality they reflect, in
order to create a personal "reality" that will carry the force of his
moral statement to the immediate attention of his reader. His is
what the Dadaists called "anti-literature," a genre that defines
traditional forms as attempts to justify the chaotic and immoral,
to compromise with the forces of violence and inhumanity in the
world. Albion Moonlight (or one of his many avatars) explicitly
makes this complaint: "In art there is ever the demand for the
distorted, for an indefinable thing termed 'magic.' But for the artist, there can only be one distortion: that which is not art. To say
it in another way, the world is in a mess precisely because a bunch
of stuffy fools insist that there is no mess." (p. 120) Consequently,
Patchen sets out on a desperate attack on form, usually conducted
by leading the reader to expect some familiar formal pattern,
denying it to him, and then breaking out of the fiction to curse or
jeer his discomfiture:

You want form, do you? I'll give you form. I'll make you
really wish for something nice and cozy — Something all
chewed and digested for you — Look, the thing's worn out
— It don't work no more. If it ain't in a pretty package, you
don't want it — Because it ain't art. Because the book critic
of The New Porker might now want to see a bit more respect
for tradition, :hrrum, hum. (*Sleepers Awake*, p. 372)

In *The Journal of Albion Moonlight*, the record of a
deranged symbolic pilgrimage, destruction of form becomes a
thematically important part of the action. Albion constantly
breaks off his journal to write other journals, novels, letters; and,

again, explicity abuses the reader who expects conventional forms. "I spit on what you call literature," he says — and interlards his narrative with confidential asides that call attention to his iconoclastic method:

> And I want you to have a sense of devotion in regard to the beginning, the middle and the end of this little chronicle of the human spirit. Perhaps this is the time to talk to you about something which causes misgivings to rise in your breast. In short, to dwell for a moment upon the novel and the problems which have faced me in it. You have only to remember one thing, and all will be clear — the perfect shape will rise to your sight. . . . (p. 145)

> You will be told that what I write is confused, without order — and I tell you that my book is not concerned with the problems of art, but with . . . the problems of life itself. (p. 200)

> By every law of this continual art, I should end this book right here. For my purposes, the end must not come at the end, but in the middle — *and then we go on.* (p. 226)

> I have a bit of a surprise for you. I am going to put another little novel right in this little novel! How will you like that? (p. 156)

By the time we have reached the end of *The Journal*, Albion and his technique have succeeded in creating a real literary mess. The last pages of the book are strewn with the rubble of exploded forms; journal entries, the table of contents of one novel and fragments of several more, snatches of poems, an assortment of catalogues, marginal musing. The closing words are:

> There is no way to end this book.
> No way to begin

But in disorder, Albion has freed himself from ordered insanity, transcended the usual human condition, and experienced truth.

Another aspect of the hostility to traditional forms, and to "literary" methods and values in general, is Patchen's constant attention to literary play, especially parody. He toys with critical terminology, calling attention to the rhythm of a particular line or the appropriateness of a sentiment; he admires his timing in introducing new themes. In *The Journal of Albion Moonlight,* he delights in providing apparently unrelated and incoherent marginal comments and parallel texts for much of his material, and in a discussion of the allegorical significance of his characters, mocks conventional modes of interpretation (pp. 30-31). All this contributes to the general shattering of form, and helps to provide the eccentric juxtapositions and distortions on which Patchen largely relies to focus attention on the material he wants perceived in a new way. He also uses parody persistently, and with obvious relish, to define and ridicule literary shortcomings. Although his chief targets are James Joyce and Ernest Hemingway — significantly, two of the most influential stylists of the century — his parodies range from the poetry of the Old Testament to the language of surrealism itself. In *The Memoirs of A Shy Pornographer,* the novel in which the tone is most comic and the use of parody most definitive, he presents the classic Freudian image, familiar from its presence in countless modern novels, in a way that makes its banal portentousness seem obvious: "There is a building on Madison in the fifties where 400 elevator boys live in a large room in the basement unknown to the superintendent, despite the fact that two old darkies go down there every night and teach them tap-dancing." (p. 12) *The Memoirs* is loaded with local parodies and burlesques of this kind, playing havoc with nearly all contemporary literary movements, and most modern standard authors. With its frequent use of literary society as a setting, and its description of the effect of publication of his commercially mutilated book upon the author-hero, it is also a general burlesque of the social and moral results of modern literature. Turning an entire body of literature in upon itself to make it define its own essential viciousness, and the rottenness of the intellectual *milieu* it reflects, is one of Patchen's applications or surrealistic destructive humor. It also relates *The Memoirs* — as well as *The Journal of Albion Moonlight* and *Sleepers Awake,* which use much the same method — to that small body of past "anti-literature" that probably comes originally from *Don Quixote*. Herman Melville's *Pierre,* for example, is another American book in which an artistic and morally admirable man

becomes so involved in the literature of his time that his life
becomes a literary role, and he is annihilated. Because of the concern with insanity, *Pierre* is more closely related in tone to *The
Journal of Albion Moonlight* than to *The Memoirs of A Shy Pornographer,* but the difference is one of tone only. The implications about the relationship of literature to human consciousness are the same.[5]

Patchen's narrative technique is also fitted to his direct
concern with the literary. The narrators of his novels are also the
authors, and are aware that they are both author and character.
This self-consciousness permits the many asides about authorial
problems (like Albion Moonlight's on form, quoted above) and,
more importantly, allows the author to turn directly to his audience with the moral truth he has to offer. These author-narrators
are not to be distinguished from Patchen himself. No indication is
given of any distance between the fictional and true authors, and
scraps of autobiographical narrative in *The Journal of Albion
Moonlight* and a bit of word-play at the end of *The Memoirs of A
Shy Pornographer* help confirm the common identity. What
results, then, is Patchen's presence at the forefront of the action,
and this presence is essential to the reality created in the novels,
and to the moral statement made. The method is the one Whitman, again, called "personalism," the attempt to create a
literature of such a texture that it carries to the reader the presence of the man writing it. Although Patchen has some qualms
about accepting the full implications of Whitman's in-
discriminate gregariousness, he describes his purpose in *The Journal of Albion Moonlight* in terms strongly reminiscent of Whitman's own:

> My purpose? It is nothing remarkable: I wish to speak to
> you. (p. 22)

> .   .   .   .

> Some of you will hate my book, for I insist on touching you.
> (p. 24)

> .   .   .   .

> But it is best that I do not become a legend, I think you will
> agree that I am alive in every part of this book; turn back
> twenty, thirty, one hundred pages — *I am back there.* That

is why I hate the story; characters are not snakes that they
must shed their skins on every page — there can be only one
action: what a man is. . . . — ah! but I am in the room
with you. I write this book *as an action*. Like knocking a
man down. (p. 261)

Patchen also shares with Whitman a concern for making
that personal touch a universal touch. His narrators are explicitly
"Everyman." Like Whitman's poetic persona, they have the
capacity for assuming identities: of becoming the murderer, the
tortured innocent, the lover. The technique attempts to bring
universal experience, through the person of the living author, to
the immediate attention of the reader. Albion Moonlight discusses
the problem: "It was my intention to set down the story of what
happened to myself and to a little group of my friends — and I
soon discovered that what was happening to us was happening to
everyone. . . . It was too late to write a book; it was my duty to
write all books. I could not write about a few people; it was my
role to write about everyone." (p. 305) Obviously, such an attempt
is extraordinarily ambitious, if not arrogant, and the demands it
makes provide an overwhelmingly difficult test of literary art. Patchen's response to these demands is remarkably successful.
Although the means by which he presents experience to the reader
involves a series of complex and involuted relationships, the impact of the experience is undiminished. Patchen's meaning is
always visceral rather than intellectual, and comes, as one of his
few perceptive critics has remarked, "by assimilation."[6]

The agency of the narrator as a means of communication
between the collective human consciousness and the individual
reader begins with the narrator's perception of what is around
him. That perception is always of an organic whole; the interaction of perceiver and perceived comprises a single life, and
there is no essential difference between an inanimate object and a
human being — they share attributes. "You have read many
books," Albion Moonlight says; "This book is reading you." (p.
202) And in *The Memoirs of A Shy Pornographer* the protagonist
is as likely to be offered advice by a cloud, or bush, or totem pole
as by another character. More important than the obliteration of
the distinction between the human and non-human, however, is
the flow of identities from one human being to another. Identity,

especially in *The Journal of Albion Moonlight,* is a community thing; Albion, with his extreme sensitivity to the natures and motives of others, takes on their characteristics and acts out their impulses. He can change, within the limits of a sentence, from lover to rapist and murderer; he records like a mirror the horrors of human existence surrounding him. In addition, in that single life created from the narrator's perception, emotional and intellectual reactions to experience are likely to take concrete form; it is a magic universe Patchen lays before us, where the word is immediately made flesh. Albert Budd, the shy pornographer, for instance, has a pleasantly corny tendency to act out puns; he comes home covered with gold paint because an angel has been "working off a guilt complex." (p. 236) And in *The Journal* the acting out of emotional reactions emphasizes the rage and terror and hatred the modern world inspires:

> At Buford, Mississippi we enjoyed a good laugh, one of the many things denied those who do not travel. Jetter was forced to get off the sidewalk every time he met a white man. What a quaint custom! Finally, after we had exhausted the humor of the situation, we started cruising up and down the main streets, machine-gun blazing like a hail storm. It was reported later — though this is open to some doubt — that we put away thirty-five hundred Bufordians, even bagging the Mayor and two councilmen. I told the Governor that, unlike his own, Jetter's skin was only black on the outside. (pp 174-5)

In this organic vision of the world, then, all things, persons, emotions, become one massive life, which is, for us, the narrative consciousness. Nothing can be irrelevant in such a vision; everything perceived has personal significance to the narrator. The implications of another's behavior, or the presence of evil in the world cannot be ignored; the individual identity, the individual response cannot be sorted out from that of humanity in general. Patchen attempts a literal personification of Donne's "Every man's death diminishes me." Although new material from outside can become part of the perception, nothing but the perception exists at any given time; the narrator's consciousness records the condition of humanity from moment to moment. This perception, however, is not in itself sufficient for communication, since the narrator, as an integral part of the single life his perception creates, is changed in his own nature by every act and emotion perceived. He must, in fact, be able to perceive himself, the only available index of mankind and its fluctuations, in order that he may be the person through whom the book "touches" the reader. Even as he is engaged in being the symbol, he must see himself as symbolic. And this is precisely what happens.

I have said that the authors of these novels are aware of themselves as characters in the fiction, and Patchen uses this literary schizophrenia to give authenticity to his universal authorial consciousness. Albion Moonlight is intensely aware that he is creating his own life, that his survival depends entirely upon his ability to write his way out of trouble. Because Albion the character is largely defined by the condition of humanity, Albion the author cannot rely absolutely upon imaginative power to keep himself from danger, but must accept the situation the world imposes — "I do not *choose* my truths," he says. He must create as an act of self-defense against that world. He knows only what is happening at the moment — "I am desperately anxious to discover what takes place next in this book" (p. 145) — and so is constantly watching Albion the character and writing madly to keep him alive. The effect is to create a split between Albion the prophetic creative consciousness and Albion the limited human being:

> I have spent ten years becoming a saint. It was not easy because always the man I was got in the way. This man's name is Albion Moonlight. He has been puzzled by my behavior. I feel that he is nearly dead now. You may ask how I happened to be in him: I do not know. One day I was there. Since then the struggle has been great. His wife has been my greatest enemy. I do not want him to make love to her because it distracts me. Her passionate nature has caused me great trouble. I cannot warn Moonlight against this orgy of the flesh: I can only be the warning. (p. 37)

This split in the personality of the author culminates, in Patchen's fictions, in an image of freedom from the usual self. The image is familiar in all mystical literature, and is one that Carl Jung would identify with his "synchronicity."[7] When these images appear, they establish the reliability of that wisdom that has freed itself from the body and transcended ordinary human limitations. These scenes also define the human identity as the legitimate spokesman for all mankind, and are among the most intensely moving in Patchen's work. In *The Memoirs of A Shy Pornographer*, Albert Budd, in the body of a man named Tony, journeys into a surrealistic landscape where from an inverted point of view he witnesses himself, in the stained yellow suit which has become symbolic of his bumbling, pathetic, meek humanity, watching a meeting he had watched in his own body some time before. As multitudes gather, and the scene becomes a celebration of man's peace and hope, Budd's familiar, often humiliated self performs the sacramental act establishing its meaning:

> And when the morning came a great shout of exultation and thanksgiving arose from every throat. A shy little man in a soiled, lemon-colored suit lifted a photograph high above his head that all might see.
> At once a voice from the highest and farthest hills was heard, and the voice said:
> "Look well upon the face which is before you, my children; for against its gentle wisdom the bondsmen of darkness and evil are as thieves and assassins who would scheme to rob the very wind of its blowing — or who would murder the sun for the heat and the light of the sun!"
> The face was the most beautiful I had ever seen.
> And every face before me there was that face. (p.90)

After this, Budd returns from "the other side of the world," with a new strength and wisdom, and records in his love and failure much of the potential of the human race.

In *The Journal of Albion Moonlight*, the split between the human and transcendent Albion is much more explicit and antagonistic, but culminates in the same kind of schizophrenic scene:

> . . . *Albion had a complete command of the room and the party below, being able to look directly down at the coffin in which his torn body rested — and, as a tear drained from his eye and fell upon the cold face which men knew as his own, "Lie still! lie still, you bastard!" he called down to his corpse. "If you stir, they'll kill you!"* (p. 252)

And the novel ends, sixty pages later, with Albion Moonlight viewing his own corpse with "indifferent pity," and seeing his own face in the "windows of all the houses on earth." This double vision permits the author, the narrator, Patchen, Everyman to be at the same time a human being experiencing the confusion, pain, and failure of his condition, and an observer, defining and pointing to that condition. Albion Moonlight, the author-character, is hopelessly insane, because he is the consciousness of the perception of an organic world in which no reference point for sanity exists; but Albion Moonlight, the author-observer, possesses in his distance from the action an absolute sanity that can diagnose his own condition and, in its living body, fling it into the consciousness of the reader so that the reader, too, may touch the madness of his brethren. By this daring use of fantasy and psychology, Patchen lifts his "personalism" far above the merely personal, and batters us with his moral statement in its starkest form.

Of course the process of using the personal vision as a means of describing human experience obliges Patchen to outline in more or less abstract terms what he feels that experience is, what the moral capacities and possibilities of the human race are. As Albion Moonlight, Aloysius Best (the author of *Sleepers Awake*) and Albert Budd, iconoclastic makers all, destroy conventional literary forms in order to release the full potential of personal contact, they rip down also the conventional definitions of "reality" that literary forms reflect. They create chaos out of apparent order, and point up the essential insanity of what is regarded as real and normal. As the familiar structure is demolished, a new definition of what is real emerges. Because Patchen regards death as a mystery that can mean, finally, either annihilation or spiritual fulfillment, and because he fluctuates between complete pessimism and joyous affirmation, it is not possible to schematize his reality in any absolute way. He does express, however, a consistent attitude toward what condition must be lived with, what limitations and possibilities characterize the universe he establishes. His reality is, because of the personalistic way of defining it, solipsistic — as Albion Moonlight, at the same time establishing the symbolic method of his novel, points out:

> ". . . I mean that there are as many worlds as there
> are human beings. And because of this, there is only one
> world . . ."
> "Eh?"
> "Because there is only one human being in the
> world."
> "And you are that one human being. I suppose?"
> "Yes, I am the world. I know of no other world but
> the one which is in me." (p. 298)

And this reality is limited to the human world. Although
he talks at length about God, Patchen resists his obvious in-
clination to posit an afterlife in which man's spiritual hunger
would be satisfied, and the trouble of this world justified. Any
religious institutionalization of this concept is for him an ob-
scenity, and the idea itself, he suggests, draws attention from the
horror around us, and encourages the moral blindness on which
the power of evil is based. The attitude is given substance in *The
Memoirs of A Shy Pornographer* when Albert Budd and his lover,
Priscilla, are being conducted through a forest by three young
men in white. Their guides stop them in a clearing and, soothing
them with the language of religion, they put a knife to Priscilla's
throat:

> "We have reached what we were seeking," said one of
> the three.
> "Soon you shall see beyond the little meanings," said
> another.
> The moon seemed to draw nearer.
> "There is more than just to live — and to die," the
> other said. (p. 162)

The scene freezes, and the horror of it is that Priscilla and Albert
are unafraid; they smile at the assassins. When Albert comes to his
senses and drives them off, he establishes the principle that
anything whatsoever that harms life is evil, is madness. The only
God is in man; Albert tells Priscilla that putting God "in the sky"
causes man to fail to see the God standing before him. In the
figure of the Roivas of *The Journal of Albion Moonlight,* the idea
of a God dissociated from man is more intensely investigated. The
novel begins as a pilgrimage to Galen, the land of Roivas (savior),

as a place of refuge from war and insanity. Roivas is a shadowy figure who becomes increasingly sinister as the implications of his presence in the human world are developed. His ways are ethically inhuman, and what divinity he may possess has no validity for man. "I am indeed the voice of God," he claims, "And I denounce you, Albion Moonlight!" "Then," Albion replies, "you are not God." (p. 31) And when Roivas finally makes a physical appearance, he is described as an obscene monster. The true God, the only God meaningful to man, Patchen insists, is a human potential: the Christ within us all, the power of the imagination to perceive beauty and joy and so transform the world around it.

The power of the imagination, however, as we have seen in Albion Moonlight's authorial problems, is not an absolute power. Patchen is not so much the mystic or idealist that he will permit his characters to establish only a subjective reality, and live in it. Escapism is as distasteful to him as any other "literary" solution to a moral problem. Albert Budd, for instance, is a visionary whose imagination can create a reality of its own:

> . . . I thought it would be nice to imagine a big snake crawling along the street — so right away I saw one poking his nose into the upper storeys of houses and lashing his tail around. Then he turned to look at me and his tail whipped out and cracked me in the leg.
> When I took off my pants for bed I was surprised to find a bruise on my left leg . . . (p. 13)

His imagination, his "faith," can create multi-colored deer that bear baskets of flowers to lovers and play in sunny fields with laughing children; but physical reality, the pressure from outside, intrudes upon and destroys this fragile human capacity. The faith that calls up the deer gives the crippled Priscilla use of her legs, until mundane circumstance crushes the momentary triumph:

> Then we heard the voice of her mother calling from the house. . . .
> And Priscilla sank to the ground, her legs twisting horribly under her.
> "Oh, God! O my God!" she sobbed.
> The little green deer was gone.
> The roses and the daffodils were gone from her hand.
> And something was dying away deep inside me.

There is in the world a potential for beauty and magnificence and joy that is tremendously important to Patchen, and is a constant impulse to celebration. For Patchen, that potential justifies man, and is his essential state. It exists, supremely, in love, the "touch" of one human being to another, and although realizable only in brief and scattered moments, although pitilessly snuffed out by the brutality of circumstance, the love of one person for another is the quality to which Patchen turns when he utters praise for the majesty of his kind. Love, too, in the outgoing spirit of man, transforms the alien things of existence into the animalistic world Patchen's narrators create and perceive, freeing the spirit and conjuring up an almost child-like wonder at the beauty and mystery of the universe — and driving Patchen to the breathless limits of his prose. Albert Budd tells Priscilla: "It amazes me to think that there are people who suppose they believe in God, and yet won't believe that there are butterflies bigger than the earth, that there are fires raging at the bottom of the sea, that there are leopards made of golden wire circling the sun —"(p.168)

But these strange exaltations exist only as flashes of consciousness. Although the essence of humanity, they are helpless in a world ordered on terror, hatred, and irresponsible power, a world of personally malevolent insanity. Human life, as it is made tangible in these pages, is surrounded by horror; the human condition is subject to the vicious structure growing, in Albion Moonlight's phrase, out of "the shitty chaos called human history." For Patchen the Second World War was a culmination of the failure of history, and even when it is only obliquely mentioned, as in *See You in the Morning*, the war is intensely in the background of all his prose. Fascism becomes the metaphor for the historical forces that have institutionalized murder and insanity, and fascism controls the writhing life with which Patchen fills his novels. Because of the personal consciousness at the forefront of the fiction, it is the effects of historical and social failure that are perceived, rather than abstract causality. Without the understanding or will of Patchen's narrators, things happen to them as in a nightmare, and they can respond only with confusion and pain. Albert Budd, on his way to marry Priscilla, is lured into the "House of the Frowning Heart," an establishment mysteriously described in institutional metaphors he does not understand.

There he is frustratingly, terribly held back from his assignation, and wrenched from the timeless exaltation his love had created so that time can destroy the idyllic pastoral landscape in which Priscilla's life was set. In *The Journal of Albion Moonlight* the causality is even more nightmarish, as familiar figures change identity, becoming agents of evil and rage; and brutal executioners materialize suddenly to humiliate utterly, torture, and kill Albion and his friends. The technique permits a more effective protest than is generally available to literary art in which attention is focused on what is outside the individual. What we think of as the literature of social protest (by which I mean literature chiefly concerned with making a statement about the helplessness of innocent individuals in relation to institutions) has typically been "realistic." Protest writers have concentrated on describing the ruthlessness and inhumanity of institutions grown out of human control, and on detailed realistic presentation of the physical surroundings such a situation begets. Because they have wanted their readers to understand how such conditions come into being, they have stood a bit above the action, and described the struggle with society of characters less knowledgeable than themselves. In Patchen's method, however, the social victim is also the narrative consciousness, so that rather then attend to the more or less abstract mechanics of social evil, Patchen directly records its impact on the human spirit, and returns protest to its original and irrevocable source: the emotional knowledge that man is in pain.

Because the structure of Patchen's universe is based on the opposition of terrible physical reality and the potential for joy in the human spirit, and because of the individual consciousness that constructs his fictional worlds, the settings, characterizations, and "plots" of his novels depend largely upon the direction and intensity of the moral statement to be made. It is for this reason that he can keep his universe operating on the same causal basis, with the same implications, finally, about human helplessness, and still create two novels of such radically different tone as *The Journal of Albion Moonlight* and *The Memoirs of A Shy Pornographer*. *The Journal* was written in response to the "plague summer" of 1940, when "the great gray plague of universal madness" threatened the human race. Told through the tortured and sophisticated mind of Albion, the novel is set in a landscape of war and insanity. In the original journal, the pilgrims start off, "slogging out of New York" on their way to Galen, followed by demonic dogs, and set upon by invisible, murderous presences that haunt the surrounding country. As their journey progresses, it becomes a series of brilliant gulliverian satires on American life, and the American countryside itself becomes the great battlefield: bombers drone overhead, damage done in bombing raids on Cleveland is listed in detail, armies slaughter one another in the forests and on the plains of the middle west, and prisoners of war (American) are taken and questioned. Later, as Albion starts one of his many novels, we learn that everything has been written in a room where he awaits execution by the companions of the pilgrimage for a murder that he both has and has not committed, that both has and has not happened. Finally, in another journal, a parallel entry for May 2 (the first day of the pilgrimage) tells us that Albion has never left home. "There is more of the world here in this room with me than I can understand," he tells those who were to travel with him. These contradictory settings — and there are many more — are not meant to cancel one another out, or to establish only a dream reality; they are all literally true. Against this background, the characters, led by the slobbering, liver-colored Riovas and the many incarnations of his mysterious daughter, are spectres called forth from the diseased collective mind of humanity, malevolent apparitions of war. The action, of course, is broken and incoherent, a patchwork chronicle of the whimpering sentience of man. Yet, even in all this fury, Patchen never permits the possibility of human dignity to be overwhelmed, never permits his reader to forget that dignity exists. It is this quality that makes the rage of the novel almost unbearably intense. Although the implications of Albion Moonlight's position are never gathered into a definitive positive statement, although he is left lonely and under attack at the end, his creative imagination, his artistic magic is, throughout the novel, a brave defiance of hopelessness:

> The great writer will take a heroic stand against literature: *by changing the nature of what is to be done,* he will be the first to do what the voice of dreaming does; he will heal the hurt where God's hand pressed too hard in His zeal to make us more than the animals. (p. 308)

and:

Thus, against murder, against hypocrisy, and for life, for
all that is most beautiful and noble in man, for the immense
joy of being alive, do I speak. I am an island in a cesspool
called History. (p. 204)

It is this potential for transfiguration in the nature of man
that informs the vision of *The Memoirs of A Shy Pornographer,*
giving that work its great humor, its whimsical delight in physical
nature, and its exuberant sense of play — even in a world which is
essentially the same as the world of Albion Moonlight. *The
Memoirs* was published in 1945, and though it is impossible to tell
exactly when Patchen wrote it, it is pleasant to speculate, at least,
that the approaching end of a decade of slaughter had some influence on his lighter tone. Albert Budd, the narrator-author, is a
naive, perfectly pure visionary who creates a world of child-like
delicacy and beauty, and makes his love manifest by calling forth
a playful green deer and an orange-colored waiter, who mat-
erializes to serve dinner in a forest, and trudges off with a burning bush in his wheelbarrow. Terrible things happen to Albert
Budd as he is forced to undergo the symbolic sufferings of
humanity, but he is not destroyed by terror. He retains his integrity, his triumph expressed in the attainment of "heaven," a
heaven made up of Klee-like (or Patchen-like, for that matter)
paintings, where life is lived precisely as it had been on earth —
except, of course, that the frightening side of human existence is
forgotten. It is a poignant comment on the failure of human
history that so little is needed to equip this utterly fictional
paradise. Like the setting, the characters in *The Memoirs* are less
terrible than those of *The Journal;* even characters who incorporate much of the failure of humanity into their persons —
George Arliss and Mr. Pinklady — are comic rather than
demonic, and some characters, such as Donald Wan, the lovable
and tubercular inventor to the universe, are figures of essential
goodness and dignity. The action of this novel is coherent and
relatively orderly, and Albert, as he develops, defines its unity. He
begins as the complete innocent who has written a book so sweet
and pure that when unscrupulous publishers replace key words
with asterisks, it seems to be thoroughly vile pornography. Budd is
established as a public figure and his adventures begin, bringing
him into contact with destructive forces that cause him to intensify

his strength, to the extent, finally, that he relives the experience of Christ and is illuminated.

This use of the personal vision of the author-narrator to establish the reality of the world, and serve as a vehicle for moral impulse, gives Patchen's prose its authority and cohesion. It also exposes Patchen to his greatest danger: sentimentality. The very preoccupation with a literary technique meant to destroy distance between author and reader practically defines sentimentality for many critics and practitioners of modern fiction who wish to keep the artist out of his surface altogether, like the creator in James Joyce's *Portrait of the Artist,* "indifferent, paring his fingernails."

Accusation of sentimentality is also, of course, one of the chief indictments of the tradition of American literature out of which Patchen works; and the accusation — against Whitman, against Miller, against Wolfe — is often justified. Patchen tries to explain the control he has set on sentimentality when he compares his purpose to Whitman's: "Walt Whitman did not want to touch people; he wanted to paw over them. A man has a privacy and a woman has another privacy. He did not know this because he always wrote as though he stood in a public room . . ." (*The Journal of Albion Moonlight,* p. 24) He is entirely aware that his method is still regarded as sentimental, however, that many readers will shrink from his touch. Keeping to his quarrel with contemporary taste, he exploits this fear of the personal by playing with critical ideas of what sentimentality is. With an audacity that is both impressive and distressing, he deliberately places himself in literary danger, choosing again and again to use plots, themes, situations which are thoroughly hackneyed, and characteristic, usually, of only the most syrupy popular fiction. In *The Memoirs of A Shy Pornographer,* for instance, the love story of Albert and Priscilla begins with the most familiar of accidental meetings in the most sylvan of forests. Its further paraphernalia includes quaint front parlors, taffy pulls, and a charming, white-haired knitting old mother. Priscilla is a hopeless cripple who is given power to walk by the force of Albert's love, and the lovers' conversations are thoroughly grounded in inconsequential small talk and inane pet names. But Patchen manages to escape the sentimentality inherent in his material, and much of the fun of the novel is in watching him do it. He saves his tone by use of all the innocent sensibility that delights in the tender and familiar, the fantasy and whimsy defining his scenes, his great ability to play with expectations and so control the reader's responses, and especially, by maintaining at all times his rich sense of humor, and being willing to chuckle over the innocence he celebrates.

Patchen's deliberate use of what is commonly regarded as sentimentalism has a purpose beyond literary play; it is instrumental also in defining his attitude toward the possibility of human joy. The trite, artistically tried situations Patchen insists upon reflect his belief that the richest fulfillment of life is not in the rare and spectacular, but in the familiar things of the everyday world. It is a man's potential to find mystery and beauty in the existence crowding about him at every moment, to discover the wonder in those situations he and every other human being have experienced many times before. Usually Patchen's attempt to exalt the familiar is successful; there is no denying the magic of Albert Budd's simple and bumbling love.

But at times Patchen loses some of the control he builds into his prose, and does become sentimental. The fault is obvious in some of his love poems, which at their worst can become a trifle giggly, and in the amazingly unsuccessful novel published in 1948, *See You in the Morning.* The plot of this novel is based on the rejuvenation, through pure and innocent love, of a young man who has been told he is soon to die, and is destroying himself with alcohol. There are some points of interest in it: a few passages that flash with Patchen's usual poetic terror, and the presence, though not developed to any great extent, of an invisible, omniscient, omnipresent narrator who is desperately frustrated because he cannot tell the lovers the truths he knows. For all this, however, the novel is conventionally developed and lacks the wild fantasy and exuberant humor that informs the others. It becomes, if not quite sticky, tedious and unbelievable. Patchen also occasionally fails to avoid the other side of sentimentality, and rages in so loud and shrill a voice that he becomes incoherent. Again, it is basically his sense of humor that more often than not keeps his prose balanced and effective, but when that fails, intelligibility may disappear completely. The tendency is most noticeable in some sections of *Sleepers Awake,* where the quality and intensity of the protest is likely to be expressed typographically rather than in the content and treatment of the material itself. *Sleepers Awake,* however, is by no means so completely disappointing as *See You in the Morning,* and it should be unnecessary to point out that these lapses are not to be taken as representative of Patchen's achievement. He succeeds far more than he fails, and the image of the author we take away from his books is not of a coy or screaming sentimentalist, but of a jauntily audacious, masterfully competent figure, cheerfully ignoring the rules others have drawn up to protect themselves.

It is a shame that Patchen's prose has not been more widely read. One of those impatient and cranky spokesmen for the American conscience that the American public typically and stubbornly chooses to ignore, he has been making statements for some time that have now become part of the popular rhetoric of the civil rights and pacifist movements, and are at least tolerated in public debate. That he has remained generally obscure seems to be the consequence not only of his unusual technique and undisguised contempt for public morality and traditional literature, but also of some pure bad luck, and one great shortcoming of his own: he has apparently nothing of the temperament needed for successful public relations. The somewhat dubious publicity he has at times received from groups that tried to claim him for themselves — the communists early in his career, and later the "Beats" — and the eccentric, often raging quality of his work, have combined to give him a vague, but widespread reputation as irresponsible. But there is nothing irresponsible about his prose. He is a master workman, and the authority of his presence in his novels is unquestionable. *The Journal of Albion Moonlight,* especially, is a large book. The reasons for Patchen's lack of popularity seem to be of the kind that are temporary — the result of our closeness to the man himself. His reputation should eventually revive.

Notes

[1]Allen Ginsberg, *Howl and Other Poems* (San Francisco, 1956).
[2]Quotations from Patchen's novels are identified as to source and pagination. Italics in quoted passages are Patchen's own. *Sleepers Awake* (New York, 1946); *The Journal of Albion Moonlight,* 5th ed. (New York, 1946); *The Memoirs of A*

Shy Pornographer (New York, 1945); *See You in the Morning* (New York, 1948).

[3]See A.N. Wilder, "Revolutionary and Proletarian Poetry: Kenneth Patchen," in *Spiritual Aspects of the New Poetry* (New York, 1940) pp. 178-195, for an example of the sympathetic treatment Patchen was beginning to receive while radicalism was still in flower. Whether or not he really belonged to this group is another question. Although his rhetoric does at times resemble that of the "proletarians" of his day, he has always been essentially an anarchist, and any political language has been incidental to his moral concern.

[4]*From Cubism to Surrealism in French Literature* (Cambridge, Mass., 1941) pp. 197-199.

[5]Kenneth Rexroth, in his "Kenneth Patchen, Naturalist of the Public Nightmare," in *Bird in the Bush* (New York, 1959) pp. 94-105, makes some drastic claims for Patchen's tradition, and his place in world "anti-literature." Rexroth's essay is largely polemical, and often aimed at his own quarrels rather than an assessment of Patchen's work; but it is vigorous, at times very perceptive, and certainly useful for balance to other critics.

[6]Hugh McGovern, "Kenneth Patchen's Prose Works," *New Mexico Quarterly* XXI (1951), 181-197. I am inclined to think McGovern's essay reflects a bit too much of the chaos he finds on Patchen's surface, and that he is insufficiently aware of the essential unity of Patchen's work. But his interest in Patchen is intelligent, and he always responds properly to the material — which makes him a lonely critic indeed. I am indebted to him for several suggestive hints.

[7]See Carl Jung, *Psyche and Symbol,* ed. Violet S. de Laszlo (New York, 1958) pp. 266-282, for a psychoanalytic discussion of the image.

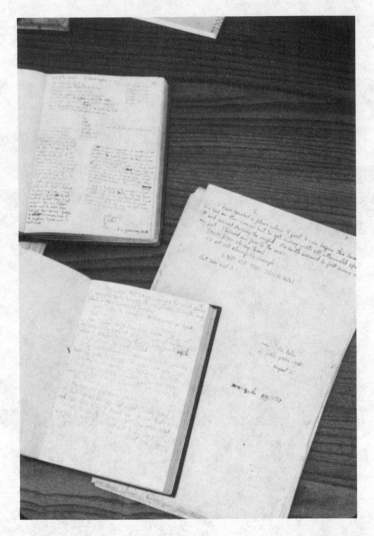

Manuscript pages from *The Journal of Albion Moonlight*.
Photograph by Richard Morgan.

Selective Bibliography and Resource Guide

PRIMARY MATERIALS

A. Books

[An asterisk indicates that the book is currently in print. the publisher's name in these cases follows the entry.]

*BEFORE THE BRAVE (1936). Poetry. Haskell House.
FIRST WILL AND TESTAMENT (1939). Poetry.
*THE JOURNAL OF ALBION MOONLIGHT (1941). Prose.
  New Directions.
THE DARK KINGDOM (1942). Poetry.
THE TEETH OF THE LION (1942). Poetry.
CLOTH OF THE TEMPEST (1943). Poetry.
*MEMOIRS OF A SHY PORNOGRAPHER (1945). Prose. New
  Directions.
AN ASTONISHED EYE LOOKS OUT OF THE AIR (1946).
  Poetry.
OUTLAW OF THE LOWEST PLANET (1946). Selection of
  published poetry, introduction by David Gascoyne.
A LETTER TO GOD (1946), with PATCHEN, MAN OF
  ANGER AND LIGHT. Introduction by Henry Miller.
  Prose.
THE SELECTED POEMS (1946). Poetry.
*SLEEPERS AWAKE (1946). Prose. New Directions.
PANELS FOR THE WALLS OF HEAVEN (1946). Prose.
PICTURES OF LIFE AND DEATH (1946). Poetry.
THEY KEEP RIDING DOWN ALL THE TIME (1946-1947).
  Prose.

CCLXXIV POEMS (1947-1948). FIRST WILL AND TESTAMENT, THE DARK KINGDOM, and CLOTH OF THE TEMPEST bound together. Poetry.

SEE YOU IN THE MORNING (1948). Prose.

TO SAY IF YOU LOVE SOMEONE (1948). Poetry. Never distributed.

RED WINE AND YELLOW HAIR (1949). Poetry.

IN PEACEABLE CAVES (1950). Poetry. Never distributed.

ORCHARDS, THRONES & CARAVANS (1952). Poetry.

FABLES AND OTHER LITTLE TALES (1953). Prose-poems.

THE FAMOUS BOATING PARTY (1954). Prose-poems.

*POEMS OF HUMOR & PROTEST (1954). Poetry. City Lights.

GLORY NEVER GUESSES (1955). Portfolio of silk-screen prints.

SURPRISE FOR THE BAGPIPE PLAYER (1956). Portfolio of silk-screen prints.

*THE SELECTED POEMS, ENLARGED EDITION (1957). Poetry. New Directions.

HURRAH FOR ANYTHING (1957). Poems and drawings.

WHEN WE WERE HERE TOGETHER (1957). Poetry.

POEMSCAPES (1958). Prose-poems.

*BECAUSE IT IS (1960). Poems and drawings. New Directions.

THE MOMENT (1960). Bound edition of the silk-screen portfolios GLORY NEVER GUESSES and SURPRISE FOR THE BAGPIPE PLAYER.

*THE LOVE POEMS (1960). Poetry. City Lights.

*DOUBLEHEADER (1966). Contains POEMSCAPES, A LETTER TO GOD, and HURRAH FOR ANYTHING. New Directions.

*HALLELUJAH ANYWAY (1966). Picture-poems. New Directions.

*THE COLLECTED POEMS (1968). Poetry. New Directions.

SELECTED POEMS [U.K.] (1968). Poetry. Introduction by Nathaniel Tarn.

*BUT EVEN SO (1968). Picture-poems. New Directions.

LOVE & WAR POEMS (1968). Poetry, prose, and drawings.

*AFLAME AND AFUN OF WALKING FACES (1970). Contains FABLES AND OTHER LITTLE TALES, and new drawings. New Directions.

*THERE'S LOVE ALL DAY (1970). Poetry. Hallmark.

*WONDERINGS (1971). Picture-poems. New Directions.

*IN QUEST OF CANDLELIGHTERS (1972). Contains PANELS
FOR THE WALLS OF HEAVEN, ANGEL-CARVER
BLUES, BURY THEM IN GOD, and THEY KEEP
RIDING DOWN ALL THE TIME. Prose. New Direc-
tions.

*PATCHEN'S LOST PLAYS [THE CITY WEARS A SLOUCH
HAT and DON'T LOOK NOW (forthcoming, 1977). Introduction by Richard Morgan. Drama. Capra Press.

B. Recordings

[All except the first and last are available from Folkways Records.
The first is out of print. The last is available from Greentree
Records, 2340 Sierra Court, Palo Alto, CA 94303]

KENNETH PATCHEN READS HIS POETRY WITH THE
        CHAMBER JAZZ SEXTET (1957)
THE JOURNAL OF ALBION MOONLIGHT (Selections) (1958)
KENNETH PATCHEN READS HIS SELECTED POEMS (1959)
KENNETH PATCHEN READS WITH JAZZ IN CANADA
        (1959)
KENNETH PATCHEN READS HIS LOVE POEMS (1961)
PATCHEN'S FUNNY FABLES (1972)

C. Manuscripts, Correspondence, and Ephemera in Public Collections

University of California at Los Angeles. Department of Special
    Collections, University Research Library.
University of California at Santa Cruz. The Kenneth Patchen Ar-
    chive. Department of Special Collections.
University of Chicago. Special Collections, The Joseph Regenstein
    Library. Amy Bonner Papers, Poetry Magazine Papers.
Harvard University. Special Collections. Houghton Library.
Huntington Library. Wallace Stevens Collection, Special Collec-
    tions.
Indiana University. Special Collections, The Lilly Library.
State University of New York at Buffalo. Poetry Collection, The
    University Library.
New York Public Library. Special Collections, Library of the Per-
    forming Arts at Lincoln Center.

Northwestern University. Department of Special Collections.
Princeton University. Firestone Library, R. P. Blackmur Archive.
University of Texas at Austin. Humanities Research Center.
Yale University. Collection of American Literature, Beinecke
    Rare Book and Manuscript Library.

SECONDARY MATERIALS

A. Bibliography

Morgan, Richard G. *Kenneth Patchen: A Comprehensive
    Bibliography*. New York: Paul Appel, due in 1978. An-
    notated, descriptive listing of all works by and about Pat-
    chen, including a detailed inventory of all manuscripts,
    correspondence, and ephemera in public collections.

B. Books (General)

Detro, Gene, ed. *Patchen: The Last Interview*. Santa Barbara,
    CA: Capra Press, 1976. 29pp. Reprinted from *Outsider*
    4/5 (1968) homage to Patchen [See Section G (below)],
    and in section two of this volume. Additional commentary,
    and a new introduction, by Detro, with a foreword by
    Miriam Patchen.
*The Argument of Innocence: A Selection from the Arts of Ken-
    neth Patchen*. Oakland, CA: The Scrimshaw Press, 1977.
    98pp. Reproductions of Patchen's picture poems, concrete
    poems, and painted books, reprints of several of his poems,
    and photographs of his papier-mache animals. Ac-
    companying commentary by Peter Veres, foreword by
    Miriam Patchen.
Tribute to Kenneth Patchen. London: Enitharmon Press, 1977.
    Collection of "appreciations" of Patchen by writers, artists,
    and friends around the world, with a new Patchen poem
    included.

C. Critical Biography

Morgan, Richard G. *Kenneth Patchen*. Authorized biography in
    progress. For information, or to supply information, con-
    tact Morgan at the Department of English, University of
    New Mexico, Albuquerque, NM 87131.

D. Dissertations

Hogue, Herbert P. *The Anarchic Mystique of Five American Fictions.* DAI 32:1514A. University of Washington, 1972. One of the five is *The Journal of Albion Moonlight.*

Nelson, Raymond J. *An American Mysticism: The Example of Kenneth Patchen.* DAI 30:5453A-54A. Stanford University, 1971.

Smith, Larry R. *The World of Kenneth Patchen: Form and Function in His Experimental Art.* DAI 35:6161A. Kent State University, 1974.

E. Exhibition Catalogs

Danese, Renato, G., Ed. *Kenneth Patchen: Painter of Poems.* Washington, D.C.: Corcoran Gallery of Art, 1969. 48pp. Catalog of the picture-poem exhibition at the Corcoran, December 12, 1969 to January 18, 1970, with additional commentary by Miriam Patchen, Richard Bowman (reprinted in section two of this volume), and others.

Reuter, Laurel, Ed. *Hallelujah Anyway! A Kenneth Patchen Exhibition.* Grand Forks, North Dakota: University Art Gallery, 1974. 30pp. Catalog of the exhibition of Patchen's picture-poems at the University of North Dakota, March 18 to April 5, 1974, with an introduction by Reuter.

F. Periodical Articles

Anon. "Warren Youth Wins Guggenheim Award." *Warren* (Ohio) *Tribune-Chronicle* (April 1, 1936): 1. Patchen one of five poets to receive Guggenheim. His name is twice misspelled in the article.

Anon. "Former Niles Man Now Rated as an Outstanding Poet." *Niles* (Ohio) *Times* (April 10, 1936): 1. Gives biographical background and records that *Before the Brave* was recently placed in the local library.

Anon. "Bookshop Notes." *Publishers Weekly* 140 (August 2, 1941): 320. Deals with the "launching" of *The Journal of Albion Moonlight* at the Gotham Book Mart in New York City.

Anon. *New York Times* (February 28, 1951): 25. "Six Poets to Read Works [to raise funds for Patchen's medical expenses]." The poets were W. H. Auden, E. E. Cummings, Archibald MacLeish, Marianne Moore, William Carlos Williams, and Edith Sitwell.

Anon. "Kenneth Patchen Wins Poetry Prize." *The Villager* (December 31, 1953): 13. The prize was the Shelley Memorial Award.

Anon. "Poetry, Art, Books, Will be Highlights of Patchen Exhibit." *The Stanford Daily* (May 3, 1963): 1. Announces exhibit at Stanford, which ran through the month of May.

Anon. *New York Times* (December 29, 1969): 27. Review of the picture-poem exhibition at the Corcoran Gallery.

Anon. "Patchen Exhibit in Gallery 'Visual Poem'." *The Dakota Student* 88 (March 20, 1974): 45. Concerns the exhibit of painting-poems in the University of North Dakota Art Gallery, March 18 to April 5, 1974.

Calmer, Alan. "Portrait of the Artist as a Proletarian." *Saturday Review of Literature* XVI, 14 (July 13, 1937): 3-4, 14. Discusses the Proletarian movement in literature, mentioning Patchen as an example.

Carlier, Marie. "Sketch of Kenneth Patchen." *Le Journal des Poetes* [France] V (June 1949): 1. Biographical notes.

Fowler, Albert D. "The Man Who Writes Letters to God." *Fellowship* XII, 10 (November 1946): 180-181 General critical essay concentrating on Patchen's humanism and hatred of war.

Frankenstein, Alfred. "Patchen's Search for a 'Beautiful World'." *San Francisco Examiner & Chronicle* (January 28, 1973): 38. An appreciation.

Glover, David. "The Horror and the Hope." *Avatar* (March 1-13, 1968): 5-7. Extended critical and biographical article centering on the picture-poems, but including other works. Reprinted in *Kaleidoscope* I, 15 (May 24-June 6, 1968): 2, 10-12.

Lesdain, Pierre. "Kenneth Patchen: Homme de Courroux et de Lumiere." *Le Journal des Poetes* V (June 1949): 4. Critical commentary.

Margolis, Barba, "Patchen." *The Staff* (December 3, 1971) Part two: 35, 37. Personalized critical and biographical essay on Patchen, concerned in large part with the picture-poems.

May, James Boyer. "Towards Print." *Trace* 26 (April 1958): 1–4. Includes a discussion of poetry-and-jazz, crediting Patchen with starting the movement.

McGovern, Hugh. "Kenneth Patchen's Prose Works." *New Mexico Quarterly* XXI (Summer 1951): 181–197. In-depth examination of the major prose.

Rigg, Margaret. "Kenneth Patchen." *Motive* XXIV, 4/5 (January–February 1964): 53–61, 76. Concerns Patchen's life and work; includes two drawings, three poems and nine picture-poems by Patchen.

Scleifer, Marc. "Kenneth Patchen on the 'Brat' Generation." *Village Voice* (March 18, 1959): 1, 7. Discusses Patchen's poetry-and-jazz readings and his feelings about the San Francisco Beats.

Spencer, Elizabeth. "Niles-Born Poet, Kenneth Patchen, Is World Famous." *Niles* (Ohio) *Daily Times* (March 21, 1958): 1.

Untermeyer, Jean Starr. "The Problem of Patchen." *Saturday Review of Literature* XXX (March 22, 1947): 15–16. General critical review of Patchen, centering on the works produced in 1946 and 1947.

G.   Periodicals: Special Issues

"A Bay Area Poet's Fight Against Pain." *Alameda County Weekender* (September 16, 1967). Special twelve-page supplement on Patchen. Includes a brief interview by Douglas Dibble, notes by Gene Detro and Ray Nelson, and work by Patchen reprinted from *Poemscapes* (1958),

Because It Is (1960), *Hurrah for Anything* (1957), and "A Letter to God" from *Doubleheader* (1965).

"Homage to Kenneth Patchen." *The Outsider* 4/5 (1968), special issue. Contains notes, appreciations and brief essays on Patchen by Norman Thomas, Brother Antoninus, Allen Ginsberg, James Boyer May, Harold Norse, Millen Brand, Hugh MacDiarmid, David "Tony" Glover, Kenneth Rexroth, John William Corrington, Bern Porter, Lawrence Ferlinghetti, David Meltzer, Lafe Young, Jack Conroy, Frederick Eckman, and Henry Miller, an interview by Gene Detro, a holograph reproduction of a letter from Miriam Patchen, and a selection of photographs of Patchen from various sources.

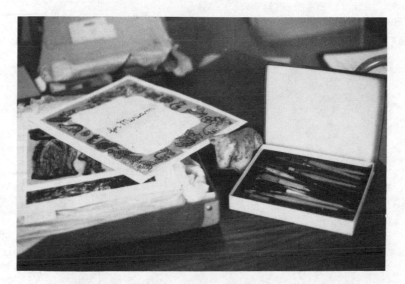

Patchen's tools, and samples of his work. On the right, the pens and brushes he used for his painting-poems; on the left, the originals of *Wonderings;* between them, one of the papier mâché animals Patchen made from scraps cut off the sheets on which he painted. Photograph by Richard Morgan.

LEARNING RESOURCES

CENTER

ILLINOIS CENTRAL COLLEGE
MCMLXVI

East Peoria, Illinois